THE LIFE OF
MARPA THE TRANSLATOR

THE LIFE OF MARPA THE TRANSLATOR

SEEING ACCOMPLISHES ALL

Tsang Nyön Heruka

Translated from the Tibetan by the Nālandā Translation Committee under the direction of Chögyam Trungpa

SHAMBHALA
Boston & London
1986

Nālandā Translation Committee

CHÖGYAM TRUNGPA, *DIRECTOR*
LAMA UGYEN SHENPEN
LOPPÖN LODRÖ DORJE HOLM
LARRY MERMELSTEIN, *EXECUTIVE DIRECTOR*

CATHRYN STEIN ABATO
DAVID COX
DANA DUDLEY
TONY DUFF
CHRISTINE KEYSER
SHERAP CHÖDZIN KOHN
DEREK KOLLEENY
ROBIN KORNMAN
JUD LEVINSON
MARK NOWAKOWSKI
REGINALD A. RAY
JOHN ROCKWELL, JR.
SUSAN SCHULTZ
ROBERT VOGLER
IVES WALDO
SCOTT WELLENBACH
GERRY WIENER

SHAMBHALA PUBLICATIONS, INC.
314 Dartmouth Street
Boston, Massachusetts 02116

9 8 7 6 5 4 3 2 1
First Shambhala edition

Printed in the United States of America
Distributed in the United States by Random House
and in Canada by Random House of Canada Ltd.

LIBRARY OF CONGRESS CATALOGING-IN-PUBLICATION DATA

Gtsaṅ-smyon He-ru-ka, 1452–1507.
The life of Marpa the translator.

Translation of: Mar-pa-rnam-thar.
Reprint. Originally published: Boulder : Prajña Press, 1982.
1. Mar-pa Chos-kyi-blo-gros, 1012–1097. 2 Bka'-rgyud-pa lamas—China—Tibet—Biography. I. Nalanda Translation Committee. II. Title.
BQ7679.9.M377G7713 1986 294.3'923'0924 [B]
86-11837
ISBN 0-87773-377-5 (pbk.)

CONTENTS

ILLUSTRATIONS

Front cover — *Marpa the Translator.* Detail from a thangka painted by Karshu Gönpo Dorje, from a series of lineage thangkas at Rumtek Monastery in Sikkim, India. Photograph used by the gracious permission of the late His Holiness the Sixteenth Gyalwa Karmapa, Rangjung Rikpe Dorje.

Page 57 — *Dagmema,* the wife of Marpa. Detail from the above thangka by Karshu Gönpo Dorje.

Page 71 — *Kālacakra Monogram.* The stylized monogram of the Kālacakra mantra, known as the All-Powerful Ten, consisting of the syllables HA K-ṢA MA LA VA RA YA-Ṃ.

Page 86 — *Hevajra,* the principal yidam of Marpa. Detail from the above thangka by Karshu Gönpo Dorje.

Page 107 — *Vajravārāhī Shrine at Phamthing.* This shrine building houses a large Vajravārāhī statue, which is said to have been located here since the time of Marpa. Phamthing is presently known as Parpheng, Nepal. Photograph courtesy of Timothy and Elizabeth Olmsted.

Page 157 — *Marpa the Translator.* This is the entire above-mentioned thangka by Karshu Gönpo Dorje. Marpa's principal yidam, Hevajra in consort with Nairātmyā, is in the upper right. Directly above Marpa is the Sekhar, built by Milarepa, and above that is Marpa's dharma center of Trowo valley. On Marpa's left is his wife Dagmema, and below her is his student Ngoktön. To the left, below, are Marpa's students Metön and Tsurtön (bottom). Below, in the middle, is the protectress Vetālī.

Page 268 *Vetālī,* an important mahākālī (protector of the dharma) of the Kagyü lineage since the time of Nāropa and Marpa. Detail from the above thangka by Karshu Gönpo Dorje.

ACKNOWLEDGMENTS

The Life of Marpa the Translator is the first translation to appear in the Biographies of the Ngetön Lineage Series. Ngetön (T: nges-don; S: nītārtha) means "direct, true, or ultimate meaning." In the Tibetan tradition, it refers specifically to the highest level of teachings given by Śākyamuni Buddha during his lifetime, in his various forms as teacher of hīnayāna, mahāyāna, and vajrayāna Buddhism. Thus the teachers of the ngetön lineage are understood to be those Tibetan masters who practiced, studied, realized, and taught these ultimate teachings of the Buddha, thereby causing the buddhadharma to flourish. The great eleventh-century Tibetan teacher, Marpa of Lhotrak, was just such a master, and embodied this ideal in his life in a direct, practical, and unusually complete way. Moreover, he did so through his efforts to "translate" (in both literal and figurative senses) the authentic buddhadharma from India to Tibet. Since this series seeks to further just that same end, rendering the buddhadharma from Tibetan into the Western idiom, it is particularly appropriate that *The Life of Marpa* is the first biography of the present series.

In accordance with the longstanding Buddhist tradition of translation, this work has been produced by a collaborative effort. Within the Nālandā Translation Committee, a core group of translators prepares a first draft, which is then carefully reviewed with Lama Ugyen Shenpen, who is a native of East Tibet and well studied in the English language and all facets of Tibetan Buddhism. Having thus prepared a second working draft, this is presented to the director, Vajrācārya the Venerable Chögyam Trungpa, Rinpoche, and with him we repeat the meticulous reading of the entire text. The Vajrācārya's accomplishment in both Tibetan and English coupled with his own realization sparks a delightful feast of language and meaning. The text is then reworked a number of times by the core group and other members of the committee—revising, editing, and polishing the English. Research into technical matters continues, and many portions of the translation are often scrutinized again by the Vajrācārya.

Following the early directives of the Buddha, we strive to translate into a modern idiom that is both accurate and useful for practitioner and scholar alike. Rather than straining often inadequate and approximate English phraseology for key Buddhist terminology and concepts, we commonly render these in the ancient lingua franca of Buddhist culture, classical Sanskrit. While this demands more from particularly the nonscholarly reader, we feel that only in this way is the precision, accuracy, and brilliance of the teachings left uncompromised. Others may criticize that the Sanskrit does not fully encompass the range of meanings of the Tibetan term; this is often true. However, we try to remedy this potential shortcoming by appending a glossary of such terms, indicating something of the rich and varied meanings given to these words by the living Buddhist tradition of Tibet. Much of the glossary to this volume was originally compiled for *The Rain of Wisdom;* this has been adapted to accord with the terminology found in this biography.

In preparing this translation of *The Life of Marpa the Translator: Seeing Accomplishes All* (T: *sgra-bsgyur mar-pa lo-tsā'i rnam-thar mthong-ba don-yod*) two complete editions were used: a modern handwritten text (Varanasi: E. Kalsang, 1970) and a reproduction of a late nineteenth-century Tengyeling (T: bstan-rgyas gling) edition entitled *Bka'-brgyud-pa Hagiographies,* compiled and edited by Khams-sprul Don-brgyud nyi-ma, Vol. 1 (Tashijong, India: Sungrab Nyamso Gyunphel Parkhang, Tibetan Craft Community, 1972). In addition, two partial editions were consulted: sections of the *Kagyü Gurtso* (T: *bka'-brgyud mgur mtsho;* translated by the Nālandā Translation Committee and published under the title, *The Rain of Wisdom* [Boulder & London: Shambhala, 1980]) and *La Vie de Marpa* (Paris: Librairie Orientaliste Paul Geuthner, 1937) edited and translated by Jacques Bacot. In all these editions, only minor variant readings were found, mainly differences in spelling—a common inconsistency—which, however, did lead to some differences between our translation and that of Bacot. Bacot's French translation has the virtues and faults of a pioneering work. He made the basic life story of Marpa accessible, yet made a number of errors, mostly due to his unfamiliarity with vajrayāna doctrine and practice. Moreover, he only translated roughly one-third of the entire biography and omitted almost all of the songs. These shortcomings have prompted our own efforts to make available in English the entire life example of Marpa the Translator.

Although other members of our committee participated in this translation, most of the work was prepared by a core group consisting of David Cox, Dana Dudley, John Rockwell, Jr., Ives Waldo, and Gerry Wiener, in collaboration with Loppön Lodrö Dorje and myself. We are deeply indebted to the Vajrācārya, Trungpa Rinpoche, and Lama Ugyen Shenpen for their close guidance, care, and wisdom throughout all aspects of this project.

Special thanks are due His Holiness Dingo Khyentse, Rinpoche, and His Eminence the Venerable Shamar Rinpoche for sharing their vast learning with us, clarifying various technical points; Robin Kornman, for his work in amending our Glossary; Reginald A. Ray, chairman of the Buddhist Studies Department of Naropa Institute, for reading the manuscript and making valuable suggestions toward both the form and content of the final presentation; Scott Wellenbach, for his close reading of the final text; Carolyn Rose Gimian, editor-in-chief of Vajradhatu, and Olive Colón, for their invaluable editorial contributions to the entire manuscript; Barbara Bash, for her elegant map drawings; Helen Berliner, for the preparation of the Index; and, in particular, to

John Rockwell, Jr., for his work on the Introduction, Notes, and Maps, as well as serving as the general editor for the entire production. As well, we would like to acknowledge the efforts of the many volunteer typists who prepared the numerous drafts and revisions of our work. Finally, we would like to thank the entire staff of Prajñā Press for their support in facilitating this book.

The richness and diversity of Marpa's life and teachings provide a genuine account of liberation. We hope that this translation will inspire a greater understanding of vajrayāna wisdom, and that it may benefit beings and lead them to the path of buddhadharma.

Larry Mermelstein
Nālandā Translation Committee

Dedicated to His Holiness the Sixteenth
Gyalwang Karmapa

May his blessings continue.
May the full moon of such a rebirth arise soon.

PREFACE

It is my great privilege and honor to present the life of Marpa the Translator. The life of Marpa is a great example of how the Tibetans of ancient times brought the buddhadharma from India to Tibet. It shows how the Tibetans conducted themselves on their journeys, and how much hardship they went through to bring the teachings to Tibet. So Marpa was not purely a translator who translated from Sanskrit to Tibetan, but he actually brought Buddhism to Tibet.

Marpa is one of the great saints in the Buddhist tradition of Tibet. He was a scholar and a practitioner as well as a very practical person, being a farmer and householder. It seems that we don't have any equivalent of him in modern days. Today, you are either a scholar who translates from one language to another, or you are a devotee of a guru who is supposed to transmit the essence of the teachings he has studied. In the West, many scholars would agree that either you become a practitioner or a scholar; you can't be both. If you are a practitioner, you lose your "objective" viewpoint, and if you are a scholar, you lose the heartfelt magic. From that point of view, there is no hope of combining the two. But here, in the life of Marpa, we have a unique story that has been handed down from generation to generation, of how translation and practice can be brought together.

The Tibetans, Chinese, and Japanese throughout history have both translated and practiced, and in these cultures, the belief is that if you don't practice, you can't translate accurately. Therefore practice and translation go hand in hand. There is no particular bias to either side; rather, the idea is that, if you have personal experience of the basic logic or dharma of the teachings, you are in a better position to translate accurately with feeling. We could say that this approach is like a human being singing, as opposed to a computer making the same sound. A computer might be a technically good singer, but we still prefer the human voice.

We hope that presenting Marpa's life and his life example—how he brought Buddhism to Tibet—will be of some use to those who are practicing Buddhism, as well as to those who are purely interested in how Buddhism comes from one culture to another. In turn, at this point, we have a further translation happening, in that Buddhism and Buddhist literature are being translated into the English language. We have done this translation in the hope that it may be able to cross the cultural gap and enlighten people through the profound and powerful messages that come across in the example of Marpa's activity. Hopefully, this work could now be translated into other European languages, as well as Chinese and Japanese.

The working style of translation that we have adopted is to combine precision and accuracy with a certain sense of devotion. Because of this, we have had no need to add anything new or omit anything as irrelevant. Working in this way, we have also found that translating together as a committee is most enjoyable.

I would like to invite the readers to share in what we have found. I am so pleased that we are able to present this work. What we have discovered could be equally yours.

Vajrācārya the Venerable
Chögyam Trungpa, Rinpoche

Tibet & Surrounding Countries

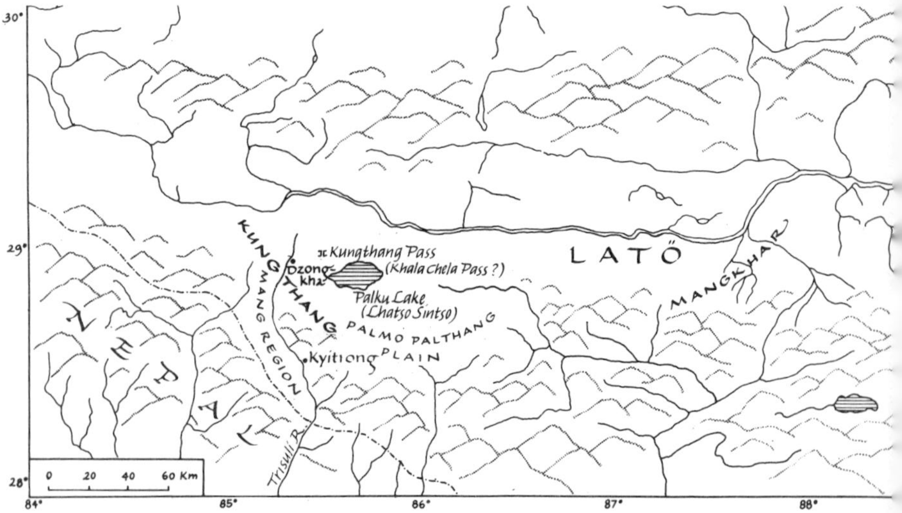

Central Tibet

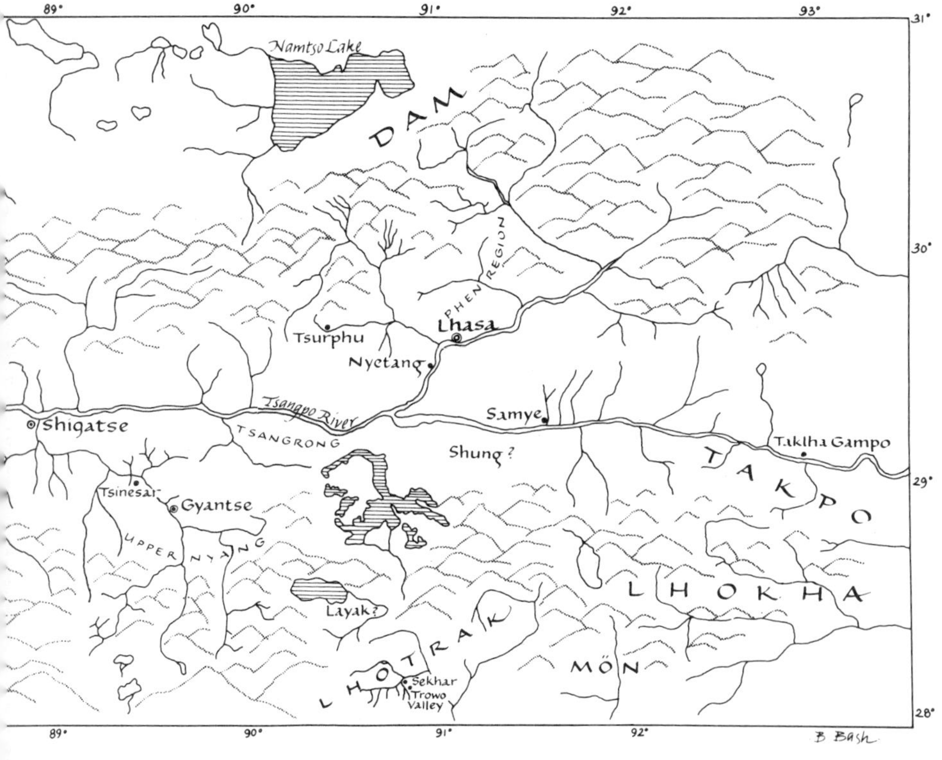

INTRODUCTION

THE *Life of Marpa* was written in Tibet at the beginning of the sixteenth century, a time when a whole school of biographical literature was coming into being. This so-called "school" of biographers originated with the author of our text, who signs his name in this work as "Trakthung Gyalpo [King of Herukas], the yogin who wanders among charnel grounds." He is more commonly known as Tsang Nyön Heruka, or simply as the Mad Yogin of Tsang. Besides his biography of Marpa, his two other biographical works concern Marpa's main disciple, Milarepa: *The Life of Milarepa* and *The Hundred Thousand Songs of Milarepa,** both of which have already been translated and published in English. One other work, *The Life and Teaching of Nāropa,*† written by Lhatsün Rinchen Namgyal, a major disciple of Tsang Nyön, has also been published in an English translation. Nāropa was Marpa's guru, and so with this publication of Marpa's biography, we have three generations of master-disciple relationship before us.

Tsang Nyön had at least four other disciples who, inspired by their teacher's example, each compiled several biographies, including works on such famous teachers as Tilopa, Nāropa, Rechungpa, their guru Tsang Nyön Heruka, and others. It is from their biographies of their teacher that we learn of the life of our author.

* *The Life of Milarepa,* translated by Lobsang P. Lhalungpa (Boulder: Prajñā Press, 1982); *The Hundred Thousand Songs of Milarepa,* translated and annotated by Garma C. C. Chang (Boulder: Shambhala, 1977).

† *The Life and Teaching of Nāropa,* translated from the original Tibetan with philosophical commentary based on the oral transmission by Herbert V. Guenther (London: Oxford University Press, 1963).

TSANG NYÖN HERUKA: AUTHOR, TEACHER, AND MAD YOGIN*

Tsang Nyön Heruka was born in 1452 in Upper Nyang in Tsang (western Tibet). At the age of seven, he was ordained as a novice monk. Later, when he was eighteen, he had a vision that urged him to go on a pilgrimage to the sacred mountain of Tsāri. On his way there, he met with his guru, Shara Rabjampa, who gave him teaching and sent him into retreat to practice. After this retreat and in accordance with his guru's instructions, Tsang Nyön entered a Sakya monastery to continue his studies of the teachings of tantric Buddhism. When he had studied for two or three years, he realized that this monastic way of life was not going to bring him to the fullest realization of these teachings.

On the occasion of a visit to the monastery by his patron prince with his court, Tsang Nyön displayed such wild and insulting behavior that he was expelled from the monastery. From that time on, he lived an eccentric, varied, and productive life. He traveled a great deal, covering much of Tibet and visiting Nepal several times. Most of his time, he spent in retreat in western Tibet, especially at the holy places where Milarepa practiced. It is obvious from the lifestyle he adopted, the places he frequented, and especially from the amount of energy he devoted to compiling the biography and realization songs of Milarepa that Tsang Nyön identified very closely with Milarepa. He completed both these works on Milarepa when he was thirty-seven (1488).†

*Our outline of Tsang Nyön's life is based on *The Life of the Saint of Gtsaṅ* by Rgod-tshaṅ-ras-pa Sna-tshogs-raṅ-grol; edited by Lokesh Chandra, with a preface by E. Gene Smith; Śata-piṭaka Series, Indo-Asian Literatures, Vol. 79 (New Delhi: 1969). Gene Smith's preface is especially helpful and informative and has three detailed appendices: one on the editions of Milarepa's biography (rnam-thar) and his collection of songs (mgur-'bum), one on the biographical works by Tsang Nyön and his school, and one listing the contents of two collections of Kagyü biographies.

†This date is based on Milarepa's biography, which was written in the Phurba year (Earth Male Monkey). Mila's collection of songs (mgur-'bum) is undated,

Later, Tsang Nyön worked for many years on a multivolumed compilation of the teachings of the hearing lineage (T: snyan-brgyud). These teachings, connected with the *Cakrasaṃvara-tantra,* were special instructions that Marpa received from his guru, Nāropa, on his last trip to India. Marpa passed them on to his main disciple, Milarepa, who in turn gave them to three of his major disciples—Gampopa, Rechungpa, and the teacher of Ngen Dzong. Tsang Nyön himself belonged to the lineage passed down through Rechungpa.

Through his travels, his writings, his attainment, and his unconventional behavior, Tsang Nyön became renowned throughout both Tibet and Nepal. He attracted many disciples and was patronized by several royal families. At one point, he was called upon to mediate between rivaling factions during these troubled political times. Requesting a highly accomplished teacher to act as an impartial mediator (T: gzu-ba) was frequently done in Tibet to settle all kinds of disputes.*

Around 1505, during his last years, Tsang Nyön dictated the biography and songs of Marpa. He did this at Chuwar, one of the famous caves where Milarepa had meditated. He died two years later, at the age of fifty-four (1507), at Rechung Phuk (Cave of Rechungpa).

The Nature and Intent of Tibetan Biography

It is interesting and helpful to examine the question of why Tsang Nyön and his disciples devoted so much time in compiling these biographies. What is the nature of these biographies that makes them so important? Why should we be interested in reading them?

The word for biography in Tibetan is namthar (T: rnam-thar, short for rnam-par thar-pa), which literally means "complete

---

but was evidently finished around the same time since both the biography and songs were first printed together as one volume.

*See R. A. Stein, *Tibetan Civilization* (Stanford: Stanford University Press, 1972), pp. 146-7.

liberation." This clearly shows the intent of Tibetan biography. The central concern is to portray the spiritual development and fruition of the person's life. This is why enlightening dreams and visions are often to be found as part of a biography. Moreover, this explains why songs are included as a central part of the biography. As we shall later discuss, spontaneous song was a traditional way of communicating an experience or teaching of spiritual significance.

Being a spiritual biography, it serves as a "supreme example for sincere beings."* Seeing the example of how Marpa or Milarepa overcame their own personal obstacles can inspire later spiritual practitioners in their own efforts to attain complete liberation. In this way, Marpa's or Mila's life story becomes a teaching to be studied and contemplated, since it can spark one's own realization. This liberating quality that comes from reading these biographies is stated in the title of Marpa's biography, *Seeing Accomplishes All (T: Mthong-ba don-yod).* The meaning of this pithy title is that merely seeing or reading this biography can accomplish one's purpose, which is to awaken enlightenment. This is the intent with which Tibetan authors write these biographies, or namthars.

In his own time, Tsang Nyön became dissatisfied with the restrictive pattern that Buddhism was taking, to the detriment of keeping the heart of the teachings alive. By the fifteenth and sixteenth centuries, monasteries in Tibet were not only the repositories of spiritual learning and practice, but were also the bastions of secular power. They had become wealthy and powerful, and so political disputes between rivaling monasteries were not uncommon. At times like these, the practice of meditation was sometimes forgotten or considered secondary.

When Tsang Nyön took up the lifestyle of the crazy yogin, the nyönpa (T: smyon-pa, "madman"), he devoted his life primarily to meditation in solitude. It seems clear that he

*This quote is from Tsang Nyön's colophon to this work (see p. 204).

wanted to break free from the busier and more regulated life of the monastic scholar and as well from any involvement in political power and wealth. In taking this step, he was not alone. During the fifteenth century, there were many other nyönpas, of whom three were as renowned as Tsang Nyön. They were Thangtong Gyalpo* (1385-1464 or 1361-1485?, also known as Lungtong Nyönpa, "Madman of the Empty Valley"), Druk Nyön Künga Lekpa† (1455-1529, otherwise known as Drukpa Künlek), and Ü Nyön Künga Zangpo (1458–?).‡ Moreover, the appearance of the nyönpa was not a new occurrence, but can be traced back to India, in particular to the tradition of the eighty-four mahāsiddhas (who will be discussed below) and probably much earlier. It seems that for as long as there have been practitioners who chose to live within the monastic structure, there also have been those who chose to live outside it. Over time, they have served to counterbalance each other in preserving the practice and teachings of the Buddha.

In Tibet, Milarepa was the exemplar of the crazy yogin who devoted his life to meditation in mountain solitudes. He epitomized the style of the nyönpa—unconventional, uninhibited, full of earthy humor, skilled in teaching through song and story-telling, and possessing great insight into the nature of the world through his intensive practice.§ In his biographies of Marpa and Milarepa, Tsang Nyön has masterfully woven many of

*Thangtong Gyalpo's life and teachings are described in an unpublished master's thesis by Cyrus Stearns, "The Life and Teachings of the Tibetan Saint Thang-stong rgyal-po, 'King of the Empty Plain'" (University of Washington, 1980).

†The best work on Drukpa Künlek is *Vie et Chants de 'Brug-pa Kun-legs Le Yogin* by R. A. Stein (Paris: G.-P. Maisonneuve et Larose, 1972).

‡As for Ü Nyön, Gene Smith in his preface to Tsang Nyön's biography (p. 3, n. 5) mentions that there is a biography of Ü Nyön by Bshes-gnyen rnam-rgyal of about eighty folia. To our knowledge, this has not yet been translated or studied.

§In a meeting with Phadampa Sanggye, a famous Indian yogin, Milarepa sang a delightful and humorous song about the craziness of himself, his lineage forefathers, and their realization. See *The Hundred Thousand Songs of Milarepa,* vol. 2, pp. 610-613.

the qualities of the nyönpa into their stories. He uses a more colloquial style of language in both the prose and songs, infuses the plot with lively humor and human pathos, and delights in describing both the details of ordinary life and the profound wisdom of the solitary practitioner. It is no wonder that these biographies have been extemely popular among all Tibetans.

Tsang Nyön has not only created masterpieces of literature, but has also portrayed the profound and heartfelt spiritual development of two great teachers and practitioners. Marpa was a farmer and layman; Mila was an ascetic, a renunciant. Each of them forged his own path based on who he was and what his resources were. Tsang Nyön held their life examples up, not as lifestyles or forms for one to imitate, but as examples of how one's life—anyone's life—could be devoted wholeheartedly to the practice and realization of the buddhadharma.

THE SPREAD OF BUDDHISM IN TIBET

Tibet, the land of Marpa's birth, has long been a country that is remote and difficult to reach. In the South, it is separated from India and Nepal by the great Himalayan mountain range. In the West and North, it is bordered by the Karakorum and Kunlun ranges. In the East, there are a series of smaller ranges and stretches of sparsely settled land. But besides mountains, Tibet was, at one time, also a land surrounded by either Buddhist countries or areas heavily influenced by Buddhism. Most notably, there were China, the Tarim Basin (where the Silk Route crossed from China to India), Kashmir, Nepal, and India. Though geographically remote, Tibet was by no means culturally isolated. Long before Tibetans actively sought to acquire the teachings of the Buddha, opportunities for contact with Buddhist and other ideas and forms were present.

According to traditional accounts,* Buddhism made its debut in Tibet when some Buddhist texts and a small stūpa fell from the sky onto the roof of the royal palace. At that time, no one knew how to read the texts, since Tibet did not even have a written form for its own language yet. A Tibetan alphabet and grammar were formulated around 632 A.D., after the model of an Indian language, and gradually, Buddhist ideas began to penetrate the Tibetan mind more deeply, beginning in the eighth century. In time, Buddhist teachers from India, such as Śāntarakṣita and Padmasambhava, and from China and elsewhere were invited to Tibet to teach, and Tibetan students were sent abroad to study. Eventually, the first Tibetan monastery, Samye, was constructed in 779, the first seven Tibetan monks were ordained, and translations of Buddhist texts were undertaken. According to tradition, by 792, the Tibetans had chosen to commit themselves solely to the Indian tradition of Buddhism over and against the Chinese tradition, which had also been taught in Tibet up to that time. The end result of all these developments was that Indian Buddhism was officially declared the state religion by King Trisong Detsen. This marked the climax of what was called the "first spreading" of Buddhism in Tibet.

The success of this first spreading was short-lived. In 836, Langdarma assumed the throne and initiated a period in which Buddhism was suppressed. The monasteries were emptied, and the monks and nuns were forced to become lay people or were exiled. Though information is scanty, it does appear that the practice and study of Buddhism did survive among the lay population, yet Buddhism ceased to exist as an organized and visible institution during this time. Even worse, after Langdarma's

*Two of the greatest Tibetan historians are Butön (1290-1364) and Gö Lotsāwa Shönnu Pal (1392-1481). Butön's *History of Buddhism* (chos-'byung) has been translated into English by Dr. E. Obermiller (Heidelberg: O. Harrassowitz, 1931-2). *The Blue Annals* by Gö Lotsāwa has been translated into English by George N. Roerich (Delhi: Motilal Banarsidass, 1976).

assassination in 842, Tibet entered a dark age of feudal fragmentation and civil war. Nevertheless, by 978, the embers of Buddhism began to be rekindled in different parts of Tibet. This was the beginning of the "second spreading" of Buddhism in Tibet, in which Marpa was to play a prominent role.

MARPA'S BIRTH AND ENTRY INTO THE DHARMA

Marpa was born in 1012 in the region of Lhotrak. This region is in the extreme south of Tibet, right above the border of Bhutan. It is a region of forests and fertile farmland, of agriculture and grazing flocks and herds. Marpa's parents were wealthy landowners, with both farmland in the lowlands and grazing pasture in the highlands. As Marpa was an aggressive child, his parents decided to entrust him to a dharmic training, lest he become too aggressive and destructive. Thus Marpa began his education at the age of twelve, and received his Buddhist name, Chökyi Lodrö (Intellect of Dharma). True to his name, Marpa quickly mastered both reading and writing. But as he had still not mastered his temper, his parents finally encouraged him to go far away to western Tibet to study the dharma further. To this, Marpa readily agreed.

At this time, there were several monastic and educational institutions in Tibet. A few Tibetans, such as Drogmi, Marpa's first teacher, had traveled to India to study with the Buddhist scholars and yogins, and had returned learned and well trained. Drogmi had established his monastery in Nyugu valley in 1043. He was well versed in vajrayāna Buddhism, but his speciality was the teachings of "path and fruition" (T: lam-'bras), which later became the philosophical foundation for the teachings of the Sakya lineage. Drogmi was also a "lotsāwa," a translator, and while in Tibet, he translated a great number of texts now found in the Tibetan Buddhist canon.

Marpa came to Nyugu valley to study with Drogmi around 1054 and stayed three years with him, learning Sanskrit and several colloquial languages of India. This was the foundation of Marpa's own training as a lotsāwa. He then became frustrated with his inability to receive the further teachings that he desired. Being a practical person, Marpa decided to go to receive teachings from the best source—India.

Here and elsewhere, the biography points out the nature of Marpa's personality. In all his activity, Marpa is shown as not holding anything back. His style is depicted as uninhibited, direct, and stubborn. When he saw what he wanted, he went after it. When he saw what needed to be done, he did it. Thus, early in his life, he saw that the dharma was true and worthwhile, and sought it wholeheartedly. Realizing that he would have to make the long and dangerous journey to India to obtain the dharma, he did not hesitate to go. Having converted most of his possessions into gold and overcome the objections of his parents, Marpa began the first of his three journeys to India.

MARPA TRAVELS TO INDIA

Making the journey to India was no easy task, as Marpa attested in several of his songs. Leaving from Lhotrak, he had to travel over three hundred miles to the western edge of Tibet, at Kungthang. Though there were many plains and mountains to cross, Marpa remembered in particular the large desolate plain of Palmo Palthang and the high, snowy pass of Khala Chela (probably over 15,000 feet) in the region of Kungthang. Then, following the Trisuli river valley down to Kyitrong and into Nepal, Marpa descended quickly into the humid and hot foothills of Nepal. This complete change of altitude and climate could be quite dramatic for a Tibetan, and often led to sickness. Therefore Marpa stayed for three years in Kathmandu to acclimatize himself to the heat, before descending further to the even hotter plains of India. It was here in Nepal that Marpa's karmic connection to his guru, Nāropa, was reawakened through meeting two of Nāropa's disciples, Chitherpa and

Paiṇḍapa. These two Nepalese teachers gave Marpa a great deal of dharma and language instruction, and then sent him to meet Nāropa in India.

On the border of Nepal and India, Marpa encountered famine and greedy tax collectors. And throughout his journey, he faced the dangers of bandits, wild animals, swollen rivers, sheer precipices, rickety bridges, and the like. Overall, he certainly traveled over seven hundred miles and descended over 10,000 feet in elevation to reach Phullahari, the place where his guru Nāropa lived.

A final danger that Marpa encountered on his first trip was a difficult traveling companion. Partway across Tibet, Marpa met Nyö of Kharak who traveled with him all the way to India, and later, in India, became Marpa's rival in mastery of the dharma. Though Marpa reaped a temporary benefit in traveling with Nyö, the end result was rather different, as we shall see below.

Buddhism of India

The situation in India that Marpa and Nyö were to encounter was quite a contrast to that in Tibet. About 1,500 years had passed since the time when Śākyamuni Buddha had first turned the wheel of dharma, at the Deer Park in Benares. Buddhism had grown from a small gathering of wandering ascetics into an array of monastic centers supported by a broad-based lay community. Buddhism had spread throughout India and beyond its borders to other countries, including Ceylon, Nepal, Kashmir, China, Korea, Japan, and elsewhere.

In India itself, Marpa arrived during a time when two developments were prominent. The first was the great importance and prestige of the monastic universities such as Nālandā, Vikramaśīla, Bodhgayā, and Otantapurī. Nālandā was the oldest of these, dating back to the sixth century. Its fame had attracted Chinese and other pilgrims for centuries. Now it was mainly the Tibetans who journeyed to study and learn. Besides teaching the Buddhist scriptures, these universities were repositories of many aspects of Indian learning. They encompassed many disciplines, including the fine arts, linguistics and philology, science, medicine, and debate.

Moreover, in these universities, and in particular at Vikramaśīla, the teachings of vajrayāna Buddhism (whose nature will be discussed below) were taught. This was the other major development taking place in India at this time. From being an esoteric development in Buddhist tradition, vajrayāna, or tantra, had been accepted and incorporated into the mainstream monastic institutions. Therefore many learned scholars, "paṇḍitas," studied and expounded on the tantras, the root texts of vajrayāna outlook and practice, and soon a vast literature of commentaries and practice liturgies came into being. It was to study the vajrayāna with these teachers at the great universities that Marpa and other Tibetans came to India.

However, because of Marpa's karmic connection to his guru Nāropa, his path took a slightly different direction than one might expect. Upon his arrival in India, Marpa went directly to study with Nāropa, who was living at Phullahari northwest of Nālandā. Nyö, Marpa's traveling companion, remarked disdainfully that Nāropa used to be a great paṇḍita at Nālandā, but now was practicing kusulu meditation under Tilopa. Tilopa was Nāropa's guru, and a kusulu was a yogin who attended to only the barest physical necessities so that he could spend as much time as possible in meditation. His activity was often unconventional in other regards as well. Rather than paṇḍitas, both Tilopa and Nāropa were considered to be mahāsiddhas, the embodiments of the highest realization of vajrayāna teachings.

VAJRAYĀNA AND THE MAHĀSIDDHA TRADITION

The vajrayāna teachings date back to around the sixth and seventh centuries, when the root texts of vajrayāna, the tantras, surfaced in India. However, since vajrayāna relies primarily on the secret oral instructions given by master to disciple, it is likely that the appearance of written instructions was a later phase, and that the actual practice probably predated this. It is said that Śākyamuni Buddha manifested as Vajradhara, the primordial buddha, to teach vajrayāna to a few advanced students. The tantras, which are records of these teachings, do not tend to present a dialogue between enlightenment and confusion, as in the early teachings of the Buddha. Instead, they present the view of fruition, of complete enlightenment.

Vajrayāna literally means "indestructible vehicle." The word vajra signifies the indestructible actuality of enlightenment. In vajrayāna, enlightenment is not regarded as something potential in the world or in oneself. Rather it is completely manifest and self-evident in all aspects of life. The world, the body, and one's state of mind are all vajra-like, primordially pure and self-liberated from dualistic confusion. The view that sees this primordial purity of experience is called sacred outlook (T: dag-snang) and it is the essence of vajrayāna practice and realization.

Vajrayāna is an indestructible *vehicle* because it uses the view of fruition, sacred outlook, as the path to enlightenment. This view of the fundamental sacredness of the world and experience is first transmitted to the disciple by his or her guru. With this uncovering of the primordial purity of phenomena, everything in one's life becomes workable and can be included as a stepping stone on the path of liberation.

Accordingly, a wide range of approaches were available to the practitioner of vajrayāna. This variety can be seen by looking through the lives of the famed eighty-four mahāsiddhas,* the Indian forefathers of vajrayāna practice and realization. A

*There are two main accounts of the stories of the eighty-four mahāsiddhas. The first was written in the late eleventh or early twelfth century by the Indian Abhayadatta. It was subsequently translated into Tibetan by the monk Smon-grub Shes-rab and was included in the Tenjur of the Tibetan Buddhist canon. Presently, it has been translated into English by James B. Robinson and published under the title *Buddha's Lions* (Berkeley: Dharma Press, 1979).

The other account comes from the great historian and scholar Tāranātha (1575-?). He groups his stories of the siddhas according to the lineage of teachings to which they belong. Thus, his work is called *The Seven Special* mahāsiddha was a "great accomplished or perfected one." The special quality of the siddhas was their ability to skillfully use any aspect of the world as a vehicle to liberate themselves and others. Because of this, they were said to possess great magical powers called siddhis, of which there are two types. Ordinary siddhis involve a fundamental mastery over phenomena. For example, Virūpa stopped the sun as he drank an enormous amount of liquor, Ḍombī Heruka rode on a tigress and could not even be scorched by a large bonfire. The supreme siddhi is enlightenment itself.

Though there were certainly more than eighty-four mahāsiddhas, the life stories of these eighty-four were widely renowned and so were written down. Amongst this group, there were wandering yogins who lived on the fringes of society, as well as many people who practiced tantra while engaging in their everyday activities and jobs. They were scholars, carpenters, monks, blacksmiths, kings, beggars, housewives, craftsmen, and so on. They were high caste, low caste, and outcaste. Their personalities also covered a wide range. Some were passionate, some were aggressive, some were ambitious, and some were just plain lazy. Yet through the sacred outlook and skillful means of the vajrayāna, they were each able to use their temperament and worldly activity as a vehicle for meditation practice and the attainment of the supreme siddhi, enlightenment.

Tilopa: The Guru of Nāropa

Tilopa is included among the eighty-four siddhas.* He began his Buddhist training as a monk and spent twelve years in strict

---

Transmissions (Bka'-babs bdun-ldan). We have utilized a translation-in-progress of this work by the Nālandā Translation Committee (from the Tibetan edition *Five Historical Works of Tāranātha* [Arunachal Pradesh, India: Tibetan Nyingma Monastery, pp. 361-499]).

Other related works in English are G. Tucci's *Tibetan Painted Scrolls* (Rome: La Libreria dello Stato, 1949). and T. Schmid's *The Eighty-five Siddhas* (Stockholm: Statens Etnografiska Museum, 1958).

*The stories of Tilopa's life as well as of the other mahāsiddhas are all quite short in both Abhayadatta's and Tāranātha's works (see note above).

meditation at Somapuri. After this, he actualized his path by engaging in the everyday world completely. For another twelve years, he continued his meditation practice as he pounded sesame seeds by day, and by night acted as the procurer for a prostitute. Unifying his meditation practice with his daily activity, he thus attained ultimate realization. He then wandered throughout India, and in particular Bengal, usually teaching with miraculous and outrageously direct methods. Tilopa was the forefather of the Kagyü lineage, that is, the particular teachings that were successively passed down to Nāropa, Marpa, Milarepa, and so on. Tilopa had no human root guru, as it is said he received transmission and instruction directly from Vajradhara, the primordial buddha. In addition, Tilopa did have four main teachers from whom he received four different lineages of teachings. These four special transmissions (T: bka'-babs bzhi)* plus some other special oral instructions are part of the legacy that he handed down to his main disciple, Nāropa.

Therefore, for the details of Tilopa's life, we have relied heavily on our forthcoming translation of Padma Karpo's account in his history of the buddhadhrma in India and Tibet, *Chos-'byung bstan-pa'i padma rgyas-pa'i nyin-byed* (vol. 2, Ka of the *Collected Works* [gsuṅ-'bum] *of Kun-Mkhyen Padma-dkar-po,* pp. 226:3-250:5) (Darjeeling: Kargyud Sungrab Nyamso Khang, 1973). Another similar and even more lengthy biography, also in progress, was written by Wangchuk Gyaltsen, one of Tsang Nyön's disciples, in 1523 at Dzari Samten Ling. It is contained in a *Bka'-brgyud gser-'phreng* from Gemur monastery in Kinnaur (Delhi: 1975).

*There are several different accounts of the four special transmissions of Tilopa. All agree that Tilopa received four sets of yogic practices from various gurus, which he transmitted to his principal disciple, Nāropa. The four special transmissions became the primary source for the six yogas of Nāropa (T: Nā-ro chos drug). Often the four special transmissions are said to comprise the yogas of illusory body, dream, luminosity, and caṇḍālī.

One of the most extensive descriptions of the four special transmissions is given by Wangchuk Gyaltsen in his biography of Tilopa (see previous note). He delineates two sets of four special transmissions, one ordinary and the other extraordinary. The ordinary four special transmissions (T: thun-mongs kyi bka'-babs bzhi), together with their respective lineage of teachers are: (1) mahāmudrā (Lord of Secret [Vajrapāṇi], Saraha, Lohipa [Lūyipa], Dārika, Dingkapa [Ṭeṅgipa]), (2) father tantra (bodhisattva Ratnamati, Nāgārjuna,

Nāropa: The Guru of Marpa

The life of Nāropa, who was also a mahāsiddha, is similar in many ways. He first trained for a long time within the traditional monastic framework, eventually rising to the apex of scholarly accomplishment. He was appointed one of the four academic gatekeepers at Nālandā and Vikramaśīla universities*

Mātaṅgī), (3) mother tantra (Sumati, Shinglopa, Thanglopa, Karnaripa), and (4) luminosity (Birvapa [Virūpa], Ḍombīpa, Bhinasa, Lavapa, Indrabodhi [Indrabhūti]). Thus Tilopa's gurus for these teachings were Dingkapa, Mātaṅgī, Karnaripa, and Indrabodhi.

The extraordinary four special transmissions (T: thun-mongs ma yin-pa'i bka'-babs bzhi) are connected with Tilopa's receiving the practices of the six yogas. They are: (1) caṇḍālī and dream yogas, from Kṛṣṇācārya, (2) illusory body yoga and father tantra, from Nāgārjuna, (3) luminosity yoga and nondual tantra, from Lavapa, and (4) ejection and pardo yogas and mother tantra, from Sumati Samantabhadrī.

Other sources for information regarding the four special transmissions include Padma Karpo's biography of Tilopa (see previous note) and his *Jo-bo nā-ro-pa'i khyad-chos bsre-'pho'i khrid rdo-rje'i theg-par bgrod-pa'i shing-rta* (fol. 2a sqq., as referred to in *The Life and Teaching of Nāropa* by Herbert V. Guenther, p. 37, n. 1) as well as Tilopa's own work, the *Ṣaḍdharmopadeśa* (Bstan-'gyur, Peking Tripiṭaka No. 4630 and *Gdams-ngag mdzod,* vol. 5, pp. 106-7).

As for the ḍākinī hearing lineage teachings that Tilopa also received, see notes on pp. 90 and 176.

*Our sources for Nāropa's life story have primarily been *The Life and Teaching of Nāropa.* According to this text (p. 20), the four academic gatekeepers were: East—Prajñākara, South—Kṛṣṇācārya, West—Ratnākaraśānti, and North—Nāropa. Moreover, these gatekeepers are said to have resided at Nālandā.

Tāranātha in his *History of Buddhism in India* translated by Lama Chimpa and Alaka Chattopadhyaya (Simla: Indian Institute of Advanced Study, 1970) mentions six gatekeepers at Vikramaśīla (pp. 295-303) East—Ratnākaraśānti, South—Prajñākaramati, West—Vāgīśvarakīrti, North—Nāropa, as well as Ratnavajra who dwells on a great central pillar and Jñānaśrīmitra who dwells on a second great central pillar.

The Blue Annals also mentions these six gatekeepers, though reversing the South and West gatekeepers (p. 206).

Thus, though the lists vary somewhat, they are all in agreement in placing Nāropa at the northern gate. Whether these gatekeepers were at Nālandā and/or Vikramaśīla monastery is still unclear. Tāranātha in his *Bka'-babs bdun-ldan* (p. 424:1) writes that Nāropa was the northern gatekeeper at both Nālandā and Vikramaśīla. In *Buddhist Monks and Monasteries in India,* (p. 360) S. Dutt also mentions the possibility of this sort of arrangement.

and was recognized as the most learned of all. Still, his great learning did not satisfy him, and one day he had a vision of an ugly hag, who questioned his understanding of the teachings. He then realized that he had not mastered the experience behind the words. Abandoning the cloistered life of the monastic university, Nāropa set out in search of a master who had experienced and could teach the true meaning behind the words.

This teacher he found in Tilopa. With this uncompromising master, he underwent twelve major and twelve minor trials. Most of these trials involved tremendous physical hardship that resulted from some outrageous action he was compelled by his guru to perform. After each trial, Tilopa rectified the physical hardship Nāropa suffered and gave him a particular instruction. Finally, after twelve years, Nāropa's pride and ego-clinging were utterly destroyed and his realization of the awakened state of mind was uncovered. Now endowed with the rigorous intellectual training of a paṇḍita and the fearless realization and skillful means of an accomplished yogin, Nāropa left Tilopa, established himself at Phullahari, and began teaching. This is where Marpa found him.

MARPA MEETS WITH NĀROPA, BECOMES HIS REGENT, AND RECEIVES TEACHINGS

Marpa's coming to India and his worthiness as a disciple had already been prophesied to Nāropa by Tilopa. Therefore, Nāropa immediately welcomed Marpa to assume the role of his regent, the future lineage holder. He then gave Marpa abhiṣekas, which are empowerments to practice certain vajrayāna teachings, and oral instructions.

The idea of lineage and devotion to a teacher is very important to examine here, especially in relation to the teachings and abhiṣekas that Marpa received. In order for a student to be trained in vajrayāna practice, he must first make a personal connection with an authentic teacher of a lineage. Belonging to a lineage means that the teacher has himself been trained properly in the practice by his own teacher, and so has the experience and realization to guide his students. Moreover, the innermost essence of the practice is always communicated personally and is rarely written down. Therefore, only a teacher who possesses the oral intructions of the lineage and who has realized their truth can fully empower a student to do this practice.

Abhiṣeka and Yidam Practice

The means by which a teacher empowers the student is abhiṣeka. Abhiṣeka literally means "sprinkling over" and signifies anointment, or empowerment (T: dbang). It is a ritual ceremony by which the vajra master, the guru, enters the disciple into the maṇḍala, the sacred world, of the guru and yidam. A yidam is a deity that expresses the actuality of sacred world in visual form. The appearance of this deity or yidam can represent different aspects or energies of enlightenment. They can be peaceful, semiwrathful, or wrathful. Peaceful yidams have gentle, smiling countenances. They are elegantly adorned with beautiful clothes and regal ornaments, and usually assume a meditative posture. Their forms communicate the open and accommodating energy of compassionate wisdom. On the other hand, semiwrathful and wrathful yidams have grimacing expressions, can hold weapons of various kinds, assume a dancing posture, and so on. They dynamically embody the uncompromising and penetrating quality of compassionate wisdom.

The teacher may empower a disciple with a certain type of yidam to suit the particular characteristics of that student. In Marpa's case, his personal yidam, Hevajra, was a semiwrathful yidam. In any case, the yidam serves as the enlightened manifestation of the student's basic being. It is not an external deity that is being worshipped so that one can be saved. Rather it is a vivid representation of one's own enlightened nature. Having been empowered by his teacher, the student identifies his body, speech, and mind completely with that of the yidam, and so progressively arouses an unshakable confidence in his own awakened nature.

Moreover, through receiving abhiṣeka, the student is not only introduced to this sacred world, but he binds himself to it irrevocably. He takes a vow, called samaya, to commit himself totally to his guru and likewise to the yidam that he has received, and is now empowered to practice. In essence, the yidam is inseparable from the guru. As the teacher not only compassionately guides the student through his practice, but is also the very embodiment of the fruition of the practice, the student naturally regards his teacher with great trust and devotion. Without the guru, there would be no teachings and no path. Therefore devotion makes possible the transmission of sacred outlook, enlightened mind, from guru to disciple. Devotion to one's guru is thus the ground, path, and fruition of vajrayāna and especially in the Kagyü lineage.

MARPA VISITS OTHER TEACHERS

Jñānagarbha and Kukkurīpā

Having received abhiṣeka from Nāropa, Marpa was spurred on by his rivalry with his former companion, Nyö, to seek out two other traditions of practice, namely the *Guhyasamāja* and *Mahāmāyā*. (These names are both the name of the yidam and of the tantra, the text that describes the practice of this yidam.) First, Marpa received the abhiṣeka and instructions on the *Guhyasamāja-tantra* from Jñānagarbha, who was also a great scholar and translator. Then he overcame great obstacles to receive the abhiṣeka and instructions on the *Mahāmāyā-tantra* from the eccentric yogin Kukkurīpā.

Kukkurīpā was another teacher of Marpa, whose life story is included among those of the eighty-four mahāsiddhas.* Previously, Kukkurīpā had spent many years meditating in a cave, accompanied only by a female puppy that he had found starving and had taken into his care. At one point, through his compassionate concern for this dog, he was freed from the blissful trap of a meditative attainment that was not complete enlightenment. The dog then transformed into a ḍākinī, a spiritual messenger or protector, and gave him instructions, thus bringing him to the highest realization. Kukkurīpā's close association with dogs became his trademark, and it is said that he lived with a large number of them on his secluded island in the center of a poison lake. This is where Marpa finally found him, and their meeting was lively and filled with Kukkurīpā's playful jesting.

It is interesting to note that though Nāropa was able to give Marpa the teachings on Guhyasamāja and Mahāmāyā, he initially declined to do so. Instead, he sent Marpa to the teacher who had specialized in that particular tantra as that person was the "pure source." Later, Marpa received these teachings from Nāropa and found them the same in essence as what he had already received. Marpa was made to work hard to obtain these teachings and so came to appreciate their preciousness and did not regard them as spiritual trophies to collect. Nyö, Marpa's antagonist, did not possess this attitude; hence, he later lacked the merit and karmic connection to find Kukkurīpā and receive teaching from him.

Marpa Meets Maitrīpa, His Other Main Guru

After returning from Kukkurīpā, Marpa received Nāropa's permission to go and study with Maitrīpa, who became Marpa's second main guru, almost as important as Nāropa. When he

* We have taken this story of Kukkurīpā from *Buddha's Lions,* Abhayadatta's biographies of the eighty-four siddhas (pp. 128-30). Tāranātha's story of Kukkurīpā is basically similar, and is found on p. 451:1-6.

first entered the dharma, Maitrīpa had been a student of Nāropa at Nālandā. Later, at Vikramaśīla, during the time when Atīśa was the head disciplinary monk, it seems that Maitrīpa was reprimanded and forced to leave for drinking liquor and consorting with women. Upon leaving, Maitrīpa placed a leather cushion on the surface of the Ganges river and departed across the water. After undergoing further training under his guru Śavari, he completely assumed the unconventional lifestyle of a mahāsiddha and was recognized by all as an enlightened master of the teachings of mahāmudrā.*

The Tradition of Dohās and Mahāmudrā

After arriving at the Blazing Fire Mountain monastery, Marpa received instruction on two important traditions from Maitrīpa. The first tradition is the vajrayāna practice of singing spontaneous songs of experience and realization, which are known as dohās. These dohās are generally sung at a gaṇacakra, a feast offering that is celebrated by a group of tantric practitioners on auspicious occasions or after special sessions of intensive practice. Traditionally, in India, these songs were often short and sung in a secret, tantric, code language, much like the one that Nāropa sang to Marpa before his second return to Tibet. With Marpa, they became more narrative and longer, using more straightforward language. Marpa eventually passed on this tradition of dohās to his main disciple, Milarepa, who also gave these songs his personal stamp. Being spontaneous, these songs reveal the inner nature of the singer and express his insight and devotion in an uninhibited and unique fashion. Because they are born out of the realization that comes from practicing the guru's oral

*Our source for this story of Maitrīpa is Tāranātha's *Bka'-babs bdun-ldan* (pp. 374:4-377:3). Maitrīpa does not seem to be included among Abhayadatta's eighty-four siddhas. In T. Schmid's book *The Eighty-Five Siddhas,* Maitrīpa is equated with the sixty-second siddha, Avadhūtipa, which is another common name for him.

instructions, they are also profound and direct in their ability to transform and awaken the mind of the listener. They direct the listener's attention to the nature of mind, at that very instant. In this way, their message is universal, even though merely giving a hint of the singer's complete experience.

The second tradition that Marpa received from Maitrīpa is the teachings of mahāmudrā, which are extremely important for both Marpa and the Kagyü lineage. Generally, there are two lineages of which Marpa was a holder. The first lineage began with Vajradhara, the primordial buddha, and was passed to Tilopa, Nāropa, and then to Marpa. This is called the direct lineage (T: nye-brgyud) and is concerned primarily with the four special transmissions of Tilopa and the six yogas of Nāropa (all of whose practices derive from the former). The teachings of mahāmudrā are also found within this lineage. The second lineage, the indirect lineage (T: ring-brgyud), has as its central focus the transmission of the mahāmudrā teachings. It also originated with Vajradhara, but then was passed down through Ratnamati, Saraha, Nāgārjuna, and Śavaripa, who gave it to Maitrīpa.

THE VIEW, MEDITATION, ACTION, AND FRUITION OF MAHĀMUDRĀ

Mahāmudrā literally means "great symbol, seal, or gesture." According to the *Cakrasaṃvara-tantra, mu* is the wisdom of emptiness, *drā* is freedom from saṃsāra, and *mahā* is their indivisibility. When reality is realized to be empty and free from saṃsāric confusion, it becomes the greatest symbol of all, a self-existing symbol of enlightened nature.

After practicing the teachings he received from Maitrīpa, Marpa sang of his realization of mahāmudrā, outlining its view, meditation, action, and fruition.* First, he sang:

*This song is found on pp. 29-30. The commentary that follows is derived in part from the teachings of the Vajrācārya Chögyam Trungpa, Rinpoche.

This unceasing dharmatā
Is unobstructed, self-luminous insight.
Within innate insight, unity,
Spontaneous wisdom is the view.

Dharmatā is the ground of things as they are. It is not created nor is it destroyed; therefore it is "unceasing." It is the ground of all, all-pervading like space. It is beyond any duality, such as confusion and liberation, saṃsāra and nirvāṇa. The awareness of this ground is insight, essentially empty, but by nature luminous. As such, it is the unity of both luminosity and emptiness. Since in emptiness no essence exists anywhere, luminosity, the expression of dharmatā, is completely unobstructed and manifests everything. This insight is innate and spontaneous, as Marpa explains. Therefore it naturally recognizes the dualistic fabrications of confusion and freedom as already self-liberated in the ground of dharmatā. Wisdom does not have to be created, but is self-existing, spontaneous. This is the view with which one practices. Basically, from the point of view of the path, it is a description of both the ground and fruition of practice.

As for meditation, Marpa sang:

Throughout the four activities of postmeditation,
Inseparable in the three times, like a flowing river,
This yoga is lucid, free from obscurations.
Free from distraction is the meditation.

In practicing the view, there is no attempt to create a special state of mind through meditation. Mahāmudrā meditation is simply to be one-pointedly aware in the moment of whatever arises in one's experience. Therefore everything that occurs is part of the path, and meditation is continuous throughout the day and in any activity. There is a constant sense of unfolding and uncovering the true state of one's mind and world. One does not churn up further turmoil through trying to attain something. Instead, letting things be as they are and not wandering in confusion, obscurations disperse by themselves. Therefore this practice is naturally lucid and unobscured. Ultimately, even the obscurations themselves are seen as manifestations of the awakened state and are not regarded as obstacles. Of course, in meditation practice, one does make an effort to see clearly, but the overall process is one of wearing through the shoes of deliberate meditation with which one walks the path. More and more, mind settles and vision clears by itself, spontaneously.

In action, the same view holds. Marpa sang:

> The dharmas of body, speech, and mind, and the three
>   times
> Are an unpredictable variety adorned with a single
>   ornament—
> Unceasing, effortless, and the same in essence.
> Like an illusion is the action.

Action is not done deliberately with some preconceived purpose in mind, but arises immediately in response to the need of a situation. Thus it is unpredictable, unceasing, and effortless. The realized yogin cares for whatever needs caring, nourishes whatever needs nourishing, and destroys whatever needs destroying. This unconditioned, compassionate activity can often appear to be outrageous to the conventional mind. It is "the same in essence," beyond the duality of good and bad. Because it is free from any fixed reference point, it is "like an illusion."

Finally, Marpa sang:

> The essence of realization is nowness,
> Occurring all at once, with nothing to add or subtract.

Self-liberation, innate great bliss,
Free from hope or fear is the fruition.

Ultimately, from beginning to end, mahāmudrā is nothing but nowness in which everything is complete. Here there is nothing to gain or lose; therefore there is nothing to hope for or fear. It is self-liberation on the spot, which is unconditioned great joy. One's mind is realized as buddha, completely awakened.

In summary, we could quote from Jamgön Kongtrül Lodrö Thaye's own song on mahāmudrā:*

Since in the view of mahāmudrā
Analysis does not apply,
Cast mind-made knowledge far away.
Since in the meditation of mahāmudrā
There is no way of fixating on a thought,
Abandon deliberate meditation.
Since in the action of mahāmudrā
There is no reference point for any action,
Be free from the intention to act or not.
Since in the fruition of mahāmudrā
There is no attainment to newly acquire,
Cast hopes, fears, and desires far away.

This is the depth of the mind of all Kagyüs.

In the union of the ground and fruition of mahāmudrā, one does not look back to one's exertion and experiences as particularly significant; rather one looks with heartfelt appreciation

*"The Self-Arising Innate Song upon Acquiring a Mere Glimpse of Certainty in the View and Meditation of the Incomparable Takpo Kagyü" by Jamgön Kongtrül Lodrö Thaye is translated into English by the Nālandā Translation Committee in *The Rain of Wisdom* (Boulder & London: Shambhala, 1980), pp. 81-90. This section of the song is found on p. 90.

and gratitude to one's guru and the lineage forefathers. This is not mere humility, but it is the profound and natural outcome of practice. Every stage of the path would not have been possible had this teaching not been practiced, assimilated, and passed down through many generations to one's present guru. Through the blessings of this lineage, which completely ripen and free one on the path, and the overwhelming generosity of one's guru, one inherits one's natural birthright, awakened mind. Thus, in mahāmudrā, devotion and realization are two sides of the same enlightenment.

MARPA MEETS NIGUMA, PRACTICES, RETURNS TO TIBET, AND BEGINS TEACHING

After attaining his first realization of mahāmudrā under Maitrīpa, Marpa returned to Nāropa. This time, Nāropa sent Marpa to receive teachings from Niguma, Wisdom (Jñāna) Ḍākinī Adorned with Bone Ornaments. She was Nāropa's wife before he renounced worldly life to enter the dharma, and later she became his student and consort. Finally, she became a great teacher herself and her lineage of teachings was taken to Tibet (though not by Marpa) and continues to this present day. Unfortunately, our story here does not tell us very much about their meeting.

When Marpa returned to Nāropa, he requested further teachings and then practiced intensively until experience and realization arose in him. Now, after twelve years of living and studying in India, Marpa had just about depleted his provisions. He therefore decided to return to Tibet to gather more gold so that he could further review his understanding of the teachings with his gurus, as well as obtain new teachings. His thirst for dharma still unquenched, he began the trek back to Tibet.

It was on his return to Tibet that Marpa's assimilation of the teachings was tested. Envious of Marpa's learning, Nyö had all of Marpa's books tossed into the Ganges, as if by accident. Marpa was not fooled by this ploy, but felt heartbroken. Now that his precious books were gone, was there anything left of all his efforts and study? This loss of his books acted as a catalyst for Marpa's inner certainty to blossom fully. He saw that his mind and the dharma had mixed. Realizing the futility of clinging to things as real, Marpa sang a spontaneous song of compassionate instruction to Nyö, whose ego-centeredness had led him to commit this harmful act. Nyö's treachery only served to give rise to "unperverted, good view" in Marpa. This was a sign to Marpa that obstacles could always be brought to the path and heighten realization.

On the road in Nepal, Marpa received further teachings from Saraha in a dream, which profoundly deepened his experience of mahāmudrā. Although dreams usually arise from habitual patterns, at times they arise spontaneously from a clear state of mind, and can deliver teaching or prophetic messages. Saraha was yet another of the eighty-four mahāsiddhas. His occupation was that of an arrow maker. He was particularly well known for the three cycles of dohās that he sang to a king, his queen, and his people.* As mentioned earlier, he was a teacher in the lineage of mahāmudrā (as well as of the dohās) that Marpa received from Maitrīpa.

There were many other occasions in Marpa's life where dreams played a fundamental role. He had significant dreams of his guru Maitrīpa, of the coming of his disciple Milarepa, and of his son Tarma Dode's death. Milarepa also had prophetic dreams, the most important one foretelling the future of the Kagyü lineage.

*Saraha's biography is found both in Abhayadatta's collection, *Buddha's Lions,* pp. 41-43 and in Tāranātha's *Bka'-babs bdun-ldan,* pp. 362:5-365:1. His "King Dohās" have been translated and extensively annotated by H. V. Guenther in *The Royal Song of Saraha.* The "Queen Dohās" are so far untranslated, but the "People Dohās" have been translated by D. L. Snellgrove in *Buddhist Texts Throughout the Ages* pp. 224-239.

After he had arrived back at his home in Lhotrak, Marpa set out to teach and gather gold for his next trip to India. In so doing, he met his first disciples—Ngoktön, Marpa Golek, Tsurtön Wang-nge, and Bawacen—and began to become renowned as a teacher. Then, for a while, he settled down at Lhotrak, married Dagmema, and began to raise his family.

MARPA'S SECOND TRIP TO INDIA

The biography says relatively little about Marpa's second trip to India, since, basically, it followed the same pattern as the first. He revisited all his gurus to review the teachings he had received previously and to receive new teachings. Accomplishing this task in six years, Marpa prepared to return once again to Tibet. At this point, Nāropa planted a seed in Marpa's mind by singing a cryptic song in symbolic code language and by promising to give Marpa some special teachings when he returned again. Marpa promised to return and then left for Tibet.

The Taming of Milarepa

In Tibet, Marpa settled down to his life as teacher, farmer, businessman, husband, and father. It was during this time that he put his chief disciple Milarepa through the arduous trial of building towers in order to purify him of his previous evil deeds and make him a worthy vessel for the teachings. As this biography of Marpa was written by the same author who wrote Mila's biography, the story of Mila's training under Marpa is very abbreviated here, and is recounted fully in Mila's biography.

Having finally accepted Mila as a disciple, given him teachings, and sent him into retreat, Marpa prepared to make his final journey to India as he had promised Nāropa. Suddenly, in a vision, he was able to solve the code of Nāropa's song and was reminded of the special teachings that Nāropa was to give him.

In retreat, Mila had a dream which confirmed Marpa's vision and which urged Marpa to leave at once. Despite the persistent efforts of his wife and students to stop him, Marpa, around fifty years of age and as stubborn as ever, departed for India alone.

MARPA'S THIRD TRIP TO INDIA

Marpa arrived in India only to find that his teacher Nāropa had "entered the action" (T: spyod-pa la gshegs-pa). Entering the action is an advanced stage of vajrayāna practice. It signifies that Nāropa left behind any fixed abode or reference point and wandered forth freely to encounter the world directly. As such, he was virtually inaccessible to the conventional world. People saw traces or glimpses of him here and there, but no one was able to approach him and study with him. He became a vajra enigma, ungraspable, beyond definition.

At this point, late in his life, Marpa for the first time had to struggle to reestablish his relationship with his guru. All previous reference points and achievements were forgotten. Although he received many prophetic confirmations that he would meet Nāropa from his other teachers, all he had to go on was his overwhelming and unshakable desire to see Nāropa. In each of the eight months Marpa spent in an exhausting search, he was confronted by a vision. These visions pointed out his confusion, doubts, attachment, and dualistic fixation—in short, everything that was preventing him from actually finding Nāropa. Thus, in searching for Nāropa, Marpa worked through his own obscurations, which prevented him from seeing his guru and the world clearly.* Moreover, he was being tested and tempered by

*After describing Marpa's eight visions, the biography states that "Up to this point, Marpa's experiences occurred in the form of these visions" (p. 85). Literally, the Tibetan says they were "experiences of mind" (T: thugs-nyams).

Nāropa in order to receive the special teachings he had been promised.

When at last he met with Nāropa, Marpa offered all his precious gold, but Nāropa simply tossed it into the forest. Marpa was shocked as he had worked hard in gathering that gold and offering it to his teachers had always been the appropriate gesture. Yet Nāropa showed him the complete sacredness and richness of the phenomenal world, which goes beyond the duality of precious gold and base metal. He touched the earth, which became gold, and proclaimed, "All the world is gold for me." This was an immediate and unconditional transmission of sacred world. As a further celebration of this sacredness, they prepared a feast offering.

Though Marpa had succeeded in finding Nāropa, there were still further obstacles for him to overcome before he received the special teachings from Nāropa and before he returned to Tibet. On returning to Phullahari, Marpa was confronted by forces obstructing his obtaining these special teachings of the hearing lineage. These forces were only overcome by Nāropa supplicating his own guru, Tilopa, on Marpa's behalf. Now blessed and protected by the lineage, Marpa received the abhiṣekas and oral instructions of Cakrasaṃvara of the ḍākinī hearing lineage.* These teachings were the innermost essence, whereas the teachings he had received before were just the outer husk. Nāropa then gave a command-prophecy to Marpa to give

---

Nāropa too experienced a similar process when he first set out to search for Tilopa. Nāropa experienced twelve visions, such as encountering a leprous woman, a dead and decaying dog, a man cutting up a corpse, and so on. When at last Nāropa met Tilopa in person, Tilopa told him, "Ever since you met me in the form of the leper woman we have never been apart, but were like a body and its shadow. The various visions you had were the defilements of your evil deeds and so you did not recognize me" (*The Life and Teaching of Nāropa,* p. 37).

*See note on p. 90.

these teachings only to Milarepa, who would thus be the future lineage holder.

As Marpa was to be the present lineage holder in Tibet, Nāropa later tested Marpa's realization. He created the maṇḍala of Hevajra, Marpa's personal yidam, in the sky and then asked Marpa if he would prostrate to the yidam or to his guru. Marpa, dazzled by the miraculous display of the yidam's maṇḍala, forgot that it was his personal connection to his human guru that was most important and which could create such a situation in the first place. He bowed to the yidam. This temporary obscuration of Marpa's realization foretold the impossibility of his dharma lineage continuing through the son of his own flesh and blood. Because of the power of this incident and of the teachings that he had received, Marpa was overwhelmed by sickness, as his karmic obscurations were flushed out and cleared away. Nāropa explained to Marpa that this sickness was actually a further blessing of his guru and the lineage, since it was the way to exhaust any further suffering that Marpa would experience due to his karmic obscurations. Thus, having faced and overcome all these personal obstacles as well as having received these special teachings, Marpa found his last trip to India the most profound and challenging, the most painful and joyous, and the most revealing and liberating. Marpa's training was completed, and sadly he left his beloved guru to return to Tibet.

At last, after twenty-one years of study in India, Marpa had received the full transmission of teachings from Nāropa. He and the other Tibetans who had traveled to India to seek the dharma were very persistent and thorough in their efforts. In a matter of a few centuries they were able to bring the vast corpus of Buddhist teachings back to Tibet, translate them, and assimilate their meaning. They were just in time. In the twelfth century, the Muslims repeatedly invaded India, and in their pillaging laid waste to the monastic centers, killing their monks and burning their libraries. Suddenly and totally, Buddhism vanished from the land of its birth.

THE FATE OF MARPA'S FAMILY AND DHARMA LINEAGE IN TIBET

The remainder of Marpa's story concerns the fruition of his dharma practice and dharma lineage and the failure of his family lineage to bear fruit. First the biography tells how Marpa attained confidence through his mastery of the transference of consciousness, which was one of the special teachings that Nāropa had given him during his last visit. This practice involved ejecting one's consciousness from one's body and temporarily transferring it into a corpse, thereby reanimating it. Marpa displayed his mastery of this practice on three occasions, to the amazement of his students, relatives, and neighbors. Thereupon, he became renowned as a siddha, an accomplished master of the teachings and the phenomenal world. Marpa passed this teaching on to his son, Tarma Dode, in the hope that his son would be his dharma lineage holder. However, as mentioned above, in accord with a prophecy given by Nāropa, Tarma Dode died an accidental death in the prime of his youth. The story of Tarma Dode's death is told at length and is one of the most moving parts of Marpa's biography. For Marpa, his wife Dagmema, and his disciples, this tragic event became a fundamental confirmation of the nature of death and impermanence and of the impossibility of clinging to anything as ultimately real.

The last part of the story tells how Marpa gave final transmission, gifts, and advice to his four major son-disciples. In accordance with Nāropa's command-prophecy and with Mila's own prophetic dream, Milarepa was recognized to be the main lineage holder of the Kagyü teachings, and so Marpa gave the most special oral instructions of all to him alone. After Mila left to visit his homeland and then to practice in the mountain solitudes, Marpa spent his final years in an effortless display of his mastery over phenomena.

For all his realization and mastery, it is said that Marpa lived in a "hidden manner." It is true that in many ways, he was very ordinary. Traditionally, he has been described as tall and stocky with a sunburnt face, crewcut hair, and a moustache and light beard. He was a householder, farmer, husband, and father. He ate good food, drank lots of barley beer, and lost his temper with his wife and children. His approach to everything was thoroughly businesslike, practical, and earthy. At home in Lhotrak, Marpa seemingly did not have much time to practice meditation. Certainly, he did not spend most of his time in intensive retreat, as did Milarepa and later disciples. Moreover, he was not even outwardly recognizable as a spiritual person since he did not wear the robes of a monk or a yogin. Even his neighbors and relatives had doubts at times about him being a spiritual teacher.

However, through his ability to completely unify his practice and realization of mahāmudrā with his ordinary life, Marpa's vision and activity were vast and precise, beyond what one would expect of an ordinary farmer or businessman. Marpa did not try to become a special or different kind of person, but simply used his ordinariness as the path, and as such, it became the expression of the ground and fruition of his realization of mahāmudrā.

In establishing the Kagyü lineage in Tibet and providing for its future, Marpa worked very hard. He traveled throughout Tibet, teaching and gathering gold to offer to his Indian gurus. He traveled to India three times, gathering the holy dharma and attending his root guru, Nāropa, for over sixteen years. Not only did he translate the texts he received, but he practiced and realized their meaning. He then trained and taught his own disciples. Thus, through his study in India and his teaching in Tibet, Marpa was able to receive and intuitively realize the heart of the teachings, actualize this heart in his everyday life, and transmit this heart-essence into the minds of his disciples. This is how the Kagyü lineage has continued unbroken and undiminished to this present day.

THE LIFE OF
MARPA THE TRANSLATOR

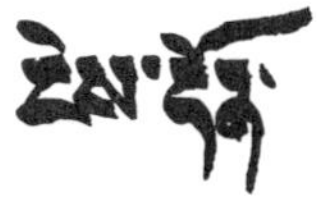

Prologue

NAMO GURU-DEVA-ḌĀKINĪ

The disciplines, vows, and aspirations of your previous lives were fulfilled at the proper time. Through not being attached to body and life, you entered the boat of good intentions for the welfare of all beings.
Rigged with the sail of the Āryan riches and right circumstances, blown by the favorable wind of exertion, you sailed to the deepest waters of the Noble Land, to Phullahari and elsewhere.
From Nāropa, king of nāgas, who blazes with glory, and from other supreme learned and accomplished ones, you received the jewel of holy dharma, which rains down whatever is needed or desired.
Now, and in time to come, you remove all the poverty of the people of Tibet and Jambudvīpa, establishing them in unconditioned virtue. Respectfully I prostrate at your feet, Marpa, the beneficial and virtuous master of the ship.

Your vajra body completely scorned weariness.
You pleased the learned and accomplished ones of India and held the regency.
In this land of snowy mountain ranges, you planted the victory banner of Śākyamuni's teaching:

To your body, Marpa the Translator, I render praise and
prostrate.

The amṛta of the speech of all the victorious ones,
Its words and meaning you drank completely,
realizing fruition.
Your lion's roar conquered perverted views and inferior
vehicles:
To your speech, Marpa the Translator, I render praise
and prostrate.

You knew the nature and extent of all that is knowable.
You benevolently cared for all sentient beings more
dearly than for yourself.
With the light of wisdom and compassion, you cleared
the darkness in the minds of many beings:
To your mind, Marpa the Translator, I render praise
and prostrate.

You body thrives with unconditioned bliss, benefiting
others.
Your speech turns the wheel of dharma, the experience
of the great yāna.
Your mind is the lord of the five wisdoms, completing
the two benefits.
Great being, Jetsün Marpa the Translator:
To your body, speech, and mind I respectfully render
praise and prostrate.

To the chief son of the victorious ones, Chökyi Lodrö,
With irresistible faith, I respectfully prostrate.

Day and night, continuously, through the three gates
and the two stages,
I exert myself in the practice of benefiting others.
Overcome by the kleśas from beginningless time,
I confess with great remorse and repentance the
degrading actions of my three gates.
You, the holy one, have undergone hardships and
asceticism for the sake of the dharma.
I rejoice wholeheartedly in your supreme actions.
In order to ripen and free myself and all beings,
Please turn the wheel of dharma for whomever
can be tamed.
Until all sentient beings are liberated from suffering,
I request you, the refuge protector, to remain, not
passing into nirvāṇa.
I dedicate the virtue so that all beings may attain
enlightenment.
May the wishes of the victorious ones and their sons
be completely fulfilled.

O great being, Marpa the Translator,
From your life of accomplishment, vast as the sky,
I will set down a brief summary of your wondrous deeds
In order to benefit beings.
Gurus, yidams, and ḍākinīs, I request your permission.
Having kindly given your permission,
Please grant your blessings.

In order to tame all ignorant beings, the supreme victorious ones conferred and sent forth their heart son, the bodhisattva mahāsattva Samantabhadra. Taking birth in India, he was known as Ḍombī Heruka, and he accomplished the welfare of many sentient beings. After that, he was sent to take birth again in order to tame beings in the Land of Snow. Rising for the glory of all beings in the snow land of Tibet, he was the excellent being who made the Buddha's teachings shine like the sun.

CHAPTER I

Marpa takes birth and later meets with the holy dharma.

THE great being Marpa Lotsāwa was born in the place of Pesar in Trowo valley in the district of Lhotrak Chukhyer. His father was Marpa Wangchuk Öser. His mother was Lady Gyamo Sa Dode. They had both fields and highland dairy farms and were very wealthy. His mother and father had three children, of whom Jetsün Marpa was the youngest son. Even from the time he was very young, Marpa was very short-tempered and stubborn.

His father said, "If my son doesn't go the wrong way, he will be very successful whether he follows the dharma or a worldly life, and there will arise great benefit for himself and others. If he goes the wrong way, he will bring disaster on himself and everyone else. Considering the potential benefits and risks, it would be good to entrust him to the dharma from the beginning."

At first, Marpa was called Tarma Wangchuk. When he was twelve years old, Marpa was sent to a local teacher,* who gave him the name Chökyi Lodrö, and he entered into the dharma. He then studied reading and writing, and through the great sharpness of his mind, he mastered them completely. But as he

*According to *The Blue Annals* (p. 399) this teacher who taught Marpa reading and writing was "an ācārya who used to worship eight nāgas." At least one other scholar, Sir Charles Bell, mentions this teacher as named Eight Serpent Spirits. His source seems to be *The Blue Annals* (*The Religion of Tibet* [Oxford: The University Press, 1931], p. 62). The teacher's name could be Lugye (T:klu-brgyad).

was aggressive and liked to fight very much, his family said, "He could cause great harm, killing himself or us, or he could do less harm such as damaging our wealth, fields, and home."

As everyone, in his home and outside, said bad and slanderous things about Marpa, his father decided that it would be best if he went to study with a good guru, far away from there. Listening to his father, Marpa decided to become a student and asked his parents for provisions. They replied, "Use these as provisions to study the dharma for a while." And so Marpa took with him two yak-loads of paper, enough for a sixteen-volume *Prajñāpāramitā,* a *sang* of gold, a silver ladle, a good horse, a saddle of teakwood, and a roll of heavy silk brocade.

As the guru Drogmi Lotsāwa had just returned from India and had become very famous, Marpa went to the monastery of Nyugu valley in the region of Mangkhar. When he met Drogmi, Marpa offered him the two yak-loads of paper and told him that he wanted to study dharma. He requested abhiṣeka and oral instructions, but Drogmi did not give them to him. So Marpa studied literary Sanskrit and the colloquial languages of India for three years, and became completely conversant in them.

CHAPTER II

Marpa travels to India three times and undergoes hardships for the sake of the dharma. Receiving the holy dharma from paṇḍitas and siddha gurus, he brings it back to Tibet.

MARPA'S FIRST JOURNEY TO INDIA

Marpa thinks of going to India and gathers the requisites for his journey. On his way he meets a companion and they travel to India.

HAVING studied with guru Drogmi, Marpa was completely conversant in the colloquial languages of India. However, he had no karmic connection to stay with guru Drogmi for a long period of time, and the time had come for awakening his good karmic connection with Mahāpaṇḍita Nāropa and other Indian gurus. Therefore Jetsünma Vajrayoginī inspired him so that he would go to meet Nāropa.

Thus, Marpa thought, "Even if I stayed a long time with this guru in order to complete the four abhiṣekas of Nairātmyā, I would have to give fifteen dris. To receive the permission-blessing of the devī Ekajaṭī, I would surely have to give at least one yak or dri. Without offerings, it is impossible to fill one's mind completely with the dharma. Even if I had such offerings and completely received the dharma in this way, I couldn't say that I had received the teachings from a great paṇḍita. In particular, I have asked again and again to borrow the *Ḍākinī-vajrapañjara-tantra* to look at briefly, but Drogmi would not give it to me. I should give this guru as many offerings as will please him, and exchange the rest of my provisions for gold. Then I should take my share of the inheritance from my parents and go to India to study the dharma.''

Marpa gave what wealth he had to guru Drogmi, so that he would not be displeased. All that remained were the horse and the teakwood saddle. He took these and went to obtain gold north of Latö in the direction of Taktse. There he exchanged both the horse and saddle for gold.

At the monastery of Shira, a student had invited the prince of Lokya from Kyerphu in Tsang to come and read the sūtras. The student made good offerings there to the prince of Lokya. While the prince of Lokya was returning to Kyerphu, he met Marpa and Marpa asked if he could accompany him. The prince of Lokya accorded Marpa full hospitality. He gave him provisions and gifts and at times let Marpa rest by riding his mule. When they arrived at Kyerphu, Marpa realized that this virtuous teacher was a person who kept his spiritual commitments.

Marpa said, ''Now I am going south to Nepal to learn translation. You have been kind to me during this visit. If there are no obstacles to my life, please remember me with kindness and receive me when I return in the future.''

The prince of Lokya said, ''I am old and I do not know if I will see you in the future. I will have my children welcome you. In any case, you should return here.'' He gave him a *sang* of gold and a bolt of white wool cloth as a parting gift.

When Marpa arrived in Lhotrak, he told his parents that he was going to India to study the dharma, and that he must have his share of the inheritance of wealth, fields, and houses.

His parents and relatives all said, ''What's the point of going all the way to India to translate and study the dharma? If you want to practice dharma, you can do that in Tibet. If you don't want to practice, stay and work on the farm.'' They raised many such objections.

Marpa said to his father, "At first you said I should be sent to a good guru a long way from here. What could be farther than India? I will definitely find a good paṇḍita guru there." He did not listen to their objections and took his share of the inheritance of wealth, fields, and houses. Except for a house and field he exchanged everything for gold. Thus he obtained eighteen *sang* of gold to take with him. Two friends were going to join him, but as they were about to leave, they were discouraged by their relatives from going. So Marpa departed for India by himself.

While he was traveling, Marpa wished that he had a traveling companion. At a place called Tsinesar in upper Nyang, he met the translator Nyö of Kharak, who was going to India.

Nyö asked, "Where did you come from and where are you going?"

Marpa replied, "I am coming from Lhotrak and going to India to study the dharma."

"Well, do you have a lot of gold?" said Nyö.

Lying, Marpa said, "Just a couple of *sho*."

Nyö said, "You can't go anywhere like that. If you go to India without lots of gold, searching for dharma will be like trying to drink water from an empty gourd. I have lots of gold; so be my servant and we'll use the gold together."

Marpa did not ask Nyö for any teachings, not knowing how this relationship would end. Hoping for some temporary benefit, he accompanied Nyö as his servant, and together they traveled to Nepal.

Having arrived in India, Marpa meets paṇḍitas and siddha gurus and receives the pith instructions of the holy dharma of the great yāna.

Marpa and Nyö then arrived in Nepal. One day, in the mountains, they saw many people milling around and they asked, "What is happening?"

Someone said, "Lord Nāropa's two Nepalese disciples, Chitherpa and Paiṇḍapa, are here. The lady devotees are performing a gaṇacakra. If you Tibetans went there, you too could get something to eat and drink."

By just hearing the name of Lord Nāropa, a connection from a former life was reawakened in Marpa and he felt immeasurable yearning. Thinking this situation was the perfect opportunity, he told Nyö, "By all means, we must go." The two of them went to sightsee and take part in the feast offering.

The Nepalese Chitherpa was giving teaching on the *Guhyasamāja,* and they listened to him. Chitherpa said to Paiṇḍapa, "All these Tibetans may not have received abhiṣeka. We might violate our samaya vows by proclaiming secrets."

Paiṇḍapa said, "They won't understand our Nepalese speech. Tibetans are like oxen."

Nyö, who understood Nepalese, became angry at this. He stopped listening to the dharma discourse, turned his back, and recited mantras.

The next day, Marpa said, "Today, let's go again to the feast offering and listen to the dharma."

Nyö said, "You can go if you want. I won't go where people say I'm like an ox. These Nepalese are the true oxen." So Nyö stayed, while Marpa went and listened to the dharma.

Chitherpa said, "Where is your friend who came yesterday?"

Marpa replied, "He understands Nepalese, and guru Paiṇḍapa's remark yesterday angered him. So today he didn't come."

Chitherpa said, "He and I have no karmic connection, but it is good that you have come."

Marpa received the oral instructions of the *Śrī Catuḥpīṭha* and the ejection of consciousness, and the permission-blessing of the devī Vetālī. He told Paiṇḍapa, "Knowing only a little Sanskrit, I would like to study translation further, but I do not have much gold." He pleased them by offering each guru one *sang* of gold.

They said, "Since you don't have much gold, you should go to the paṇḍita Lord Nāropa. He is the only guru who will teach you the dharma without demanding gold." They spoke of the virtues and greatness of Lord Nāropa and then said, "We will send you to our guru, who is just like a second Buddha. Stay here for a little while to get used to the heat." They gave him much kind advice.

Marpa felt immeasurable faith in both gurus. He thought, "I must abandon hope and fear as to whether I live or die, and go to Nāropa." As the two gurus had advised him, Marpa stayed three years at Svayambhūnāth to get used to the heat. During that time, he learned all the dharma that he needed to know, solely from the lineage of Nāropa.

When three years had elapsed, the two dharma brother gurus gave him a letter to give to Prajñāsiṃha, one of Nāropa's śrāmaṇeras, which said, "You should explain the dharma to this Tibetan. Be certain to take him to Lord Nāropa." After they had given him further advice, Marpa left with a dzoki traveling companion and Nyö. They traveled to India, undergoing great hardships.

When they arrived at the vihāra of glorious Nālandā, Marpa said to Nyö, "Here dwells the guru of Chitherpa of Nepal, the learned mahāpaṇḍita known as Nāropa. Would you like to receive teachings from him or not?"

Nyö replied, "Previously, Nāropa was a learned paṇḍita. But later he went to that Tilopa, gave up his scholarship, and is now doing kusulu meditation. I won't go to someone like him. If you continue as my attendant, we will use my gold together. But if you don't come with me, I won't give you a single grain of gold. In the East, West, South, and North of India, there are many learned paṇḍitas as famous as the sun and moon, and I am going to meet them." As he had no karmic connection with Nāropa, Nyö did not give Marpa even one grain of gold, and departed to see the gurus he wished to see.

Marpa sought out and met the śrāmaṇera Prajñāsiṃha. He gave him the letter from the two dharma brothers in Nepal and told him the whole story.

The śrāmaṇera said, "Guru Nāropa has now gone to Labar in West India and isn't here. He will return very soon. Meanwhile, stay with me. As the dharma brothers from Nepal have requested, I will care for your needs."

Marpa planned to stay there, but a paṇḍita disciple who possessed the higher perceptions came to śrāmaṇera Prajñāsiṃha and said, "Very soon, today or tomorrow, the guru, who has arrived at Phullahari, will send us a message here."

At dawn, an atsara arrived and delivered Nāropa's message: "There is a Buddhist from Tibet staying with you; you should bring him to Phullahari." Having said this, the messenger left.

Accompanying Prajñāsiṃha, Marpa went to the city Fields Adorned with Flowers and to the Golden Mountain monastery of Phullahari. There the śrāmaṇera introduced him to Nāropa. Upon meeting glorious Mahāpaṇḍita Nāropa, Marpa offered many full prostrations and then offered many flowers made of gold.

Lord Nāropa said:

> In accordance with the guru's prophecy,
> My son, the worthy vessel Marpa Lodrö,
> From the northern Land of Snow,
> Is welcome to assume the regency.*

Thus Nāropa said and felt supreme joy.

Marpa said to Lord Nāropa, "I had a friend with much gold. Relying only on an unwise remark of the Nepalese Paiṇḍapa, he has gone to see other gurus."

"I have no dharmic connections with him," Lord Nāropa replied.

*This prophecy by Tilopa, Nāropa's guru, is given in full on p. 88. It is also found in Nāropa's biography, p. 95

Lord Nāropa first gave to guru Marpa the abhiṣeka of Śrī Hevajra and the second section of the *Hevajra-tantra,* and completed this with the *Vajrapañjara* and the *Sampuṭa.* Marpa studied these for a year and then took some time off and went to a city, where he met Nyö.

Nyö said, "What did you study?"

Marpa answered, "I studied *Hevajra.*"

Nyö said, "Today we should compare our understanding." They did so, and Marpa proved to be more learned about *Hevajra.*

Nyö said, "*Hevajra* is already well known in Tibet. There is a father tantra better than this, called the *Guhyasamāja.* It enables the prāṇa to flow through your fingertips and enables you to hold buddha in the palm of your hand. That is what we need."

When Nyö began to use the dharma terms of the *Guhyasamāja,* Marpa had nothing to say. Therefore he returned to Nāropa and said, "Today, when I went into the city and met with Nyö, we compared our understanding of *Hevajra,* and I prevailed. But Nyö said that what we need is the *Guhyasamāja.* Please give me this teaching."

Nāropa said, "In the monastery of Lakṣetra to the West, in the vihāra Pūrṇacandra, there is a master of the father tantra, a paṇḍita called Jñānagarbha who is an exponent of svatantra-madhyamaka and who has attained siddhi. You should go there and request the dharma. You will not have any obstacles."

Marpa journeyed to Lakṣetra. From glorious Jñānagarbha, he requested and received the abhiṣeka and oral instructions of Śrī Guhyasamāja, as well as the ritual traditions of the kriyā and yoga tantras and the various yogic applications. Complete realization of the meaning of the secret mantra arose in him.

Then he thought, "I came to Nepal from Tibet and there I met the two Nepalese lords. Although I received advice and oral instructions from them, it is only through the blessings of the great guru Nāropa that I now have certainty in these."

At dawn, he felt very joyful and offered to the guru Jñānagarbha this maṇḍala of vajra song:

Lord, you are the equal of all the buddhas;
I prostrate to the gurus.
Pure realm, Mahāpaṇḍita Nāropa
And glorious Jñānagarbha, I pay homage at your feet.

I was born in Lhotrak in Tibet through the power of karma.
My father and mother raised me.
This one known as Marpa Lodrö
Has been established in the dharma through
their kindness.
To my father and mother, I prostrate with devotion.
Grant your blessings so that their kindness can be
repaid with the dharma.

On the maṇḍala of unborn nature
I arrange the flowers of manifold phenomena.
I make offering to the body of the gurus.
Grant your blessings to my body.

On the maṇḍala of completely pure space
I arrange the flowers of unceasing coincidence.
I make offering to the speech of the gurus.
Grant your blessings to my speech.

On the maṇḍala of the mind of great bliss
I arrange the flowers of abruptly cut thoughts.
I make offering to the mind of the gurus.
Grant your blessings to my mind.

On the maṇḍala of the jeweled ground
I arrange the flowers of Mount Meru and the
four continents.
I make offering to the body, speech, and mind of
the gurus.
Grant your blessings to my body, speech, and mind.

On the universal ground of the pure realm,
From the five elements arise
Drinking water, flowers, incense,
Light, perfumed water, food, music, and other such
offering substances.
Whatever is excellent
I offer to the lord gurus.
Grant your blessings so that I may be free from obstacles.

As limitless as space,
Parasols, victory banners, music,
Canopies, drapery, and the like
Emanate from my mind and I offer them.
Grant your blessings so that my realization may increase.

From the buddha Jñānagarbha
I listened to the great tantra, the *Guhyasamāja.*
I understood it as the union of upāya and prajñā.
I understood it as the key of dharma.
I understood it as the ocean of tantra.
I received both material gifts and the dharma.
The tree of my heart was made to grow
And the leaves of spotless dharma words flourished.
Possessing the five wisdoms,

I benefit all beings.
It is pleasant to travel the supreme path of the five stages.
Luminosity, illusory body, and dream—
All these precious oral instructions you have given to me.

Jñānagarbha, you are so kind.
From now until the culmination
Of unsurpassable enlightenment is attained,
Please adorn the top of my head as the crown jewel
of great bliss.
You are never separate from the center of my heart.
Free from sadness and fear, I take refuge in you.
Holding the radiant hook of compassion,
Please clear away the darkness of ignorance.
Please accept my body, speech, and mind.

Thus Marpa supplicated.

When Marpa finished learning the father tantra, he made offerings to repay the kindness of the guru, and pleased him by practicing with body, speech, and mind.

Then Marpa departed for Phullahari. In a temple on the road, he met Nyö Lotsāwa, who said, "Marpa, what have you studied since our last meeting?"

"I've studied father tantra."

"Well then, let us compare our understanding."

So they compared their understanding and Marpa prevailed.

Nyö said, "What we need is the mother tantra called the *Mahāmāyā,* which contains oral instructions on the stillness of the nāḍīs, the movement of prāṇa, and the placement of bodhicitta. The *Guhyasamāja* is already well known in Tibet."

When Nyö began to use the dharma terms of the *Mahāmāyā,* Marpa had nothing to say. Therefore Marpa returned to Lord Nāropa. He prostrated to Nāropa and Nāropa said, "Did you fully understand the *Guhyasamāja?*"

"I received the *Guhyasamāja* to my satisfaction. However, I met my friend on the way back. We discussed the dharma and in the *Guhyasamāja* I prevailed, but in the discussion on the *Mahāmāyā* I had nothing to say. Please teach the *Mahāmāyā* to me."

"I could have taught the *Guhyasamāja* to you, but it wasn't the appropriate time, so I sent you to Jñānagarbha. Later, when the time is right, I myself will teach you the *Guhyasamāja.* I also know the *Mahāmāyā,* but on an island in a poison lake is a master of the mother tantra, called glorious Śāntibhadra, also known as Kukkurīpā. My son, I should send you to him."

When the disciples were performing a gaṇacakra, Nāropa pointed in the direction of a charnel ground with the threatening mudrā. Instantly, from the charnel ground of Sosadvīpa arrived three charnel ground yogins. Nāropa said, "I am sending my son Marpa to the island in the poison lake in the South. You three should grant your blessings so that he has no obstacles."

One of the yogins said, "I can protect him from the danger of poisonous snakes."

Another said, "I will protect him from the danger of ferocious animals."

The last said, "I will protect him from the danger of spirits."

Then Nāropa said, "From here to the island in the poison lake is half a month's journey. The poisonous water at first is ankle deep; then by stages it reaches the knees, then the thighs, and finally you have to swim. Swim from tree trunk to tree trunk. If there are two together, pass between them. When you come to some cleared ground, camp there. Kukkurīpā has a body covered with hair. His face is like a monkey's. His color is unpleasant, and he can transform himself into anything. Tell him without hesitation that you were sent by Nāropa, and request him to give you the *Mahāmāyā* and other teachings." Having given Marpa prophecies and presents, Nāropa sent him off.

Guru Marpa took half a month's provisions and traveled toward the mountain island in the boiling poison lake in southern India. As the road was difficult to travel, he followed the instructions of his guru. Except for one day when two birds were flying ahead of him, he saw no other animals along the road. When Marpa arrived at the mountain island in the poison lake, the local spirits magically filled the sky with thick clouds. Lightning flashed, thunder resounded fiercely, and many thunderbolts struck the ground. There was a great tempest with rain and snow. Though it was the middle of the day, it became pitch black. Marpa experienced such anguish that he wondered whether he was dead or alive. Remembering the pledges that the three yogins had made before Nāropa, he called out to Mahāpaṇḍita Nāropa by name and supplicated him. The sky then became clear.

Marpa wondered, "Where is guru Kukkurīpā?" and began to search for him. Under a tree was a human figure covered with the feathers of a bird. His face was tucked into the crook of his arm. Marpa hesitated, thinking, "Is this he or not?" He asked, "Have you seen Kukkurīpā?"

The figure jerked up, his eyes glaring, and said, "Well, well, you flat-nosed Tibetans! Even a route as difficult as this doesn't keep you away. Where do you come from? Where are you going? What do you want with Kukkurīpā? Though I live here, I have never seen any kind of Kukkurīpā, nor have I ever heard of one." And he tucked his head under his arm again.

Marpa searched elsewhere for Kukkurīpā without finding him. Then he remembered his guru's words and became certain that the man he had met before was Kukkurīpā. Going before him again, Marpa prostrated and said, "Mahāpaṇḍita Nāropa sent me. I have come to request the *Mahāmāyā.* Please teach it to me." Marpa then offered him gifts.

The man raised his head from the crook of his arm and said, "What did you say? This so-called Nāropa has no wide learning. A mahāpaṇḍita who has no meditation experience is laughable. He knows the *Mahāmāyā* and he could teach it himself, but he won't leave a person in peace." Though he spoke in a mocking manner, Kukkurīpā was pleased. "Oh well, I'm just joking. He is a paṇḍita of inconceivable learning and accomplishment, and my intentions are pure. We two have exchanged our teachings. Though he knows the *Mahāmāyā,* I also hold the transmission. Through his sacred outlook, he has sent you to entreat me. I will teach you completely. Later, you can request it from Nāropa and see if there is any difference. When you were coming here, did you see two men along the road?"

"I didn't see them."

"Did you see two birds?"

"Yes, I did."

"Then you saw the two men as birds."

First Kukkurīpā performed the abhiṣeka. Then he gave Marpa the transmission of the three yogas* by means of the greater muteness, the lesser muteness, and the ornament. By the inferior yoga of form, one is brought to the path of the subtle, vivid, and concentrated. By means of the profound yoga of mantra, one is brought to the yoga of the three insights. By means of the ultimate yoga of dharma, one is bound by the five essential techniques. Kukkurīpā also explained at length the meanings of the twenty-four main sampannakramas and others.

Marpa completed his studies without any obstacles. He then arranged a feast to give thanks to the guru Kukkurīpā for receiving these teachings completely. During the gaṇacakra, Marpa felt great joy, and requested permission from the guru and the dharma brothers and sisters to offer this song:

*According to Tāranātha in his *Sgyu-'phrul chen-mo'i khrid-yig rgyal-ba'i lam-bzang,* one can do this practice based on either the expanded, intermediate, or abbreviated sādhana written by Kukkurīpā. Tāranātha then goes on to present a brief but detailed synopsis of the three yogas. The inferior yoga of form (dman-pa dbyibs kyi rnal-'byor) involves visualizing oneself as Mahāmāyā, who appears as inseparable appearance and emptiness, like a rainbow. The profound yoga of mantra (zab-pa sngags kyi rnal-'byor) uses the complex practices of the illusory body of nāḍī, prāṇa, and bindu. The ultimate yoga of dharma (mthar-thug chos kyi rnal-'byor) concerns the ordinary and extraordinary bringing of whatever occurs to the path. See the *Bka'-brgyud sngags-mdzod,* vol. 3, no. 11, pp. 281-293.

Lord, heart son of all the buddhas,
Vajradhara for all beings,
Holder of the treasury of the secret tantras,
Glorious Śāntibhadra, I pay homage at your feet.

Seeing your body crumbles my mountain of pride.
Hearing your speech frees my being from petty mind.
Remembering your mind dispels outer and inner darkness.
These days I am fortunate.

I came to the land of India from Tibet.
I am a man who has traveled a long way.
I requested the holy dharma from paṇḍitas.
I received the holy dharma of the direct lineage.
I touched the feet of the lord who possesses siddhi.

Having pacified obstacles of humans and spirits,
I received the father and mother tantras of the
secret mantra.
I am a teacher who has received the great oral instructions.
Glorious Śāntibhadra has accepted me.
I am the only son of the good guru.

Without obstacles I traveled south to Nepal.
I am a Buddhist of fortunate karma.
The king of tantras, *Cakrasaṃvara,* seems to be easy,
As this holy dharma was accomplished in a short time.
Having heard an auspicious prophecy,
I realize the value of obtaining a human birth.

My umbilical cord was cut in Lhotrak in Tibet.
My fortunate karma was reawakened in India.
Meeting siddhas and paṇḍitas,

Receiving abhiṣekas, expositions of tantra, and
oral instructions,
My body, speech, and mind were blessed.

At the feet of the lord of ḍākinīs,
I learned the meaning of the three yogas
And met the mother Great Miracle.
Attending the father, All-Good,
I sharpened my experience of samādhi on the path
of passion.
Brightening the lamp of the three kinds of prajñā,
Dispelling the darkness of the three delusions,
Burning up the fuel of the three obscurations,
Emptying the graves of the three lower realms,
Oh, how very kind is the lord guru!
Oh, how happy is Chökyi Lodrö!
Oh, how joyful to be with all the dharma brothers
and sisters here!

Since Marpa sang this song in Tibetan and there were no fellow Tibetans present, or anyone who understood Tibetan, Dharaśrī and some other dharma friends asked, "Is this Tibetan crazy?"

Marpa said, "I have particularly good fortune and family, but through the power of some dense habitual patterns in this life, this song came out in Tibetan." He translated the song into their language, and they thought it was wonderful.

Later Marpa thought, "I must quickly return to Nāropa."

In general, Marpa had indestructible faith in the famous Master Maitrīpa, and so continually thought, "I must by all means receive teachings from him." In particular, the night before a farewell gaṇacakra to be performed by the guru Kukkurīpā, Marpa vividly remembered the guru Maitrīpa again and again, and supreme faith was born in him. Mentally he offered a maṇḍala and performed the sevenfold service; then he supplicated Maitrīpa.

In a dream that night, a beautiful maiden holding a vase in her hand appeared, and said she was a messenger of Maitrīpa. She placed the vase on top of Marpa's head. When Marpa awoke, he experienced immeasurable joy.

The next day, as Jetsün Marpa was preparing to depart, glorious Śāntibhadra performed a farewell gaṇacakra for him and gave him scriptures of the teachings that he had bestowed upon him. He placed his hand on top of Marpa's head and said, "The path to this place is difficult to travel. By coming here you have received great benefit. Because he knew you were a worthy person, Nāropa sent you to me. Now you will also be sent to Maitrīpa. Nāropa himself has accepted you through his kindness. After he has given you whatever oral instructions you want, he will empower you as his regent to tame disciples in the Land of Snow. I knew you were coming beforehand, and sent two protectors transformed into men to escort you. You did not see them as men, but as birds. Now, having given you oral instructions and scriptures, I bestow on you the auspicious empowerment. Take delight in this." Thus Kukkurīpā was very pleased.

All this accorded with Lord Marpa's dream and prophecy. He experienced irreversible faith in guru Kukkurīpā, and immeasurable, great joy. As a parting gift, Marpa offered this song of realization to the guru and the dharma brothers and sisters:

Jetsüns who reside here,
Heart friends, brothers and sisters, please listen.
I, stubborn Marpa the Translator,
Went south to Nepal when my karmic link
  was reawakened.
From the Nepalese who possess siddhi,
And from Jñānagarbha and Śāntibhadra,

I received the *Catuḥpīṭha, Guhyasamāja,* and
Cakrasaṃvara.
The treasury of tantras and oral instructions was opened.
Now, in the presence of the master,
I requested and was given oral instructions
And received auspicious prophecies at the same time.

The other night,
I mentally arranged a maṇḍala,
Supplicated Maitrīpa, and then fell asleep.
In the confused habitual patterns of dream,
A messenger of Master Maitrīpa,
A maiden of radiant beauty,
Arrived holding a vase in her hand.
I dreamt that she touched it to my head.
I thought, "This must be a blessing of Maitrīpa's
kindness.
It is the result of former aspiration and a karmic link."
Therefore, with intense longing and faith,
I will go into the presence of the venerable father.

To you, the jetsün who resides here,
Unceasing devotion arises.
I take refuge so that we will be inseparable.
Grant your blessings so that the lower realms
may cease to exist.

All you vajra brothers and sisters,
Friends with whom I am joined in this life and the next,
Cast behind you the deceptive seductions of saṃsāra.
Practice the holy oral instructions.
Keep samaya free from hypocrisy.

Always meditate on the guru on the top of your head.
Enjoy the ten virtues.
Abandon the ten nonvirtues like poison.
Practice continually without interruption.

Thus Marpa offered this song.

Guru Śāntibhadra put his hand on top of Marpa's head, granting a blessing so that Marpa would be free from obstacles.

Now guru Marpa knew the aspects of the *Mahāmāyā.* In three days he arrived back at Phullahari. The great Lord Nāropa was in the process of giving private oral instruction to the śrāmaṇera Prajñāsiṃha. He made a sign to Marpa not to approach. Marpa waited and prostrated continually until they had finished. When the teaching session was over, he presented himself and requested Nāropa's blessings. Nāropa asked, "Did you receive the teachings?"

"Yes, I received them."

"And didn't he ridicule me?"

"There was some joking."

"What did he say?"

Marpa repeated what was said and Nāropa said, "This is he, indeed. Since he is without virtue, he lives on an unpeopled island in the poison lake. As he has the face of a monkey on a human body, he could not find a human consort, so he has to resort to bitches. Who but Kukkurīpā would do such a thing?" Nāropa laughed and continued, "I'm only joking. That's what makes him great. There is no one like him. He received the *Hevajra* from me, and because he has attained the siddhi of *Mahāmāyā,* I received the *Mahāmāyā* from him." Nāropa then gave Marpa the *Mahāmāyā* in one session. The meaning was no different from Kukkurīpā's, though Nāropa's words were somewhat more extensive.

Marpa asked him, "Why did the guru, knowing this teaching so well himself, make me undergo such hardship in going to the island in the poison lake?"

"Because Kukkurīpā is the master of the mother tantra and has achieved certainty in the oral instructions. I sent you because he is the pure source of *Mahāmāyā.*"

Later guru Marpa went east to see the temple in Bengal where the statue of Khasarpaṇa had miraculously appeared. At that time, he thought of having a discussion with Nyö on the *Mahāmāyā,* and he went to Nālandā where Nyö was receiving the teaching of the guru Balimṃtapa. At the market, Marpa bought a good deal of food and liquor, and then met with Nyö. During their meal, they compared their understanding of the *Mahāmāyā* and Lord Marpa was the victor. Nyö said to him, "What master taught you the mother tantra?"

Marpa, keeping the guru a secret, replied:

My guru possesses the three yogas.
His form is inferior, but his mantra is profound.
He is a yogin of the ultimate dharma,
Known as the One Who Shows the Path to Liberation.
At this moment, he is in the city of Kapilavastu.

Nyö went to Kapilavastu and looked for him, asking, "Where is the guru known as the One Who Shows the Path to Liberation?"

He was told, "All the gurus show the path to liberation. Which one do you want?"

He realized that this was true and that the guru had been kept secret from him. Still, Nyö looked for Kukkurīpā, but could not find him at first. Later, he located him, but it is said that Nyö was unable to cross the poison lake and did not meet glorious Kukkurīpā.

Lord Marpa returned to glorious Nāropa and said, "I met my friend. We compared our understanding of the mother tantra and I was the victor. He asked me what master taught me the mother tantra, but I did not tell him."

Nāropa said, "You did not need to keep the name of the guru secret. He may have a lot of gold, but that is not sufficient. What one needs is merit and a karmic link."

Then Marpa supplicated Nāropa to permit him to go and meet Maitrīpa. Nāropa joyously granted him permission. Marpa gave offerings to please guru Nāropa and offered feast torma to the ḍākas, ḍākinīs, and vajra brothers and sisters. He supplicated that he be free from obstacles, and many wondrous signs arose. Then Marpa departed.

On his way, he asked some other travelers where Maitrīpa was living. They replied, "He resides at the monastery of Blazing Fire Mountain. That path is difficult to travel; you had better not go."

Marpa thought, "I'm not looking for wealth in this life. Whether I die or not, I must seek the dharma." He continued without hesitation, and in half a day arrived at the place where Maitrīpa was residing. He met Maitrīpa sitting in the shade of a nyagrodha tree. He felt great joy, just like that of the bodhisattva Sadāprarudita when he met the bodhisattva Dharmodgata. He offered full prostrations seven times, a gift of gold and other things, and sang this song praising the body, speech, and mind of the guru:

In order to benefit beings in Jambudvīpa,
You took birth in a royal family.
You know the variety of outer and inner sādhanas.
I prostrate to you, Maitrīpa.

Ārya Tārā gave you prophecies
And unobstructed blessings.
You touched the dust of Lord Śavari's feet.
I praise you, Avadhūti.

Your body is a mountain of precious gold.
Your wisdom, aspiration, and the like are pure.

You quell the disease of the kleśas.
I praise you, sun of dharma.

The śūnyatā vajra of your mind
Crumbles the great mountain ranges of belief in a self.
You see the quality of all dharmas.
I praise you, unequaled lord guru.

Nirmāṇakāya, ornament of all Jambudvīpa,
Essence of Vajrasattva,
Refuge of beings, possessing the treasure of kindness,
I praise you, crest ornament.

Amongst the hordes of humans, spirits, and demons,
All vicious ones without exception
Obey your command through the power of your
yogic discipline.
I praise you, vajra holder.

Kind sugata gurus,
You gave up your subjects to act for the holy dharma.
From Mahāpaṇḍita Nāropa and other gurus
I received instructions
And finished this study of the tantras.

At the mountain island in the boiling poison lake
in the South,
While I was staying at the feet of glorious Śāntibhadra,
You, holy one, kindly accepted me.
Not concerned for my life, I came to see you.

At the monastery of the Blazing Fire Mountain,
In the cool shade of a nyagrodha tree,

Master, Prince Maitrīpa,
Father Buddha, now I meet you.

Faith arises like the sun
And I am so moved by faith that I even dare to die.
I supplicate without hypocrisy.
Please bless me continuously.

You hold the tradition of the Great Brahman
And stayed with the emanation, Lord Śavari.
Please give me the holy dharma, well taught by them,
The essential meaning of the pinnacle of all yānas,
The mahāmudrā free from extremes,
Which is like space.

Thus Marpa supplicated.

The Master accepted him and gave him complete abhiṣekas and the secret name Vajracitta. At that time, Marpa made offerings to please the guru and arranged feast tormas to please the ḍākinīs. Thus, many wondrous signs arose. The guru gave him the oral instructions and transmission of mahāmudrā, the *Āryamañjuśrī-nāma-saṅgīti* along with its commentary, and the dohās along with their explanation. Marpa's doubts were completely cleared away. When he practiced these teachings, excellent experiences and realizations arose in his mind, and so he was very pleased. At a gaṇacakra which he offered as thanksgiving to the guru, Marpa offered in song his realization and experience:

In the palace of great bliss on top of my head
On a spotless lotus, sun, and moon
Dwells the guru Master, the loving protector.
Please bless my mind.

All the buddhas of the three times
And the countless hosts of yidams and devas
Are inseparable from you, glorious Avadhūti.
Please remain on the lotus in my heart.
Grant me mastery over speech.

In the pure realm of India
Dwell Mahāpaṇḍita Nāropa and others.
The dust of the feet of those siddhas
I touched to the top of my head.

Listening to many words of the tantras
I was not satisfied even by these.
Therefore, I came to the jetsün Master
And properly requested the blessing of the holy dharma.

In particular, I requested the mahāmudrā.
Doubts about the teachings I knew were cut.
Teachings that I did not know, I studied.
Blessings and realization
In the tradition of Lord Saraha occurred at once.

I sing a song offering my realization to the lord.
All the various outer and inner schools
Are realized and unified in mahāmudrā.
All the limitless deceptive appearances
Arise as manifestation of the unity of equality.

This unceasing dharmatā
Is unobstructed, self-luminous insight.
Within innate insight, unity,
Spontaneous wisdom is the view.

Throughout the four activities of postmeditation,
Inseparable in the three times, like a flowing river,
This yoga is lucid, free from obscurations.
Free from distraction is the meditation.

The dharmas of body, speech, and mind, and the
three times
Are an unpredictable variety adorned with a single
ornament—
Unceasing, effortless, and the same in essence.
Like an illusion is the action.

The essence of realization is nowness,
Occurring all at once, with nothing to add or subtract.
Self-liberation, innate great bliss,
Free from hope or fear is the fruition.

Regardless of how many words one hears,
At last the ground of mind is understood as dharmakāya.
At last my doubts are exhausted.
At last the ground and root of confusion are destroyed.
I do not hope for enlightenment through sophistry.

Thus, in the presence of the great lord Master,
Through the fruition of practicing the essence
And through the blessings of the lineages,
I offer this understanding, experience, and realization.*

*Understanding, experience, and realization (T: go, nyams-myong, rtogs) are three stages in the practice of mahāmudrā. They are also called "the three stages of birth" (T: skye-lugs gsum). In the *Nges-don phyag-rgya-chen-po'i sgom-rim gsal-bar byed-pa'i legs-bshad zla-ba'i 'od-zer* (fol. 329A), Trashi Namgyal writes:

According to Lord [Tsangpa] Gyare,
"Understanding arises from analytical
investigation; the experiences are

May the jetsün guru and dharma friends
Gathered here rejoice!

Thus Marpa offered this song.

Master Maitrīpa then sang this vajra song of twelve instructions to Marpa:

O son, if the root of faith is not firm,
The root of nonduality will not be firm.

If you do not develop unbiased compassion,
The two rūpakāyas will not be attained.

If the three prajñās are not practiced,
Realization will not arise.

If you do not attend the jetsün guru,
The two siddhis will not be attained.

If you have not cut the root of mind,
Do not carelessly abandon awareness.

If you cannot strike phenomena with mudrā,*
You should not retreat into great bliss.

If thoughts of desire arise,
You should act like a joyful elephant.

---

strong and weak bliss and luminosity;
realization is recognizing things as they
are.''

See also Guenther's *The Royal Song of Saraha,* pp. 116-7, n. 42.

*Striking phenomena with mudrā (T: snang-ba rgya-yis-thebs): this refers to an awareness that abruptly brings one back to sacred outlook, the view of mahāmudrā. Phenomena are not regarded as something separate from mahāmudrā, therefore there is no dwelling on any experience of great bliss.

If occasionally the kleśas arise,
Look at the mind and meditate without distraction.

If the mind is harmed by unfavorable conditions,
Practice the four abhiṣekas continually.

If kleśas arise in your being,
Remember the guru's instructions.

If you do not supplicate one-pointedly,
How can you fulfill the intentions of the holy ones?

If you do not meditate in the union of utpatti and
sampannakrama,
How can you realize the inseparability of saṃsāra
and nirvāṇa?

This is a vajra song of twelve instructions.
Remembering these makes thirteen.

If these yogas are practiced,
You will remain on the thirteenth bhūmi.

Thus Maitrīpa sang.

Marpa was delighted with these instructions and assimilated them. With unwavering faith in Maitrīpa, he departed and returned to Nāropa at Phullahari.

Nāropa said, "On the shores of the poison lake in the South, in the charnel ground of Sosadvīpa is Jñānaḍākinī Adorned with Bone Ornaments. Whoever encounters her is liberated. Go before her and request the *Catuḥpīṭha.* You can also request of the kusulus there whatever teachings you desire."

Having arrived in the charnel ground at Sosadvīpa, Marpa met this yoginī, who was living in a woven grass dome. Offering her a maṇḍala of gold, he supplicated her. She joyfully gave him the full abhiṣeka and oral instructions of the *Catuḥpīṭha.* Moreover, Marpa received abhiṣekas and oral instructions on utpatti and sampannakrama from some authentic kusulu yogins —glorious Siṃhadvīpa and others dwelling in the charnel ground or under trees. From time to time, he also requested oral instructions for various practical uses. Thus he became a treasury of oral instructions.

Finally, Marpa returned to Nāropa. Having prostrated, he inquired about Nāropa's health. Nāropa asked, "What certainty did the abhiṣekas and oral instructions arouse in you?" Marpa told him what had happened and Nāropa was very pleased.

Lord Marpa supplicated glorious Nāropa, saying, "I want the abhiṣeka of Cakrasaṃvara and instructions on the commentary to the tantra."

Nāropa gave him the full abhiṣeka, as well as the reading transmission and instructions on the commentary to the tantra, and said, "Practicing them is of great importance."

Having been given the renowned oral instructions of the four special transmissions, the six yogas of Nāropa, and the mahāmudrā transmission showing the mind as innate coemergent wisdom, Marpa meditated. In general, many special experiences and realizations of the unsurpassable secret mantra were born in his mind. In particular, while practicing caṇḍālī, he actualized the unity of bliss, luminosity, and nonthought. For seven days, he was unable to move the gates of body, speech, and mind, and he established confidence in this. The ten signs arose, and in a joyful state of mind the days and nights passed.

Later, Marpa thought to himself, "I have spent about twelve years in Nepal and India. Not only have I received abhiṣekas and oral instructions, I have also studied and practiced both their words and meaning. Therefore I have no regrets, and I do not have to emulate others' explication and meditation.

"Now that my gold is almost spent, I will return to Tibet for a little while and obtain as much gold as I can. Then I will return to India and please my gurus by offering it to them. I will thoroughly review with them the teachings previously obtained, and I will obtain whatever I did not receive before. Now, in general, I must by all means spread the teachings of Buddha in Tibet, and in particular, the teachings of the Practice Lineage." He then assembled the necessary provisions, using the remainder of his gold, and kept just enough for expenses on the road.

Having summoned brahman Sukhamati and yoginī Sukhadhari and others, Marpa offered a gaṇacakra of thanksgiving and celebration to Mahāpaṇḍita Nāropa. At the feast, he thought to himself, "Fulfilling my purpose in coming to India from Tibet, I have met many gurus who are learned and who have attained siddhi. I have received and studied many tantras along with their commentaries. I have become the model of a learned translator who knows the languages. Unperverted experiences and realizations have arisen in my being. Now, as I am returning to Tibet without obstacles, there is no happier day than today."

Marpa then sang the first of eight grand songs to glorious Nāropa, a long song in a voice with the drone of a tamboura. This is the song in which he offered his realization:

Lord, authentic precious guru!
Because of the merit accumulated by your previous
practice,
You met the nirmāṇakāya Tilopa in person.
The suffering of existence, which is difficult to abandon,
You scorned throughout your twelve trials.
Through your practice of austerities,
You saw the truth in an instant.
I prostrate at your feet, Śrī Jñānasiddhi.

I, the translator, a novice from Tibet,
Through the karmic link of previous practice

Met you, Mahāpaṇḍita Nāropa.
I studied the *Hevajra-tantra,* famed for its
profundity.
You gave me the essence, Mahāmāyā.
I received the inner essence, Cakrasaṃvara.
In general, I extracted the inner essence of the four
orders of tantra.
As granted by the mother Subhaginī,
Whose river of blessings is continuous,
You transmitted the four abhiṣekas to me.
I gave birth to undefiled samādhi
And established confidence in it in seven days.
The sun and moon, the life force and descent,*
Were locked in the home of still space.
The experience of self-existing coemergence—
Bliss, luminosity, and nonthought—dawned from my
heart.
The confusion of habitual sleep
Was realized as the nature of the path of luminosity.
The movements of the mind, both grasping and
fixation,
Dissolved into the simplicity of dharmakāya.
Outer appearance, this illusory contrivance,
Was realized as unborn mahāmudrā.
Inner fixation, this mind consciousness,
Like meeting an old friend,
Realized its own nature.
Like a dream dreamt by a mute,
An inexpressible experience arose.
Like the ecstasy experienced by a maiden,

*Life force (T: srog-rtsol) and descent (T: 'pho-ba) refer to different aspects of caṇḍālī practice. Life force refers to the inner heat that is generated and that blazes up, causing the bodhicitta to descend as great bliss.

An indescribable meaning was realized.
Lord Nāropa, you are very kind.
Previously, you gave me blessings and abhiṣekas;
Please continue to accept me with your kindness.

Thus Marpa offered his realization.

Mahāpaṇḍita Nāropa placed his hand on top of Marpa's head, and sang this song of oral instructions:

You, Marpa the Translator from Tibet!
Do not make the eight worldly dharmas the goal of your life.
Do not create the bias of self and other, grasping and fixation.
Do not slander friends or enemies.
Do not distort the ways of others.
Learning and contemplating are the torch that illumines the darkness.
Do not be ambushed on the supreme path of liberation.
Previously, we have been guru and disciple;
Keep this with you in the future; do not give this up.
This precious jewel of your mind,
Do not throw it in the river like an idiot.
Guard it carefully with undistracted attention,
And you will accomplish all needs, desires, and intentions.

Nāropa said many kind things, at which Marpa greatly rejoiced. Marpa made a vow that he would return to see Nāropa, and he then left for Tibet.

Having received abhiṣekas and oral instructions, Marpa returns to Tibet.

Marpa's provisions had run out, as had those of Nyö. They met at a mutually prearranged time and traveled together on the return route. Nyö began to think, "Although I had more gold, he seems to be the more learned," and evil, jealous thoughts arose in him. Nyö had with him two paṇḍita friends, an atsara, and some others who carried his books and his baggage. Marpa carried his own books in a bundle. Nyö said to him, "It isn't right that we great lotsāwas should carry baggage. Let this atsara carry your bundle." Later, Nyö secretly bribed this atsara, saying, "Throw Marpa's books into the water, as if by accident."

When their boat came to the middle of the Ganges, the atsara threw Marpa's books into the water. Marpa knew that this was the work of Nyö. He thought, "In Tibet, searching for gold is hard work. In India, searching for gurus is hard work. Nothing was more precious than these teachings and oral instructions, and now they are gone. Should I throw myself into the water?" He considered this seriously, but remembering the oral instructions of his guru, he calmed his mind a little. Although he had no intention of seeking revenge, he told Nyö, "This was your doing."

"I didn't do it," Nyö replied.

As soon as the boat landed, Marpa grabbed the atsara and said, "I am going to talk to the king about this." The atsara fully recounted all that Nyö had told him to do. Then Marpa spontaneously sang to Nyö this song of shame:

> Listen to me, companion met through the power of karma.
> You are the man I agreed to travel with.
> In general, you have entered the gate of dharma.
> In particular, you are known as a lotsāwa, paṇḍita,
>   and guru.
>
> With perverted intentions you entered the boat.
> Even though you cannot benefit someone,
> In general, you should not cause harm to another.
> In particular, by harming the teachings of Buddha,

You have injured me and all sentient beings.
How could you possibly cause such harm?

By the thought and deed of the five poisonous kleśas,
Along with my books
You threw the fame you cultivated,
Your gold, and the holy dharma into the water.
It is not the material value I am thinking of,
But these special teachings were precious for others.
I am sad that others will not be benefited.

However, by my earnest application and questioning,
The dharma and my mind have mixed.
I clearly recall their words and meaning.
Returning to India again,
I need only ask for them
From Mahāpaṇḍita Nāropa and other siddha gurus.

Today, you should abandon
The name of guru, dharma teacher, and lotsāwa.
With remorse and repentance, return to your country.
Confess your evil deeds and do rigorous penance.
Thinking and acting as you have done
And boasting that you are a guru,
Though you might deceive a few fools,
How can you ripen and free those who are worthy?
With your precious human body so difficult to gain,
Please do not cultivate the three lower realms.

Thus Marpa sang.

Nyö said, "Don't worry about it. I will lend you my original texts and you can copy them."

Marpa said, "I don't know whether you will lend me the originals or not, but even if you did, our gurus and oral instructions are different so it would be of no use. I prefer what I have in my mind to your books."

Though Marpa thought of returning quickly to India, he then said, "Lend me your originals later, as you suggested."

When they arrived in Nepal, Marpa thought, "Accompanying Nyö, I will only accumulate evil deeds," and he told Nyö that he intended to go no further with him.

When they parted, Nyö said, "Don't spread the story of how your books were lost in the water. Come to my house and ask for my books," and Marpa promised that he would. Nyö went first from Nepal to the Nepalese-Tibetan border. There he sent a messenger instructing that attendants meet him. When they arrived, he went with them to Kharak.

Marpa met guru Chitherpa and the dharma friends headed by his friend White Hadu, who gave Marpa a fine reception. They said, "It was wonderful to hear that you sang a song to Nyö without being angry, even though he threw your books in the water out of jealousy. Your meditation practice is taking effect; it is the sign that you have given birth to unperverted, good view. Not relying on the words of texts, but arising out of your own mind, please sing us a song of the ultimate view."

In answer, Marpa sang this song:

O holy guru who is the guide,
And you who are headed by White Hadu
And who have completed your study of the sūtras and
 tantras,
Listen for a moment to a Tibetan's song.

The ultimate view is very special,
Indivisible and nondwelling.
It is the mind of the victorious ones of the three times.

Those who want to separate upāya and prajñā
Must be prevented from falling into extremes.

To speak to such learned ones as you is difficult.
I have not sung this song before, so it may not go well.
Nonetheless, listen and I will sing you a song of the
śāstras.

Preventing the grasping onto things as real
Is said to be the only way to conquer the hordes of Māra.
Understand that grasping in this way causes obscuration.
As for the glory of servants and personal virtues,
Abandon special attempts to gain it.

Ignorant ones believe that "emptiness" is nihilism.
The extreme of nihilism undermines the accumulation of
virtue.
Those who desire flowers in the sky
Destroy the harvest of virtue
With the hail of perverted views.

One should know the characteristics of space.
All those who do not know emptiness
Claim nonexistence is existence.
The perverted regard a mirage as water.
Ignorance about the truth is the cause of saṃsāra.
Cittamātrins and heretics like the Sāṅkhyas and
the rest
Maintain that upāya and prajñā are separate.
Each has his own theory.
This is the same as maintaining that a dead tree has
flowers.

Free from all assumptions
Is nondwelling truth.
Knowing this fully is prajñāpāramitā.
Not dwelling in the extremes of saṃsāra and nirvāṇa,
Compassion possesses the essence of emptiness
And unifies upāya and prajñā.
This is self-existing coemergence.
In the same way, I understand
Bliss-emptiness and insight-emptiness
As not being different.

Nonconceptual compassion
And the primordial nature of emptiness
Are inseparable in the nature of simplicity.
You should understand all dharmas like this.

As for the view that is merely shown by words,
See this as an object of clinging.
In accord with the common view,
Have confidence in the cause and result of karma.
It does not wear out in a hundred kalpas,
Just as the supreme wise one has said.

People without compassion
Are like sesame seeds burnt by fire.
How could further seeds come from that?
If there is no ground, how could there be any
  characteristics?
Therefore, these people cannot enter the mahāyāna.
Thus said the supremely wise Nāgārjuna.

If there is not a proper view of the objects of mind,
It is useless to give the holy dharma.

It is like chaff with no grain.
Thus says Marpa Lotsāwa.

You whose minds are vast with the truth of wisdom,
If I have the wrong meaning, please forgive me.

Thus Marpa sang.

The Nepalese guru, his friend White Hadu, and the others were very joyful.

Marpa's Dream of Saraha

On his way to Tibet, Marpa came to a village on the border between Nepal and Tibet called Liśokara, where the people collected many custom taxes. Lord Marpa was forced to stay there several days. His last night there, he had a dream in which ḍākinīs lifted him up in a palanquin and carried him to Śrī Parvata in the South. There Marpa met the Great Brahman Saraha, who blessed his body, speech, and mind. Saraha gave him the signs and the meanings of the dharma of the essential truth, mahāmudrā. Undefiled bliss dawned in his body, and unperverted realization dawned in his mind, so that Marpa's dream was filled with immeasurable delight. Even after he awoke, he did not forget what Saraha had said. In a state of delight, Marpa went to the province of Mang where he stayed at Langpokhar about two months and taught the dharma.

In Tsang at Kyerphu, the prince of Lokya had passed away, leaving his eldest son as prince. Hearing that Marpa was nearby, the prince sent a messenger to Kyitrong to invite Marpa to Kyerphu. Marpa accepted, set a time for the meeting, and sent the messenger back. The people of Palkhü escorted him from the lake of Lhatso Sintso, and he was welcomed warmly when he arrived at Kyerphu. For a month, Marpa taught a good course on the dharma.

On the tenth day of the waxing moon, the festival of the ḍākas, a gaṇacakra was held. During the feast, the prince said to guru Marpa, "Guru, my father and I received you warmly before. Now I alone am doing so, and today I request you at this gaṇacakra to please sing a song not sung before, a song unifying words and meaning."

Marpa answered, "Last spring, I traveled from central Nepal to a place the time of one meal's journey from there. In that uncivilized border town called Liśokara, the people collect many custom taxes. I stayed there a few days. One night, in a dream, women of authentic being dressed in the clothes of a brahman's daughter came to me and said, 'Let us go to Śrī Parvata in the South,' and they took me there. It seemed in the dream that I met the Great Brahman in person. At that time, I heard the essential truth which is not fabricated by the mind, sung by the Great Brahman."

Marpa then sang, in the melody of the outstretched wings of a soaring garuḍa, this grand song, a vajra dohā that pierces to the pith of mind:

> On this glorious and auspicious day of the waxing moon,
> The holiday of the tenth day,
> At the gaṇacakra feast of the ḍākas,
> A son who is unswerving in samaya,
> You, the prince of Lokya, have requested, "Sing a
> song never heard before."
>
> I have traveled a long way on the road,
> And my body is overcome with weariness.
> Therefore, this song will not be melodious nor
> ravishing to your mind,
> And I am not even skilled in composing songs.
> But because there is no one more important than
> you, my friend,

And since I cannot refuse an important man,
I will sing a wondrous song which has never been
heard before,
A song of the sayings and thoughts of the Lord Brahman.
You, the many monks and tāntrikas who fill these seats,
Listen carefully and consider this in your hearts.

In the third month of last spring,
I came up from the land of central Nepal.
After being on the road the time of one meal,
I arrived at the Nepalese custom-tax station
In a town of lower caste people.
The custom-tax collectors exploit any man they meet,
And detain defenseless traveling Tibetans.
I, too, had to stay several days against my will.

One night, while dreaming in a light sleep,
Two beautiful brahman girls of authentic being,
Wearing the brahmanical thread,
Smiling coyly, and glancing out of the corners of
their eyes,
Came before me and said,
"You must go to Śrī Parvata in the South!"
I said, "I have never gone there before;
I don't even know the way."
The two girls replied,
"Brother, you don't have to do anything difficult;
We shall carry you on our shoulders."
They put me on the seat of a cloth palanquin
And lifted it into the sky like a parasol.
Like a flash of lightning, in a mere instant of time,
I dreamt that I arrived at Śrī Parvata in the South.

In the cool shade of a grove of plakṣa trees,
On a tira corpse seat
Sat Lord Saraha, the Great Brahman.
I had never before seen such majestic brilliance.
He was flanked by two queens.
His body was adorned with charnel ground ornaments.
His joyous face was beaming.

"Welcome, my son!" he said.
Seeing the lord, I was overwhelmed with joy.
The hairs of my body stood on end, and I was moved to tears.
I circumambulated him seven times and I offered a full prostration.
I received the soles of his feet on the top of my head.
"Father, accept me with kindness," I supplicated.

He blessed my body with his.
The moment he touched his hand to the top of my head,
My body was intoxicated with undefiled bliss.
Like an elephant drunk with liquor,
There dawned an experience of immovability.

He blessed my speech with his.
With the lion's roar of emptiness,
He spoke "that without letter."
Like a dream dreamt by a mute,
There dawned an experience beyond words.

He blessed my mind with his.
I realized the coemergent dharmakāya,
That which neither comes nor goes.

Like a human corpse left in a charnel ground,
There dawned an experience of nonthought.

Then the pure speech of great bliss arose
From the vase of his precious throat.
With sign speech in the melody of Brahmā,
He sang this vajra song which points out things
as they are,
The meaning of an empty sky free from clouds.
Thus I heard this unborn self-utterance:

"NAMO Compassion and emptiness are inseparable.
This uninterrupted flowing innate mind
Is suchness, primordially pure.
Space is seen in intercourse with space.
Because the root resides at home,
Mind consciousness is imprisoned.
Meditating on this, subsequent thoughts
Are not patched together in the mind.
Knowing the phenomenal world is the nature of mind,
Meditation requires no further antidote.
The nature of mind cannot be thought.
Rest in this natural state.
When you see this truth, you will be liberated.
Just as a child would, watch the behavior of
barbarians.
Be carefree; eat flesh; be a madman.

"Just like a fearless lion,
Let your elephant mind wander free.
See the bees hovering among the flowers.
Not viewing saṃsāra as wrong,

There is no such thing as attaining nirvāṇa.
This is the way of ordinary mind.
Rest in natural freshness.
Do not think of activities.
Do not cling to one side or one direction.
Look into the midst of the space of simplicity."

Going beyond the exhausting of dharmatā is the essential truth,
The summit of views, mahāmudrā.
This sign meaning, which pierces to the pith of mind,
I heard from the mouth of the Great Brahman.

At that instant, I awoke.
I was caught by the iron hook of this unforgettable memory.
Within the dungeon of ignorant sleep,
The vision of insight-wisdom opened up
And the sun dawned in a cloudless sky,
Clearing the darkness of confusion.
I thought, "Even if I met the buddhas of the three times,
From now on, I would have nothing to ask them."

This was a decisive experience.
Discursive thoughts were exhausted, what a wonder!
E ma! The prophecies of yidams and ḍākinīs
And the profound truth spoken by the guru,
Although I have been told not to speak of these things,
Tonight I cannot help but speak them.
Except for this very occasion,
I have never said this before.
Listen with your ears and repeat it at a later time.

I am a man who has traveled a long way
Without intimate friends and relatives.
Now, when my body becomes tired and hungry,
Son, what you have done will be in my mind.
I will not forget this; it is impressed deeply in
my mind.
My heart friend, your kindness is repaid.

The lords who dwell above, the gurus,
The divine yidams who bestow siddhis,
And the dharmapālas who clear obstacles,
May all these please not scold me.
Please forgive me if there is any confusion in
what I have said.

Thus, this song was sung, and the guru Marpa was seen as the buddha in person by the prince of Lokya.

On the way to Lhotrak, Lord Marpa went to Nyö's house in Kharak to see if Nyö would lend him the books to make copies. "I need the copies of the texts," he said.

Nyö offered Lord Marpa one *sang* of gold and a maṇḍala and said, "You are very knowledgeable about the *Mahāmāyā*. You have no need for these texts. You expound the *Mahāmāyā* and other teachings of the mother tantra. I will expound the *Guhyasamāja* and other teachings of the father tantra." Speaking in this way, Nyö refused to let him copy the texts.

Feeling intense longing to return soon to India, Marpa traveled to Lhotrak. His father and mother had both passed away. His teacher and older brother gave him a good welcome. Since Marpa had been a former pupil, the teacher did not request teachings from him, but he respected Marpa's learning in the dharma. Furthermore, none of his relatives, servants, or any of the local folk requested teachings from him or prostrated to him. However, they all held him in high esteem and trusted him. Some people came to Lhotrak from far away to request teachings and abhiṣeka. There were many who offered him prostrations and some token gifts.

This ends the first section, Marpa's First Journey to India.

MARPA'S SECOND JOURNEY TO INDIA

Marpa goes looking for gold and meets with disciples.

Thinking that he should bring along some attendants in his search for gold, Marpa gave instructions on the words and meaning of various sādhanas, as well as on their ritual traditions, to some students in Lhotrak who had requested teaching from him. He brought these students along as attendants and also brought some fine abhiṣeka implements and shrine objects.

Riding on a horse, he went to Central Tibet south of the Tsangpo river. He had stopped by a river bank for a meal when two tantric priests who looked like teachers came by. The chief one said, "Reverends, where do you come from and where are you going?"

One of the students who was eloquent answered, "Your reverences might have heard of this lord; he is the close disciple of the siddha, Mahāpaṇḍita Nāropa of India. This guru is known as the translator Marpa Lotsāwa. We, master and disciples, are here to ripen and free those worthy ones who have fortunate karma and to establish a virtuous karmic connection to those who are less fortunate. In order to benefit the teachings and sentient beings, Lord Marpa is collecting offerings of gold and provisions to return to India again." Continuing in this way, the student gave a complete and detailed account.

The priest said, "Yes, I have heard of the fame of this guru before and thought of meeting him. Please come and stay at my house tonight."

In this way, he invited them to the monastery Soaring Garuḍa Mountain in the region of Shung. This priest was the first of Marpa's chief disciples. He was known as Ngoktön Chödor of Shung. Ngok received Marpa at Shung and served him well. He requested teachings and Marpa gave him the abhiṣeka and sādhana of the bhagavat Hevajra according to the teacher Padmavajra. Ngok made many offerings of good clothing and other things. Moreover, he urged his own disciples and many patrons to request teachings. They supplicated the guru and received abhiṣeka. Marpa taught the dharma for two months. He received many gifts and his fame spread.

Then Marpa stayed at Sesamar in the region of Phen. He healed nine women of the condition of "infant death" by means of the *Kīla,* and received eleven *sho* of gold for each cure. He performed the permission-blessing of the devī Remati as well as several yogic applications. He taught several dharma courses and all present became very devoted.

One day, Marpa gave the abhiṣeka of Hevajra to many people at Sesamar. At that time, from Nyingtrung in the Damshö district in the North, the merchant Marpa Golek arrived in Central Tibet on business. He asked who the many people milling about on the hillside were and what they were doing. They said, "Jetsün Nāropa's disciple, Marpa Lotsāwa, has conducted an abhiṣeka and is now performing a gaṇacakra."

Marpa Golek thought, "He might be my relative and a good guru as well. I should receive teachings from him." Thus he offered Marpa four sides of yak meat and one sack of rock salt.

While they were conversing, faith arose in Marpa Golek and he thought, "I should invite this guru to my house." He told Marpa, "If you are looking for gold to offer to the gurus of India, you won't find it in the region of Phen. According to the proverb: 'In the dry region of Phen they count the portions of poultry. In the eight districts to the North they count the quarters of a wild yak.' The people of the region of Phen are not honest. They have little faith and they are crude and thick-headed. If you go with me to the North, you will ride on horseback, wear a fine robe, and sit on fine cushions. You will have plenty of meat, butter, and cheese."

"Well then, I should go with you," said Marpa.

"When you receive our invitation, please come," Marpa Golek said.

Marpa Golek finished his business and departed again for the North. There he sent back a welcoming party to meet Marpa, with a horse for the guru to ride and with dzos loaded with fine clothing and provisions. When he heard Marpa was near, Golek himself mounted his horse and went to receive him. He met the guru at the border near Tsül in Dam. He noticed that Marpa was wearing his old clothes and had packed away the new clothes that Golek had given him. "For us highlanders in the North," Golek said, "physical appearance is very important. I would like to request you to put aside your old clothes and put on the new ones."

Marpa replied, "In general, it is said that demons do not harm what you really own. In particular, the great and glorious Nāropa blessed these clothes of mine. It would be a great loss if I threw them away, so I will save them to bring back to Lhotrak." He then packed them away in his baggage. "I will please you," he said, and he put on the new clothes offered by Ngok, and by Golek as well.

Golek offered him his own saddled horse. As they were going along the road, Golek thought, "Besides all the clothes I offered him, he has other new ones he hasn't worn. He seems to be miserly. Generally, the actions of a holy person cannot ultimately be fathomed; however, if this is greed for material wealth, it is a great fault. Therefore, I must test this guru."

Golek asked, "Besides the new clothes I offered you, you have others. Why did you not wear them from the start?"

"It would be very inconvenient to take all these clothes to India and when they get old they can't be exchanged for gold. Exchanging these new clothes for gold, I plan to offer the gold to glorious Nāropa. Now, in order to please you, I have worn them. If I do not have gold in India, I cannot obtain teachings,'' Marpa answered.

Marpa Golek thought, ''Such desire for material wealth is not a fault but a virtue,'' and his karmic connection was awakened further. He burst into tears, his hairs trembled, and extraordinary faith was born in him. In the presence of the guru, he took a vow to practice wholeheartedly and to attend him constantly.

Then they arrived at Nyingtrung in the Damshö district. At the urging of Golek, who was the chief of this province of highlanders, his family and servants gave Marpa a good welcome. In accord with his vow, Marpa Golek entered the gate of dharma and requested abhiṣeka and oral instructions. He urged his servants, relatives, and friends also to receive teachings. Marpa healed the condition of ''infant death'' many times, and received much gold. About ninety people received teachings and offered him gold and much wealth. All the gifts that were not gold were exchanged for gold.

Then Marpa went to the gold rock of Mera in the North and received much gold. In particular, Golek himself gave eighteen *sang* of gold, many dzos, horses, cattle, sheep, suits of armor, and his own horse, called White Headed Turquoise Dragon. When Marpa was content with the gifts of gold and other things, he thought, ''Now I should go to India.''

With Golek and some other dharma practitioners following as attendants, guru Marpa departed for Lhotrak. When they were north of the Tsangpo river, Tsurtön Wang-nge of Töl invited them to his house. Thus, the master and disciples went to Töl and were welcomed. Tsurtön supplicated for the abhiṣeka and oral instructions of *Guhyasamāja*.

Marpa gave him the abhiṣeka and said, ''I'll give you the oral instructions later; now I'm in a hurry.'' After Tsurtön had made many offerings, he followed the guru as an attendant in order to receive the oral instructions.

Ngokpa invited Marpa again to Shung and gave him many gifts of gold and other things. Then he also departed with Marpa, as his attendant. As soon as the master and disciples arrived in Trowo valley, Bawachen of Parang invited them to South Layak. He received the abhiṣeka of *Mahāmāyā* and offered many gifts. Marpa accepted the gifts, and those who had received teachings attended him.

In Trowo valley, the guru gave the abhiṣeka of *Hevajra* in order to repay the disciples for their service and devotion. Marpa gave the *Hevajra* especially to Ngokpa. To Tsurtön and Marpa Golek, he gave the *Guhyasamāja* according to the root text and the direct instructions of the five stages. To Bawachen of Parang, he gave the explanations on the *Mahāmāyā*.

For the farewell feast, Marpa invited his older brother and organized an excellent gaṇacakra. At the feast the students asked, "Precious guru, how many gurus did you have in India? Among them, who possessed the wondrous mark of siddhi? What abhiṣekas and oral instructions did you receive from them? What kind of companions did you travel with?"

In response, Lord Marpa gave them an extensive account. Then, being more concise, he sang this song in verse:

> Lord Vajradhara of this age of strife,
> Supreme being who has accomplished ascetic discipline,
> Carried by everyone like a crown on his head,
> Glorious Nāropa, I respectfully pay homage at your feet.

> This Marpa Lotsāwa of Lhotrak
> Met with dharma when twelve years old.
> This certainly reawakened the predispositions from former training.
> First I learned the letters of the alphabet.

Then I learned the translation of words.
Finally I went south to Nepal and India.

I stayed three years in central Nepal.
From blessed Nepalese gurus
I heard the *Catuḥpīṭha,* renowned as a powerful tantra.
I received the devī Vetālī as a protector.

Not satisfied by this alone,
I went to India for further teachings.
I crossed poisonous and deadly rivers.
My skin shed like a snake's.

Daring to abandon my life for the sake of dharma,
I arrived at that wonderful place prophesied by the
ḍākinīs,
Phullahari in the North.
At this monastery imbued with siddhi,
From the gatekeeper Mahāpaṇḍita Nāropa
I received the tantra of *Hevajra,* renowned for
its profundity,
And the oral instructions of the union of mixing
and ejecting.
I especially requested the karmamudrā of caṇḍālī
And received transmission of the hearing lineage.

At the monastery of Lakṣetra in the West
I touched the feet of glorious Jñānagarbha.
I listened to the father tantra, the *Guhyasamāja,*
Received the instructions of the illusory body
and luminosity,
And learned the meaning of the path of five stages.

I went to the island in the boiling poison lake in
the South.
In the middle of the day, it grew as dark as midnight.
Sometimes the path was clear and sometimes it
disappeared.
Abandoning my fear of death, I searched for the jetsün.
I met glorious Śāntibhadra in person.
He gave me the mother tantra, the *Mahāmāyā.*
I learned the meaning of the three yogas, form
and so on,
And received the instructions of the tantra of three
illusions.*

In the East I crossed the Ganges, the river of siddhis.
At the monastery of the quaking mountain
I touched the feet of the lord, Master Maitrīpa,
And received the profound tantra, the
Mañjuśrī-nāma-saṅgīti.
Living in the realization of the dharma of mahāmudrā,
The nature and workings of actual mind were resolved.
I saw the essence of the meaning of ground dharmatā.

Renowned throughout all Jambudvīpa,
These are the lineage gurus of the four directions.

Also from wandering yogins in charnel grounds
And kusulus dwelling under trees,
Some of whom are completely unknown,

*According to Tāranātha's commentary on the *Mahāmāyā,* the three illusions are: (1) illusion of phenomenal appearances (T: snang-ba sgyu-ma), (2) illusion of dream (T: rmi-lam sgyu-ma), and (3) illusion of pardo (T: bar-do sgyu-ma). See *Bka'-brgyud sngags-mdzod,* vol. 3, no. 11, Sgyu-'phrul, pp. 291:3-292:5.

I received many short instructions in sampannakrama,
Wondrous sādhanas,
And countless oral instructions of yogic applications.

On the way back to Tibet, Nyö of Kharak
accompanied me.
When we arrived in central Nepal
I, Marpa Lotsāwa of Lhotrak,
And Nyö Lotsāwa of Kharak
Discussed which lotsāwa was more learned and had
greater oral instructions.

When crossing the border from Nepal to Tibet,
Nyö was richer in wealth and material goods.
When I arrived in the four parts of Latö,
I had attained equal renown as a translator.
When I came to the center of Ü and Tsang in Tibet,
I was famed for oral instructions.
Since I have met siddha gurus,
There is no question as to the greatness of these
oral instructions.
Since I do not hope for enlightenment from sophistry,
Those expounders of texts may do as they please.

Thus Marpa sang.

Even his older brother felt great devotion and offered Marpa any property or valley he desired. Thus Marpa's dignity, wealth, property, and renown increased greatly. When he had gathered many disciples and much wealth, he married Dagmema and took other authentic consorts possessing good qualities, and Tarma Dode and other sons were born.

Marpa goes to India a second time, meets with his gurus, and receives teachings.

Marpa prepared an excellent thanksgiving feast for the gurus, yidams, dharmapālas, and protectors for their past favor. Supplicating them and entrusting them with his future success, he arranged elaborate offerings and torma for the feast and performed a good gaṇacakra. Taking about fifty *sang* of gold, he prepared to depart for India. Though a few students requested to go as attendants, Marpa did not grant his permission and said he would go alone. Thus he left and arrived in Nepal, where he met Chitherpa and Paiṇḍapa. He offered them gold and they were pleased. The Nepalese dharma brothers arranged for some trustworthy companions to accompany him, and so Marpa went with them to India where he arrived without mishap.

Marpa offers gold to his gurus, headed by Nāropa, to repay their kindness, thus pleasing them, and he again receives teachings.

In the presence of glorious Nāropa, Marpa requested the abhiṣeka of *Hevajra* in the extensive, intermediate, and abbreviated versions, the second section of the *Hevajramūlatantra,* the extraordinary explanation of the *Ḍākinī-vajrapañjara-tantra,* and the ordinary explanation of the *Sampuṭa-tantra,* all of these together with their commentary and oral instructions.

Then Nāropa said, "Go meet with your other former gurus as well. Thoroughly review the teachings you received earlier. Later, when you have no doubts concerning these, request other teachings that you have not yet received and discuss them. To whom would you like to go first?"

Marpa replied, "First I will go to Maitrīpa." Marpa went to stay with Maitrīpa, pleased him with an offering of gold, and carefully reviewed the teachings he had received earlier. Then he requested the abhiṣeka and commentary of the *Guhyasamāja* and the tantra of the *Mahāmudrā-tilaka,* and copied their texts.

After a brief return to Nāropa at Phullahari, he went to Nālandā where he met the Kashmiri paṇḍita Śrī Bhadra. At a welcoming gaṇacakra, Śrī Bhadra asked, "You have heard Master Maitrīpa expound the pith instructions. Which do you think is more profound, the intention of the lineage of Lord Śavari, the disciple of the lord Great Brahman, or the intention of our own guru Nāropa, the disciple of Tilopa?"

Marpa thought, "A gaṇacakra always involves song and dance; therefore there is no harm in revealing some aspects of Maitrīpa's intention in a song." Then he sang this song:

Listen, heart friend Śrī Bhadra!
I am a Buddhist called Marpa.
As you asked which is more profound,

The intention of Nāropa or Maitrīpa,
This song is my reply.

Lion-like Nāropa
Is the most precious of all.
His great intention
Is to fulfill all needs and desires.
Lord Dharmadhara, please accept us with kindness.

The lotus feet of this mahāpaṇḍita
These days are my crest ornament.
His intention is as follows.
Please pay attention and listen carefully.

The sky of dharmakāya is thick with rain clouds of
wisdom.
The continuous rain of emanations spreads over all beings.
To the supremely born guru of the uninterrupted lineage
I respectfully prostrate with body, speech, and mind.

The dharmakāya like the sky
Is the buddha, great Vajradhara.
The thick rain clouds of wisdom
Are the two bodhisattvas.

The amṛta rainfall of buddha activity
Is the jetsün, Brahman Saraha.
The emanation who works for the benefit of beings
Is the Lord of Hermits, Śavari.

The holder of this unbroken lineage
Is the Master, Prince Maitrīpa.

I received kindness from this holy one.
This is how to understand his intention.

Self-luminous unchanging insight
Is described as unborn dharmakāya.
Unceasing self-born wisdom
Is described as the multiplicity of nirmāṇakāya.

These two unified in coemergence
Are described as the sambhogakāya.
These three free from origin
Are described as the svabhāvikakāya.

All these, beyond conditions
Are described as the mahāsukhakāya.
These are the five ultimate kāyas.
Does this gladden your minds, heart friends?

Thus Marpa sang and described how the five kāyas function.

Śrī Bhadra said, "Now please describe the view, meditation, action, and fruition."

So Marpa sang this song:

Please listen without your minds wandering.
Though I am not skilled in composing songs,
This is the way to understand the true oral instructions.
Keep this in mind and ponder it.

The three worlds are primordially pure.
Ultimately, there is nothing more to understand.
Not negation, unceasing continuity,
Unchanging—such is the view.

The innate essence is naturally luminous.
Unconditioned, meditation is unceasing.
Not negation, beyond losing and gaining,
Without desire or attachment—such is the
meditation.

Arising from the natural occurrence of various
coincidences,
The play of illusion is unobstructed.
Not negation,
Things are unpredictable, abrupt—such is the action.

Mind shines as bodhicitta.
There is no attainment of the three kāyas of buddha.
Not negation, beyond hope and fear,
Without ground or root—such is the fruition.

Thus Marpa sang.

Again Śrī Bhadra asked, "Did Maitrīpa give the practitioners oral instructions all at once, or did he instruct them gradually by way of techniques?"

In reply Marpa sang this song:

O you superior dharma friends!
My Jetsün Maitrīpa
Touched the feet of Śavari,
The heart son of Nāgārjuna, protector of beings,
Who was foretold by Avalokiteśvara.

Śavari gave him the full teachings of the three yānas.
He received the secret name Advayavajra.
He holds the keys of all the orders of tantra.
He accomplished the techniques of the secret mantra.

Victory banner of dharma, treasury of dharma,
Lion of dharma, king of dharma—
He is widely learned in philology, madhyamaka,
and logic.
He attained the mastery of a paṇḍita.
He knows faultlessly the reality of things as they are.

He abandoned his royal domain as if it were weeds
And attained the supreme state in one life.
Jetsün Ḍākinī revealed herself to him
And so he received all the ordinary siddhis.
In this way he attained immeasurable virtues.

Now these are the intentions of the father:
To ordinary people who are receptive to the gradual
path
He gives the oral instruction of caṇḍālī for
life force,
The oral instruction of illusory body for nonattachment,
The transmission of luminosity for clearing away darkness,
The transmission of existence as sambhogakāya,
The transmission of birth as nirmāṇakāya, and so on.
Thus he guides them through the supreme means of
ground, path, and fruition.

To those who are receptive to the sudden path,
He transmits naked mahāmudrā.
Seeing this father fills one's body, speech, and
mind with faith.
Hearing him purifies karmic obscurations.
Meeting him liberates one from the terrors of the lower
realms.
If requested, he places buddha in the palm of one's hand.

Holding the lineage of the glorious Lord of Hermits,
Mahāpaṇḍita Nāropa's heart son,
The precious second Buddha,
Lord Maitrīpa possesses these virtues.

These days people are extremely jealous.
If this is repeated to anyone other than you, friends,
Virtue will not flourish and defilement will increase.
Therefore, keep this secret from ordinary people.
These are the actions of the guru.
Isn't this good, fortunate vajra friends?

Thus Marpa sang.

Paṇḍita Śrī Bhadra, the leader, and the rest were very pleased and said, "Translator, you have done well in accomplishing your purposes."

After this, Lord Marpa returned to glorious Nāropa. As Nāropa suggested, he went to his gurus with offerings of gold. First he went to the island in the poison lake, where he met Kukkurīpā and Yoginī Adorned with Bone Ornaments. Then he went to Lakṣetra in the West, where he met glorious Jñānagarbha and Siṃhadvīpa. He offered gold to all the gurus, which pleased them very much. Once again, in order to clarify his understanding, he requested the abhiṣekas, reading transmissions, and oral instructions already received, as well as those not yet received. He translated all the teachings he received, edited them carefully, and returned with them to Phullahari.

From glorious Nāropa, he received scrolls of the text and oral instructions on the *Cakrasaṃvara* of the lineage of King Indrabhūti and on the *Buddhakapāla-tantra* according to the tradition of the Great Brahman Saraha. Then Marpa began translating and writing down all the teachings he had previously received.

One day while Marpa was having a meal with Nāropa, a learned paṇḍita from Labar in Kashmir, a peaceful, gentle bhikṣu named Ākarasiddhi arrived. Even Nāropa greeted him as an equal. Ākarasiddhi supplicated Nāropa, saying, "Please bestow on me the abhiṣeka, reading transmission, commentary, and oral instructions of the *Guhyasamāja.*" Lord Marpa supplicated for these as well.

Nāropa said, "Now, because the time has come, I will definitely do this."

Together with Ākarasiddhi, Marpa received the abhiṣeka of the elaborate and simplified maṇḍalas of the *Guhyasamāja,* as well as the great tantric commentary called *Advayasamatāvijaya* in 3,500 ślokas and the *Pradīpoddyotana-nāmaṭīka.*

When the teaching was completed, Ākarasiddhi prepared to leave. Marpa saw him off, and asked, "Where are you going now?"

He replied, "I am going through Tibet on a pilgrimage to Wu-t'ai Shan in China."

Marpa thought, "After this learned paṇḍita goes through Tibet, it may be that fewer people will request the *Guhyasamāja* and other teachings from me."

Through his higher perception, the paṇḍita instantly knew what Marpa was thinking. Then he left for Tibet.

When Ākarasiddhi arrived in Khap Kungthang he met Naktso Lotsāwa who was teaching the *Pradīpoddyotana* on a rooftop. The lotsāwa said, "Who are you, dzoki? Where are you going?"

"I am a paṇḍita. I am going to Wu-t'ai Shan in China."

Naktso scornfully said, "These so-called Indian paṇḍitas wander around with their dirty bare feet looking for gold. They make me laugh. By the way, do you know the paṇḍita Ākarasiddhi?"

"That is I."

"In that case you are certainly not looking for gold. You are wonderful." Naktso invited him inside and offered him every hospitality. In general, Naktso requested the profound and vast teachings of the sūtras and tantras, and in particular, the *Guhyasamāja.*

While giving these, the paṇḍita realized through his higher perception, "Although I have arrived in Tibet and taught the dharma, no one here is karmically connected to me as a disciple except for this lotsāwa. All those presently in Tibet who have faith in the mantrayāna will be disciples of Marpa Lotsāwa, an emanation of Ḍombī Heruka. He alone will tame them. If I go to China, my life will be in danger. It is my destiny to perform buddha activity for disciples in Uḍḍiyāṇa." Therefore he decided to return to India.

After he had received the teachings, Naktso offered considerable gold as well as necessities for traveling in Tibet and said, "Since you are thinking of going to China, you will first have to pass through Tibet. I will send however many guides and servants you need as far as Lhasa."

Because he had great renunciation and because he had in mind what Naktso said earlier about barefoot paṇḍitas looking for gold, Ākarasiddhi said, "Now I am going to return to India. I don't need gold or companions," and he would accept nothing.

Naktso asked, "What is your reason?"

Ākarasiddhi told him what he had realized through his higher perception. Naktso said, "If you are returning to India, you must accept some gold in order that I may perfect the accumulations." With tears streaming from his eyes, he insisted that Ākarasiddhi accept.

"Well, in order for you to perfect the accumulations, I shall take a little." Ākarasiddhi took one *sang* of gold and departed.

Because of his conversation with Ākarasiddhi, Naktso Lotsāwa experienced sacred outlook and realized that Jetsün Marpa was certainly a great bodhisattva dwelling on the bhūmis.

When the paṇḍita arrived in India, he said to Lord Marpa, "My friend, I did not do as you feared. As you wish, the buddha activity of taming disciples in Tibet will be yours."

Marpa thought, "This good paṇḍita knew my trivial bad thoughts through his higher perception. Fundamentally, there was no breach of trust on my part. I don't have to feel ashamed.

Generally, I must be aware of my own mind. I must not give rise to bad thoughts.'' Marpa related his thoughts to the paṇḍita.

The paṇḍita said, ''Ah well, I am just joking. Because of your good intentions in former lives, now the guru accepts you in his heart. In the future you will be the glory of the teachings and sentient beings.'' Then Ākarasiddhi departed for Uḍḍiyāṇa.

After this, Lord Marpa translated all the texts of the abhiṣekas, reading transmissions, and oral instructions that he had received from his gurus. With exertion, he finished these compositions quickly.

Marpa returns to Tibet.

Marpa accomplished the activities intended to benefit the teachings and sentient beings. Satisfied, he prepared to return to Tibet. During a thanksgiving gaṇacakra that Marpa offered to Nāropa, the mahāpaṇḍita put his hand on top of Jetsün Marpa's head and sang this song:

A flower blooming in the sky,
The son of a barren woman rides a horse
Wielding a whip of tortoise hair.
With the dagger of a hare's horn
He kills his enemy in the space of dharmatā.
The mute speaks, the blind man sees.
The deaf man hears, the cripple runs.
The sun and moon dance, blowing trumpets.
The little child turns the wheel.

Then Nāropa said, ''Furthermore, I have the transference of consciousness, some profound oral instructions of the hearing lineage, and other teachings. You should definitely come back once more.'' Thus Nāropa urged Marpa strongly, but did not say anything more, and Marpa did not ask about the meaning of the song. Keeping Nāropa's words clearly in mind, Marpa vowed that they would definitely meet once again. Making this prayer, he departed.

Arriving in Nepal, Marpa stayed only briefly and then went to Tibet. When he arrived in Tsang, the great Metön Tsönpo of Tsangrong requested the abhiṣeka and oral instructions of Cakrasaṃvara. While Marpa stayed there and performed the abhiṣeka, his disciples in Trowo valley heard the good news of the guru's arrival in Tibet and that he was in good health. Marpa Golek and some other disciples went to welcome him. In the mountains of upper Nyang, they met the guru, who was coming from Tsangrong. They all returned and stayed in Lhotrak.

There Jetsün Mila and many other worthy disciples soon gathered. Marpa's splendor, fame, and buddha activity of taming disciples expanded greatly. During this time, the taming of Jetsün Mila and the building of the tower called Sekhar were completed.*

Tarma Dode Comes of Age

One day, during his son's coming of age and consecration ceremony, Lord Marpa and his son Tarma Dode had a debate, which the son won. The son said, "As they say, 'The stirring spoon did the hard work, but the ladle takes the juice.' The father performed the hard work, but I have the practices. The

*This line refers to the difficult hardships that Marpa put Milarepa through in order to purify him of his previous evil deeds and make him a worthy vessel for the teachings. Marpa promised to give Mila teaching after Mila had built a small castle, or tower, for his son, Tarma Dode. (The name Sekhar literally means "the son's castle.") However, Marpa changed his mind two times and each time he had Mila take down his construction, which was partially completed, and start over again. In building these towers and continually anticipating his receiving the teachings only to be disappointed, Mila was pushed to the limits of physical and mental exhaustion.

When at last the Sekhar was completed, Marpa hosted a large ceremony in which his son's coming of age was celebrated and the Sekhar was consecrated. (In fact, the song on pp. 69-70 is included in Mila's biography). It was the day after this celebration that Mila finally gave up hope of ever receiving teachings and was ready to kill himself. At this point Marpa openly accepted Mila as his disciple. See *The Life of Milarepa,* pp. 47-74.

father should sit quietly and eat his porridge." Saying this, Tarma Dode was quite amused and laughed.

The father said, "Son, as they say, 'The water of virtue cannot stay on a ball of arrogance.' The son is learned and great because of his father's kindness. I still wish you well, but don't be proud. Listen to this song."

Then Marpa sang this song of urgent command to his son:

Listen noble son, Dodebum.
Though you say you are learned and great,
All that is the noble father's kindness.
Gathering vast accumulations through former lives,
I created wealth of yellow gold.
Thus I pleased the guru.

Listen noble son, Dodebum.
Nāropa, Maitrīpa, and Path of Liberation*
Are the three holy root gurus.
Thus the oral instructions are profound.

Listen noble son, Dodebum.
Because I never irritated the gurus,
The ḍākinīs were pleased and cared for me like a child.
Thus I was free from obstacles and bad circumstances.
I trained my mind in the holy dharṃa of mahāyāna.
Arousing bodhicitta, I encompassed all beings.
Thus I spread the holy dharma in Tibet.

Listen noble son, Dodebum.
Since I went forth to greet the guru on his arrival
  and escorted him on his departure,
The soles of my feet were marked with dharmacakras.
Thus I traveled through India.

*Path of Liberation refers to Kukkurīpā. See p. 25.

Listen noble son, Dodebum.
As for the tantras, commentaries, and oral instructions,
I learned their words and meanings thoroughly,
without error.
Thus I spread the teachings.

Listen noble son, Dodebum.
Metön, Ngoktön, Tsurtön, and Golek
Are the four heart sons.
Thus I taught the tantras and commentaries.

Listen noble son, Dodebum.
He who accomplished whatever the guru said
Is Mila Dorje Gyaltsen.
Thus I bestowed the oral instructions on him.*

Listen noble son, Dodebum.
I, the lord father, am getting old.
I have arrived at the exhausting of dharmatā.
Dode, your time has come.
By your great learning, propagate the teachings.
Fulfill the wish of this old man.

Thus Marpa sang. Everyone there felt unwavering faith in Lord Marpa.

Then, when he performed the consecration and the invocation of auspiciousness, Jetsün Marpa sang this song of the benediction of auspiciousness:

I supplicate the kind gurus.
This precious lineage of mine

*This contradicts the sequence of events as described by Tsang Nyön in *Life of Milarepa.* In Mila's biography, Mila had not received any oral instructions from Marpa until the day after this consecration service had taken place.

Is auspicious, free from degradation.
May the goodness of this auspiciousness be present.

The direct path of the profound oral instructions
Is auspicious, free from corruption or confusion.
May the goodness of this auspiciousness be present.

I, Marpa Lotsāwa,
Have the auspicious profound pith.
May the goodness of this auspiciousness be present.

Gurus, yidams, and ḍākinīs
Have auspicious blessings and siddhis.
May the goodness of this auspiciousness be present.

Great sons and assemblies of disciples
Have auspicious faith and samaya.
May the goodness of this auspiciousness be present.

Benefactors from countries near and far
Have the auspicious harmonious occasion to gather merit.
May the goodness of this auspiciousness be present.

All deeds and activities
Are auspicious, enlightened, and benefit beings.
May the goodness of this auspiciousness be present.

Gods and demons of the phenomenal world
Are auspiciously under powerful command.
May the goodness of this auspiciousness be present.

The crowds of gods and men gathered here
Auspiciously aspire to bliss and happiness.
May the goodness of this auspiciousness be present.

Thus Marpa sang.

Afterward, guru Ngokpa and other disciples and benefactors offered gifts. Marpa accepted them and dedicated the virtue for the enlightenment of all.

That was the second trip to India.

MARPA'S THIRD JOURNEY TO INDIA

Marpa goes to gather gold and other things of value.

Having accepted Jetsün Milarepa, Marpa gave him abhiṣekas and oral instructions and sent him into retreat at Taknya in Lhotrak. In accordance with the vow he made in the presence of glorious Nāropa, Jetsün Marpa intended to return once more to India. Together with Marpa Golek and many other disciples, Marpa went again to northern Üru to gather offerings of gold. Because of Marpa's fame, many people requested teachings, and therefore he received many gifts of gold. Afterward, Marpa performed an abhiṣeka at Marpa Golek's residence. When he had completed the abhiṣeka itself and was about to chant the concluding liturgy, Lord Marpa passed into a state where sleep and luminosity mix, and had this vision:

Three lovely maidens clothed in silks and wearing ornaments of bone walked toward him, side by side. In order to decipher the coded verses of Mahāpaṇḍita Nāropa, which Marpa had not understood previously, the maidens on the right and left accompanied the leader in this song:

The ḍākinī is the flower blooming in the sky.
The son of a barren woman riding a horse is the hearing lineage.
The whip of tortoise hair is the inexpressible.
The dagger of a hare's horn is the unborn.
This kills Tilopa in the space of dharmatā.
Tilopa is the mute, beyond word, thought, and expression.
Nāropa is the blind man, liberated in seeing the truth of nothing to see.
Nāropa is the deaf man, the dharmakāya mountain of dharmatā.
Lodrö is the cripple, who runs on the mountain with the gait of luminosity, free from coming and going.
The moon and sun are Hevajra and consort.
They are two dancers, but one taste.
The trumpets proclaiming fame in the ten directions
Sound for worthy vessels.
The wheel is Cakrasaṃvara.
Its turning is the hearing lineage wheel itself.
O child, turn it without attachment.

At that moment Marpa woke up. He joined his palms and tears ran from his eyes.

"What is it?" his disciples asked.

"I must go quickly to glorious Nāropa; I will go tomorrow," Marpa replied.

Then he performed the concluding liturgy. Afterward, Marpa Golek supplicated Marpa, "Please tell us your reasons in detail," and Marpa told them at length. Marpa Golek said, "Well then, I and the other disciples will give you gold and make other offerings that can be exchanged for gold." As Marpa Golek said, the other gifts were exchanged for gold.

Then Marpa, together with Marpa Golek, traveled to Lhotrak. Marpa remained here for a few days, thinking that he must go to India.

At the same time, Jetsün Mila was staying in strict retreat at Taknya in Lhotrak. One night, Mila dreamt that a lady appeared, sky blue in color, beautiful with clothing of silk and ornaments of bone, and having eyebrows and moustache of bright yellow. She said, "You have the mahāmudrā and the six yogas of Nāropa, which bring buddhahood through prolonged practice; but you don't have the special teachings of the ejection and transference of consciousness, which bring buddhahood with little effort."

When he awoke, Mila did not know whether this was a revelation or an obstacle. He thought, "If this is a revelation, then my guru, who is the buddha of the three times, must have these teachings." Thus, he left retreat, told the story to Marpa, and requested the teachings.

Marpa said, "This is a message from the ḍākinīs. When I was about to return from India, Mahāpaṇḍita Nāropa spoke of the transference of consciousness and the hearing lineage. I don't think that I received these instructions, but we can look through my texts." Both master and disciple looked through the Indian texts. There were many texts on ejection, but they did not find any texts on transference.

"The coded verses deciphered in northern Üru also urged me to request this teaching. Moreover, I don't even know what kind of oral instructions there are of the hearing lineage. I will go quickly to India,'' Marpa said.

His wife, Dagmema, and the disciples opposed him insistently, citing his old age and many other reasons as objections.

''No matter what you say, I vowed to meet glorious Nāropa once again. Nāropa himself advised me to come. Therefore, whatever the consequences may be, I am going to India.'' Saying this, Marpa refused to listen. Since there was nothing else to do, they hid the gold and provisions needed for the trip to India.

Marpa said, ''If I don't have the strength to do this, it can't be done. I would rather die than break my vow to go to the guru.'' Getting angry, he went to bed.

The next morning, his bedroom was disordered and empty. The disciples ran in all directions to look for him, and Jetsün Mila found him. Some others came to that place and offered supplication. Marpa said, ''Now, even without gifts, I will not break my vow; even without gold, I will go to India.''

''Well all right, but you must come home to Trowo valley for a while. Then you can go to India.'' They urgently requested this and Marpa returned.

When Marpa was about to leave for India, once again all his disciples and servants prostrated and said, ''You are growing older now. On the road to India, there is a great plain called Palmo Palthang, where even a horse breaks down from fatigue. The snow pass called Khala Chela is so terribly cold that it is frozen even in the summertime. The tropics of Nepal are very hot, and the great Ganges river is very fearsome. In the small districts along the road through the primitive borderlands of India, great famine and wild bandits abound. All this has been said by the guru himself and must certainly be true. Now, if in spite of these dangers you were to go to India and were to lose your life, we who are students and disciples would have no one to look to with hope. What would we do?

''If anyone is able to practice the dharma, what has already been brought to Tibet is enough for their needs. Meditating on the guru who dwells inseparably in the center of your heart, and supplicating him, his compassionate blessings are beyond near and far; therefore, you should stay here.

"In any event, if you must bring more dharma teachings to Tibet, give the directions and instructions to your son Tarma Dode and his attendants. Send him to ask for the dharma. Guru, this time, have consideration for your disciples in Tibet and by all means stay. Please accept us with your kindness." Thus they supplicated.

The guru replied, "Although the guru's compassion is beyond near and far, I promised to go to meet him again. Because of my affection for my Tibetan disciples and because there are special oral instructions I have not yet received, now that I have solved the ḍākinīs' code and have followed their urging stage by stage, I have achieved certainty. Therefore, I should go.

"Suppose I were to send Tarma Dode. Generally, he is so young that everyone could not help but worry. In particular, I told my guru I would come myself, and I never said I would send my son. As is said in the proverbs, 'Although an old merchant's body is feeble, he knows the way well.' Although my body is a little old now, I am not so old that I cannot travel to India, and I have the greatest knowledge of the customs of India.

"From now on, whatever the consequences may be, I am going to receive the dharma. There are dangers on the road to India, but I have these indomitable confidences. Now, even at the cost of my life, I am going to India."

Marpa then sang this song of going to India:

I pay homage at the feet of glorious Nāropa and Maitrīpa.

The vow I have taken in the presence of Nāropa
Makes it supremely necessary that I go.
Since I have been encouraged to go by solving the
ḍākinīs' code,

I have been overwhelmed by the memory of my guru.
Whatever the consequences may be, I am going to India.
Even at the cost of my life, I am going to India.

Although the great plain Palmo Palthang is vast,
I have the oral instructions in how consciousness rides
prāṇa.
No ordinary steed is a match for this.
Whatever the consequences may be, I am going to India.
Even at the cost of my life, I am going to India.

Although the snow pass Khala Chela is very cold,
I have the oral instructions of the blazing fire of caṇḍālī.
Ordinary woolen clothing is no match for this.
Whatever the consequences may be, I am going to India.
Even at the cost of my life, I am going to India.

Although Nepal is very hot,
I have the oral instructions in equalizing the elements.
The ordinary six precious substances are no match for this.
Whatever the consequences may be, I am going to India.
Even at the cost of my life, I am going to India.

Although the Ganges river is wide and deep,
I have the oral instructions of consciousness soaring
in space.
No ordinary boat is a match for this.
Whatever the consequences may be, I am going to India.
Even at the cost of my life, I am going to India.

Although the primitive borderlands of India have
great famine,

I have the oral instructions in how to live on the
water of asceticism.
Ordinary food and drink are no match for this.
Whatever the consequences may be, I am going to India.
Even at the cost of my life, I am going to India.

Although there are great dangers on the road and in the
small outlying districts,
I have the oral instructions in mamos who paralyze bandits.
Ordinary escorts are no match for this.
Whatever the consequences may be, I am going to India.
Even at the cost of my life, I am going to India.

The gurus Nāropa and Maitrīpa live in India.
Śrī Śāntibhadra lives in India,
And the shrine of Mahābodhi is in India.
Whatever the consequences may be, I am going to India.
Even at the cost of my life, I am going to India.

Thus Marpa sang when he made his decision to go.

With the gold he had gathered from previous offerings and the gold that he had received in exchange for his students' offerings, he filled a large porcelain bowl. He rejected the offer that others accompany him as attendants, and left by himself for India.

Marpa searches for guru Nāropa and receives the dharma.

Lord Marpa arrived at Langpona in Sheng in upper Nyang, where he met Lord Atīśa who had arrived in Tibet. Atīśa had been in charge of discipline at Nālandā during Nāropa's time there. He was a peaceful and gentle paṇḍita of kṣatriya caste and had received many teachings from Nāropa; so Marpa knew who he was. Atīśa had not tolerated Master Maitrīpa's partaking of samaya substance and had criticized him a little. Although he had criticized Maitrīpa, Atīśa did this in order to maintain the monastic discipline of the saṅgha and not for selfish reasons. He was very peaceful and gentle, and because he was going to Tibet to propagate the teachings of Buddha, Marpa was very glad and experienced sacred outlook. Since Atīśa was giving the Vajramālā abhiṣeka, Marpa supplicated him and received it.

Marpa asked him for news of Nāropa's whereabouts and Atīśa said, "Nāropa has entered the action. He presides over the gaṇacakra of spiritual beings and does not receive humans. I don't know if you will meet him. Rather than going to India, it would be of more benefit to beings if you went with me as a translator."

Though Marpa thought, "It is not possible that I won't meet Nāropa," he said, "Even if I don't meet him, I must, by all means, go to India one more time." Then Marpa departed.

When he arrived in Nepal, Marpa learned from gurus Paiṇḍapa and Chitherpa that Nāropa had entered the action as Atīśa had said. This news was so painful that Marpa felt as though his heart was being torn out. He asked, "Will I not meet him now?"

They said, "Since you are a disciple who keeps samaya and the jetsün has the eye of dharma, you will certainly meet him. Therefore, you should offer gaṇacakras and supplicate."

"I must do as they say," thought Marpa, and he departed for India.

In India, Marpa met the śrāmaṇera Prajñāsiṃha, who said, "You have come too late; last year on the full moon of the New Year, Nāropa entered the action. Why did you stay so long in Tibet?"

"I was traveling in Tibet gathering gold when the ḍākinīs urged me to request the hearing lineage," Marpa said, and told his story at length. "Encouraged by these signs, I came quickly. Now it seems that my merit has not brought about a meeting with the guru. Since the jetsün is not here, do you have the teachings of the hearing lineage? Was there any message or advice for me?" Crying out Nāropa's name, Marpa shed many tears.

The śrāmaṇera said, "I have never heard of such a thing as the hearing lineage. Nāropa said you would be coming and spoke about you again and again with great affection. As he was leaving, he said, 'Marpa will certainly come. Give him these.' Nāropa left his own vajra and ghaṇṭā and an image of a yidam. The vajra and ghaṇṭā were stolen. I kept this image with me at all times."

The śrāmaṇera gave Marpa the painting of Hevajra. Marpa longed for the guru with heartfelt desire and, overwhelmed, he shed many tears. The śrāmaṇera said, "Since your intense and devoted longing for the guru and the compassion of the jetsün, who possesses the eye of dharma, are in harmony, you will surely meet him. Therefore, you should make a feast offering using golden implements, and supplicate him. First, go to Master Maitrīpa who was also your guru before, and who is a disciple of the jetsün, and supplicate with him."

Marpa went to Maitrīpa. There he made feast offerings for a month and received this prophecy that he would meet Nāropa. Maitrīpa said:

> I dreamt that the victory banner with a jewel finial
> fluttered,
> A dancing girl looked at a mirror out of the corner of her
> eye,
> A victory banner fluttered above a soaring bird,
> And a captain sailed a ship.
> You will definitely meet glorious Nāropa.

Then Maitrīpa advised Marpa, "Go to your teacher, Jetsün Śāntibhadra, who is both Nāropa's master and disciple, and supplicate with him for a month." Marpa departed and reached the island in the poison lake where he found Śāntibhadra under a tamarind tree.* Marpa supplicated for a month and received this prophecy. Śāntibhadra said:

I dreamt that the jetsün, glorious Nāropa,
Gazing like an elephant,
With his eyes the sun and moon,
Sent light rays to Tibet.
You will meet Nāropa.

Then Śāntibhadra advised Marpa, "Go to Nāropa's disciple, Yoginī Adorned with Bone Ornaments, who lives in a charnel ground, and supplicate with her for one month."

Marpa went there, supplicated, and received this prophecy. The yoginī said:

I dreamt that trumpets sounded from three mountain peaks
And guided you from the confluence of three valleys.
A lamp burning inside a vase
Filled Jambudvīpa with light.
You will meet Nāropa.

Then the śrāmaṇera Prajñāsiṃha said, "I have not been unimportant to the jetsün. Supplicate with me for one month." Marpa supplicated and received this prophecy. Prajñāsiṃha said:

I dreamt that on the great plain of misery
I led a blind man and handed him over to someone else,
Who opened his ignorant eyes.
He looked at himself in the mirror of his mind.
You will meet Nāropa.

*This identification is not certain. The Tibetan shing ting-ting 'khun-pa, literally means "a panting tree." However, a tamarind tree is called tintiḍīka in Sanskrit and ting-tu-ka in Tibetan, so this seemed the closest possibility.

Then Prajñāsiṃha advised Marpa, "Go to Nāropa's vajra brothers Riripa and Kasoripa and supplicate with them." Marpa went to Riripa, supplicated with him for one month and received this prophecy. Riripa said:

> Just as formerly the Kulika Dharmarāja
> Supplicated the Brahman Bhadrika,
> Witnessed by Kalyāṇa and Bhadra,
> Just so you will attain the fruition of meeting Nāropa.

Then Riripa explained the meaning of this. "Through the powerful combination of guru Nāropa's kindness and your strong yearning as a devoted disciple, this morning I remembered and understood an incident of a former life of mine. Nāropa was the Brahman Bhadrika. You, the translator, were Kulika Dharmarāja of the northern direction. I was the Ṛṣi Kalyāṇa and Kasoripa was the Brahman Bhadra. We were the two witnesses. You supplicated Bhadrika to meet you again and he promised to do so."

Then Marpa supplicated with Kasoripa for a month and received this prophecy. Kasoripa said:

> At immovable Phullahari,
> The pure maṇḍala of the moon,
> Nāropa will show you
> The dharmakāya mirror of mind.

Thus, all prophesied that he would meet Nāropa, and Marpa felt joyous and confident.

Longing with heartfelt desire for the jetsün, Marpa was unable to remain there. Sometimes he searched with friends and sometimes he searched alone, wandering over mountain sides and through jungles and cities. Once he lost his way and came to a city of outlaws in the East ruled by an evil king. Because the king desired Marpa's gold, he asked Marpa to be one of his priests, but kept him a prisoner instead.

Marpa said, "I am going to look for my guru, Nāropa. I don't have time to stay here," and prepared to go.

The king said, "You are very amusing; take these provisions and go." He gave Marpa a large white-bellied fish and six dre of rice, and said, "You should go straight east from here." Marpa went as advised and searched for eight months.

The first month, Marpa saw Lord Nāropa in a dream, riding on a lion flanked by two consorts called Jñānamati and Guṇasiddhi. They all were singing and dancing on the sun and moon. Marpa supplicated and the two yoginīs said:

Nāropa is nondual unity.
Flanked by two consorts,
He rides a lion
And sings and dances on the sun and moon.
Are you not deceived by the confusion of dream?

The second month, guru Paiṇḍapa arrived in India, and Marpa took him along on his search. Sometimes he also took a brahman boy Suvarṇamāla with him. They searched, but could not find Nāropa. When they were exhausted and sluggish, a voice from the sky said:

If the horse of continual devotion
Is not urged on by the whip of exertion,
Like the deer of grasping and fixation
Are you not caught in the trap of reality, wandering
in saṃsāra?

The third month, Marpa left his companions and searched alone. He questioned a man who looked like a herdsman and who said that he had seen Nāropa. Marpa rewarded him and searched on. He saw Nāropa's footprint and touched some dust from it to his head. As he searched farther, a voice said:

The footprint is like the imprint of a bird in the sky.
If you do not recognize this free from reference point,
Like a dog chasing the shadow of a flying bird
Won't you stray into the abyss of futility?

The fourth month, Marpa searched farther. He saw a yogin clad in a yellow robe, walking on a mountainside. Marpa stopped and thought, "Is it he or not?" Nāropa said:

If you do not loose the snake knot of doubt
In the dharmakāya, the dharmatā of mind
In which all is unborn,
You will not accomplish your purpose with a double-pointed needle.

Then Nāropa disappeared.

The fifth month, Marpa searched, saw a glimpse of Nāropa's face, and attachment arose in him. Nāropa said:

Like a rainbow, the body is free from attachment.
If you do not recognize this free from reference point,
Like a blind man sightseeing
How can you understand the truth?

Then Nāropa disappeared.

The sixth month, Marpa searched and had a vision of Nāropa sitting in a sandy barren place. Marpa supplicated him, offered a maṇḍala of gold, and requested teaching. Nāropa said:

Since apparent existence is primordially pure,
If you do not offer the maṇḍala of dharmatā

But rather this maṇḍala of precious metal to which
you are attached,
Are you not chained by the eight worldly dharmas?

Then Nāropa disappeared.

The seventh month, Marpa searched and had a vision of Nāropa in an earthen cave. Nāropa disemboweled the body of a human corpse and opened the skull. He was taking out brains, intestines, ribs, and the rest, and eating them. Marpa supplicated him and requested oral instructions. Nāropa gave him a handful of ribs. Marpa felt nauseated and could not eat them. Nāropa said:

In the great vessel of great bliss,
Great bliss and enjoyment are pure in equal taste.
If you do not enjoy this as great bliss,
The enjoyment of great bliss will not arise.

Then Nāropa abruptly disappeared.

Marpa looked around, but the corpse was no longer there except for a bit that was smeared on the side of the wall. Marpa licked this; the taste was wonderful and good samādhi arose in him.

The eighth month, Marpa searched farther. He had a vision of Jetsün Nāropa and chased after him, but could not catch him. When Marpa was exhausted, the jetsün sat down. Marpa supplicated him and requested oral instructions. Nāropa said:

If the horse of nonaction, dharmatā, and luminosity
Does not gallop free from coming and going,
Like a deer pursuing a mirage
Are you not wandering on the plain of futility?

Then, in his vision, Marpa conversed with Nāropa further. Up to this point, Marpa's experiences occurred in the form of these visions.

When the eighth month had passed, Marpa was very depressed. While he was sadly looking at his books, suddenly he remembered Mahāpaṇḍita Nāropa. Overwhelmed, he immediately stopped reading and went to search for Nāropa on the Dark Forest Mountain. He questioned a herdsman who said he first wanted a reward. Marpa gave him some gold and asked him again. The herdsman showed him Nāropa's footprint on a crystal boulder. Marpa experienced immeasurable joy, as if he had met the jetsün.

He supplicated with intense yearning* and saw clearly a manifestation of Nāropa's mind. At the top of a sandalwood tree luxuriant with foliage was a sphere of dense rainbow light, almost touching the branches. Within it he saw the maṇḍala of bhagavat Hevajra of nine emanation devīs, with all their colors, scepters, ornaments, and other attributes vividly clear. Realizing that this was a manifestation of the guru, Marpa prostrated, made offerings, and supplicated. From the heart center of the consort Nairātmyā, from the aṣṭamantra wheel, drawn as if with the tip of a single hair, light streamed forth, dissolving into Marpa's heart center. By this he received the blessing of body and the empowerment of speech, and he realized that this was Mahāpaṇḍita Nāropa's kindness. He rejoiced, but still filled with intense yearning for the guru, he wept and cried out in a wailing supplication. Suddenly Mahāpaṇḍita Nāropa appeared, adorned with the charnel ground ornaments and manifesting gracefulness and the rest of the nine moods of a heruka.

Nāropa said, "Now the father has arrived in front of the son," and he revealed himself in person. On seeing him, Marpa experienced inconceivable joy, as if attaining the first bhūmi. Words of deep feeling and many tears poured forth from him.

*According to the song on p. 138, Marpa supplicated Nāropa for a week after seeing this footprint and before meeting with Nāropa.

He placed Nāropa's feet on top of his head. Not content with that, he embraced Nāropa. He fainted, and when he regained consciousness, without hesitation he arranged an abundant maṇḍala of gold and offered it.

Nāropa said, "I don't want gold," and would not accept it.

Marpa said, "Lord, though you do not need it, you must accept this gold for the sake of perfecting the accumulation of myself, those who helped gather these offerings, and all sentient beings."

As Marpa insisted again and again, Nāropa said, "In that case, may this be an offering to the guru and the three jewels," and threw all the gold into the forest. Although joyful at meeting the guru, Marpa recalled with what hardship he had gathered the gold in Tibet and felt great loss. Nāropa beckoned with his hands, joined his palms, and then opened them and returned the gold—complete and unspoiled—saying, "If you feel a loss, here it is again. I don't need gold. If I needed it, all this land is gold." He struck his foot on the earth and the ground turned to gold.

Then Nāropa said, "I shall arrange a welcoming feast for the arrival of my son, Chökyi Lodrö." He looked into the sky with a yogic gaze and a large, fresh, beautiful fish landed in front of them. Nāropa said, "You should cut open this fish."

Marpa did so and from within the fish arose the five meats, the five amṛtas, and innumerable other exotic and excellent gaṇacakra substances. Many offering devīs appeared and offered these substances to the gurus, yidams, ḍākinīs, and dharmapālas, thus pleasing them. The master and disciple also partook of it with great delight.

Then Marpa supplicated for teaching. Nāropa said, "You have been drawn here through Tilopa's kindness. As Tilopa gave a command-prophecy, I will give you oral instructions at Phullahari."

Marpa said, "Please tell me this command-prophecy."

Nāropa said:

With the sun of self-liberated wisdom,
At the monastery of Phullahari
Dispel the darkness of Mati's ignorance.
Let the light of wisdom pervade everywhere.

While master and disciple were on the way to Phullahari, ḍākinīs possessive of the dharma created huge magical attacks of obstructing spirits. Whether Marpa went in front of or behind the guru, he felt great fear. Particularly, when they arrived at Phullahari, his fear became greater. Marpa circumambulated and supplicated Nāropa, saying, "Jetsün, please protect me," but the ḍākinīs and obstructing spirits boldly showed their terrifying forms and came to seize Marpa. Marpa went through a rock mountain as if passing through a cloud as he followed after Nāropa, but the obstructing spirits chased after them unhindered. Though he could have protected Marpa, Nāropa supplicated Tilopa, saying:

This son prophesied by the guru
Is the worthy vessel, Marpa Lodrö.
Please bless him by removing the obstacles
Caused by these she-māras, so-called ḍākinīs.

Manifestations of Tilopa, immeasurable hosts of wrathful deities wielding various weapons, came instantly and the obstructing spirits could not follow after Marpa. Unable to bear the radiance of the wrathful deities, they fled in all directions. The wrathful deities pursued them through crevices in the rocks. At that time, Marpa also saw part of Tilopa's form amidst heaps of clouds and light. Seeing him, Marpa danced with joy. Between the gaps in the rocks, Lord Marpa's footprints and the footprints of the fleeing obstructing spirits can still be seen these days at Phullahari.

When the wrathful deities had subjugated the obstructing spirits, the terrified ḍākinīs joined their palms together and said:

This terrifying body with terrifying speech
Is well armed with terrifying weapons.
In this great terrifying body, we take refuge.
We will do no harm.

You are as bright as two moons.
We will drive you in a great chariot.
Jetsün, glorious Nāropa,
According to prophecy, we will receive you in the
  self-liberated celestial realm.

Saying that, they disappeared.

In general, Lord Marpa requested from Lord Nāropa the hearing lineage and, in particular, the ejection and transference of consciousness. Nāropa asked, "Did you remember to request the transference of consciousness yourself, or did you receive a revelation?"

Marpa replied, "I neither received a revelation, nor did I think of it myself. I have a student called Thöpaga who received a revelation from a ḍākinī."

Nāropa said, "How wonderful! In the dark country of Tibet there is a being like the sun rising over the snow." Nāropa placed his joined palms on top of his head saying:

In the pitch-black land of the North
Is one like the sun rising over the snow.
To this being known as Thöpaga
I prostrate.

He closed his eyes and bowed his head three times. All the mountains, trees, and greenery in India bowed three times. Even now the mountains and trees of Phullahari bow toward Tibet.

Nāropa said, "I will grant you special teachings known only to a few before—the *Cakrasaṃvara* of the ḍākinī hearing lineage." By means of sand maṇḍalas, Nāropa performed the abhiṣekas of *Cakrasaṃvara* with sixty-two deities, thirteen deities, five deities, as well as the coemergent father alone. By means of sindūra maṇḍalas, he performed the abhiṣekas of the consort Vajravārāhī with fifteen devīs, seven devīs, five devīs, and the coemergent mother alone. Then by means of the maṇḍala of the guru's body, speech, and mind, Nāropa gave Marpa the sign abhiṣeka, as well as the oral instructions for everything.

"If you attend to the oral instructions of these special teachings, the oral instructions given to you previously will be like the outer husk. These supreme oral instructions are the innermost essence. It should be a teaching restricted to a single lineage holder for thirteen generations.* Give it to your student

*In general, the ḍākinī hearing lineage teachings were first received by Tilopa when he went to Uḍḍiyāṇa and received teachings from Vajrayoginī. This is why they are referred to as the "ḍākinī" hearing lineage—Vajrayoginī being the principal ḍākinī and consort of Cakrasaṃvara. Tilopa received this transmission directly from this ḍākinī, rather than from a human guru.

Nāropa received these teachings from Tilopa and then transmitted the supreme oral instructions on the innermost essence of Cakrasaṃvara and Vajravārāhī (Vajrayoginī) to Marpa and restricted this teaching to a single lineage holder (T: gcig-brgyud) for thirteen generations. A text that seems to summarize these teachings that Marpa received is the *Karṇatantra-vajrapada,* authored by Nāropa. Milarepa received these teachings from Marpa and gave them to Gampopa who gave them to Tüsum Khyenpa. This continued up to Trungmase (Rma-se rtogs-ldan blo-gros rin-chen), who was a disciple of the fifth Karmapa, Teshin Shekpa. Trungmase belonged to the thirteenth generation and thus became the first guru to transmit this particular lineage of mahāmudrā teachings to more than a single dharma successor. In fact, he taught it widely. The first Trungpa, Künga Gyaltsen, was one of Trungmase's disciples who received this teaching, and hence this teaching has been passed called Thöpaga and buddha activity will spread and flourish. Are these oral instructions different from the previous ones?" Nāropa asked.

Marpa thought, "Basically, they are the same, but there are differences in the profundity of the methods of bringing about actualization, and differences in the speed of bringing about confidence, actual experience, and actualization without too much effort. Especially, both the three teachings on mixing and ejecting of consciousness and the teaching of mixing and equal taste* are special teachings that no one else has.

"Knowing one thing liberates all. Therefore, since this king of teachings alone is enough, it would have been sufficient to give me this in the beginning."

Marpa told Nāropa what he had thought, and Nāropa said, "When you visited on the two previous occasions, it was not yet the appropriate time to give this teaching to you. In particular, if you had not made sacrifices for the dharma, you would not have realized the rarity and great value of these teachings and you would not have been able to practice them properly. Even if you had attempted to practice them, their virtues would not have arisen in you. As I told you before, under Tilopa I underwent twelve great trials and twelve lesser trials of body and life in order to receive and practice this teaching. Now, since I have attained power over phenomena, I go to the twenty-four sacred places and the buddha fields and I am well received in the gaṇacakra gatherings of ḍākas and ḍākinīs. Sometimes I am even the master of the gathering.

---

down through the Trungpa lineage to the present day. Chögyam Trungpa, the Eleventh Trungpa tülku, received this transmission from Rölpe Dorje, the regent abbot of Surmang monastery, and one of his main tutors.

*Detailed commentaries on the teachings and practices of mixing and equal taste are found in *The Life and Teaching of Nāropa,* pp. 47-49. (Professor Guenther translates these terms as "attunement and one-valueness."), and as well in Padma Karpo's *Jo-bo nā-ro-pa'i khyad-chos bsre-'pho'i khrid rdo-rje'i theg-par bgrod-pa'i shing-rta* and *Jo-bo nā-ro-pa'i khyad-chos bsre-'pho'i gzhung-'grel rdo-rje-'chang gi dgongs-pa gsal-bar byed-pa.*

"Undergoing great difficulties in collecting gold and paying no attention to dangers on the journey, you endured hardships for the sake of dharma. Tilopa saw that you would be a worthy vessel for these teachings and gave me a prophecy. Out of my irresistible love for you, I thought that I must give you this teaching. When you came this time, numerous auspicious signs coincided. Because I requested and urged the ḍākinīs and dharmapālas, you arrived here. In order to receive the blessings of the lineage, you were delayed and made to undergo hardships."

Although at that time Nāropa gave Marpa the abhiṣeka and oral instructions of Cakrasaṃvara, Marpa's personal yidam was Hevajra. Therefore glorious Nāropa thought, "Since Marpa Lotsāwa of Tibet is very loyal to me, he has repeatedly visited me, bringing gold. Because he is so good, I should see what auspicious coincidences arise concerning his ability to hold the lineage, and in accordance with these I should make a prophecy." Then glorious Nāropa gave a gaṇacakra for Lord Marpa.

That night they slept near each other and at dawn Mahāpaṇḍita Nāropa manifested the maṇḍala of Hevajra with the nine deities, bright and vivid in the sky. He said, "Son, teacher Marpa Chökyi Lodrö, don't sleep, get up! Your personal yidam Hevajra with the nine emanation devīs has arrived in the sky before you. Will you prostrate to me or to the yidam?" Marpa prostrated to the bright and vivid maṇḍala of the yidam. Nāropa said, "As is said,

> Before any guru existed
> Even the name of Buddha was not heard.
> All the buddhas of a thousand kalpas
> Only come about because of the guru.

This maṇḍala is my emanation." Then the yidam dissolved into the guru's heart center.

"The main point of this incident is that the lineage will not last long within your family. This is the lot of sentient beings. However, your dharma lineage will last as long as the teachings of Buddha remain. Therefore rejoice."

Marpa thought, "Previously, I studied and contemplated that seeing and hearing the guru is greater than witnessing the yidam. When meditating, one always visualizes the guru above the yidam's head. The other day when searching for the guru, I saw the yidam Hevajra at the top of a sandalwood tree, but I wasn't satisfied and continued to search for the guru. That I made this mistake must be the result of my former karma." After this incident, Marpa felt very upset. He began having nightmares and, at the same time, he became sick with fever and came near to death thirteen times. He also went into a coma three times.

Glorious Nāropa said, "Since these hearing lineage teachings are very powerful and sensitive, various obstacles of Māra are occurring. Since you and I cherish the Buddha's teachings, I will supplicate the three jewels. They will protect you from the harm of the māras; I assure you that your life will not be endangered. Since this is the way of exhausting the suffering due to evil karma, you should realize that this illness is the blessing of the three jewels. Continue to be mindful of the practice of friendliness and compassion for sentient beings." With these loving words, Nāropa extended his kindness.

Marpa replied, "Whether I live or die, I will think of nothing other than the kindness of the three jewels. Just as you have extended your kindness to me, please extend it to all sentient beings." When Marpa said this, Nāropa was pleased.

While Marpa was ill, some vajra brothers and sisters close to him practiced their sādhana and set up a boundary of protection around him. They came again and again, discussing what medical treatment, rites of aid, and supplications to the three jewels would be most effective.

Marpa said, "All my belongings are dedicated to the guru. I have no personal possessions. It would not be appropriate to use the guru's possessions for a rite of aid for myself. Therefore this should not be done. As for medical treatment, if the merit of the sentient beings of Tibet does not suffice, I will die in any case. If it does suffice, I will recover from my illness even without medical treatment. Therefore there is no need for it. There is no greater protection than supplication to the three jewels and the kindness of glorious Nāropa. Therefore I will continuously supplicate the guru. It all depends on whether the dharmapālas protect the teachings or not." So without medical treatments or any rites of aid, Marpa recovered completely from his illness through the power of his guru and his dharma brothers and sisters.

Although Marpa recovered from his illness, his sadness was not dispelled. The vajra brothers and sisters consoled him with a thanksgiving feast for his recovery from illness. Glorious Nāropa also gave a thanksgiving feast for his recovery from illness. At that time, in order to console him by means of oral instructions for practice, Nāropa sang this vajra song summarizing the six yogas:*

*There are actually seven practices that Nāropa sings about here. Traditionally, the practice of transference (T: grong-'jug) has been considered to be part of the ejection practice (T: 'pho-ba) and has not been counted separately. However, it is interesting to note that Nāropa in his *Karṇatantra-vajrapada* lists the six yogas, including transference (T: grong-'jug) as one of the yogas and places the pardo (T: bar-do) practice outside the six yogas as a separate topic.

Guenther notes this discrepancy in *The Life and Teaching of Nāropa* (p. 201). However, whatever Nāropa's intention may have been in listing pardo as separate from the six yogas, Tilopa clearly includes it as one of the six yogas in his own work, the *Ṣaḍdharmopadeśa* (Bstan-'gyur, Peking Tripitaka No. 4630; *Gdams-ngag mdzod,* vol. 5, pp. 106-107). Here, transference (T: grong-'jug) is mentioned as part of the ejection (T: 'pho-ba) practice.

H. H. Dingo Khyentse, Rinpoche, has explained that "One should consider that transference is part of the ejection practice in the six yogas. The practice of transference is quite special. If someone is very old and will not live much longer, but still wishes to continue his dharma practice and help others,

I bow at the feet of the kind lord.
You, Marpa Lotsāwa of Tibet,
With a free and well-favored body
And a mind of sadness this summer,
hear these words.

The method of resting the mind is confidence in the view.
The method of resting the body is the pith of meditation.
Outside is only the illusory form of devas.
Inside is just the three nāḍīs and four cakras.
Below is the A stroke, caṇḍālī.
Above is the form of the letter HAṂ.
Above and below are the wheels of prāṇa.*
Practice holding the life force in a vaselike manner.
In between the letters, experience bliss, emptiness,
and luminosity.
This we call the oral instructions of caṇḍālī.
Lotsāwa, have you captured prāṇa with precision?

Outer appearance is only illusion.
Inner experience is inexpressible.
Day and night, experiences are simply nirmāṇakāya.
This we call the oral instructions of illusory body.
Lotsāwa, have you experienced revulsion toward
attachment?

When experiencing the confusion of dreams,
Visualize at the throat the syllable OṂ radiating light.

---

then he can enter a fresh corpse that is young, strong, and healthy. If he cannot find this, he should then apply the ejection practice."

*"above and below" here refer to above the letter A (which is below one's navel cakra at the secret center) and below the letter HAṂ (which is at the top of one's head).

Through the creation of habitual thoughts:
If you dream of a man, he is said to be a male ghost;
If you dream of a woman, she is a female ghost;
If you dream of animals, they are regarded as nāgas;
If your dream is happy, you feel exalted;
If your dream is unhappy, you feel unhappy.
If you do not realize that ghosts arise from the root of mind,
You will not exhaust the ghosts of discursive thought.
Self-liberating good and evil is the meaning of this teaching.
This we call the oral instructions of dreams.
Lotsāwa, have you realized their nature?

In the period between falling asleep and dreaming,
In that state of delusion, which is the essence of dharmakāya,
Inexpressible bliss and luminosity are experienced.
Then, seal that with luminosity
And the deep sleep of luminosity occurs.
This we call the oral instructions of luminosity.
Lotsāwa, have you realized mind as unborn?

The eight doorways are the openings of saṃsāra.
The one doorway is the path of mahāmudrā.
When the eight doorways are closed and the one doorway is opened,
With the bow of prāṇa, the arrow of mind
Is propelled by the bowstring HIK
And so consciousness is shot through the aperture of Brahmā.

This we call the oral instructions of the ejection of
consciousness.
Lotsāwa, can you stop your prāṇa at the right time?

When the time to leave the body comes,
One finds another body as an authentic sacred object.
Then the seed syllable rides the horse of prāṇa.
By means of the wheels of prāṇa,
One abandons one's body like an empty house
And enters the other body, which is the essence of
nirmāṇakāya.
This we call the oral instructions of the transference of
consciousness.
Lotsāwa, is your prāṇa workable?

The mind at the time of dreaming
Should be mixed with the mind of pardo.
Its essence is sambhogakāya.
Both the pure and impure aspects of the two kāyas of form
Are attained when the time of the pardo comes.
The pith of dream pardo is the mixing and ejecting
of consciousness.
This we call the oral instructions of pardo.
Lotsāwa, are you trained in the pardo?

It is necessary to study the outer and inner teachings.
Comprehending them will enable you to overcome the two
extremes.
When uncertainty as to existence and nonexistence is cut,
That is the one path from which one does not stray.
On this path, how could there be sadness?

Thus Nāropa sang.

Marpa's mind was set at ease and his depression was dispelled. Later, whenever he was moved, he spoke of the guru and these other experiences.

When Lord Marpa's sickness had ceased and his mind was relieved of depression, Nāropa said, "From among the seven yogas,* we should do the bathing yoga," and Marpa went with him as an attendant. While bathing in a pool possessing the eight qualities, Marpa took off his powerful protection yantra and set it down. A crow snatched it and carried it away. Nāropa thought, "This is an obstacle created by spirits." With the threatening yogic gaze and mudrā, he paralyzed the bird and it fell from the sky. He picked up the protection yantra and returned it to Marpa, saying, "From now on, you are victorious over the obstacles of Māra."

Marpa's Farewell to Nāropa

The great and glorious Nāropa said, "I establish this Marpa Chökyi Lodrö as my regent."

As they were celebrating the farewell gaṇacakra, Nāropa gave this command-prophecy. "You, the translator! Previously, I gave you the transmission of the five skandhas as the five buddha families, and the five kleśas primordially existing as the five wisdoms. Since, in essence, they are free from accepting and rejecting, all the dharmas of the phenomenal world are the essence of the five buddha families. Recognizing these as the manifestation that dawns as unobstructed dharmatā, there is not a single dharma beyond this unity.

"Therefore, practice in the space of dharmatā, unobstructed, like a bird flying in the sky. This is turning the dharmacakra of

*In the *Karṇatantra-vajrapada* written by Nāropa, the seven yogas are explained thus. "One performs these excellent activities in a harmonious fashion—(1) eating food, (2) wearing clothes, (3) sleeping, (4) walking, (5) talking, (6) bathing, and (7) offering torma (*Gdams-ngag mdzod,* vol. 5, p. 90:4). See also *The Life and Teaching of Nāropa,* p. 46.

what has been realized, like a cakravartin king. You naturally turn the dharmacakra of what has been told, just as a universal monarch possesses the seven royal treasures. In general, you hold the teachings of the Buddha, both the sūtras and tantras, by means of what has been told and realized. In particular, you make what has been told and what has been realized of the mantrayāna teachings shine like the sun.

"Although in this life your family lineage will be interrupted, your dharma lineage will flow on like a wide river as long as the teachings of the Buddha remain. In the view of some impure ordinary men, you will appear to gratify yourself in this life with sense pleasures. Your desires will seem unchanging, like a carving in rock, so solid and so great. On the other hand, since you yourself have seen dharmatā, saṃsāra will be self-liberated, like a snake uncoiling. All the future disciples of the lineage will be like the children of lions and garuḍas, and each generation will be better than the last.

"Because of our love, yearning, and intimacy in this life, we are beyond meeting and parting in the realm of luminosity. In the next life, I will receive you in the pure celestial realm, and then we will be inseparable companions. Therefore, rejoice!"

After Nāropa said this, Marpa requested, "Please be so kind as to prophesy for me the way in which our dharma lineage will expand and flourish. Since ultimately there is no difference between the sūtras and tantras in their view and realization, one can hold the teachings—what has been told and what has been realized—of both. Is it necessary that in external appearance one adopt the robes of a śrāvaka and practice the prātimokṣa? It isn't, is it?

"I have seven sons of my own blood, headed by Tarma Dode. If my family lineage is to be cut, please prophesy the means by which it could not be cut."

Mahāpaṇḍita Nāropa replied, "In the future of your dharma lineage, there will be many who assume the external appearance of a śrāvaka. Inwardly, they will realize the meaning of mahāyāna, dwell on the bhūmis, and be surrounded by bodhisattvas.

Some others of varied appearance will make the teachings of the Practice Lineage flourish and expand.

"Not only if you have seven sons, even if you have thousands of sons, your family lineage will go no further. Nevertheless, without regret, father and sons should practice the sādhanas of divine yidams in strict retreats, exerting themselves in making feast torma offerings to the ḍākinīs and dharmapālas.

"Because you have the karmic stream of good practice in former lives, you are a mahāsattva dwelling on the bhūmis, and you will benefit many sentient beings. Therefore, in order to tame students of the snow land of Tibet, I empower you as my regent."

Placing his right hand on top of Marpa's head, Nāropa sang this song prophesying the future:

Possessing the karma of proper training in previous
  lives,
You are a yogin who has realized the innate truth.
You, Marpa the Translator from Tibet,
Are a bird of the five families soaring in the
  space of dharmatā.
You will hold the royal treasures of a universal monarch.
The sky flower of your family lineage will vanish,
But your dharma lineage will flow on like a wide river.
Though your desires appear vivid, like a carving
  in rock,
The ripples of saṃsāra's waters will vanish by themselves.
Your sons will be like the children of lions and garuḍas.
Later disciples will be even better than the previous ones.
Having realized the meaning of the mahāyāna,
Those of good karma will be ripened and freed.
You are the king of those worthy students.

Now depart to Ü in Tibet.
In the northern Land of Snow,

A place abundant with a variety of fragrant trees,
On a mountain slope blooming with various herbs,
Is a fortunate disciple who is a worthy vessel.
Son, go there and perform benefit for others.
You will certainly accomplish this benefit.

Because of our love, yearning, and intimacy in this life,
In the realm of luminosity we transcend meeting and
  parting.
In the next life, in the completely pure celestial realm,
I will receive you.
There is no doubt that we will be inseparable companions.
Son, rest your mind in this.

Thus Nāropa sang.

Then Nāropa said, "Now go to Maitrīpa from here and persistently request the teachings you desire. Your understanding will be even deeper than before."*

Marpa was preparing to return to Tibet. Having slept under a tree in a mango grove west of Phullahari, at dawn he thought, "In this life, I have come three times to India from Tibet—the first time for twelve years, the second time for six years and this

*According to the *Rdo-rje rnal-'byor-ma lhan-cig-skyes-ma'i bskyed-rim gyi lha-khrid rnam-bshad zab-mo rnam-'byed kyi snying-po bsdus-pa* by Dpa'-bo gtsug-lag rgya-mtsho (third Pawo incarnation, 1567-1633), Nāropa gave Marpa the teachings on Vajrayoginī (the utpattikrama of the coemergent consort and the sampannakrama of nondual prāṇa and mind) and then told him: "Seven days from now, on the winter solstice, the tenth day of the waning moon, go to the Sosadvīpa charnel ground. You will be accepted by the coemergent consort." Marpa went there and met the coemergent consort who manifested as a young woman. She gave him the blessing of the utpatti and sampannakrama. With a crystal hooked knife, she cut open her heart center and revealed the mantra circle. Then she told him, "Go to the Vajrāsana (Bodhgayā) and see the tooth of the teacher (Buddha). Then go to Tibet and accept worthy disciples."

time for three years. Twenty-one years have passed, and I have stayed for sixteen years and seven months before glorious Nāropa. I have practiced the dharma and have met with siddha gurus. I realize that I have completed my education in language and learning.'' Thinking this, Marpa rejoiced.

As for departing to Tibet and leaving his guru and dharma brothers and sisters, he felt sad. As for the dangers of rivers, steep cliffs, and bandits on the road, he felt apprehensive. Having obtained the special oral instructions after completing his education, he felt very proud in departing to Tibet. As a parting gesture he gave a gaṇacakra for Mahāpaṇḍita Nāropa. In that gathering, when Nāropa and he were conversing and reminiscing, Marpa sang, in the melody of a bee buzzing in the distance, this ''Long Song of the Journey,'' a grand and renowned song which he offered to his guru and dharma brothers and sisters:

Lord, kind leader of beings,
Gurus of the siddha lineage,
Please dwell as ornaments on the top of my head.
Dwelling there, please bless me.

Both Mahāpaṇḍita Nāropa of India
And Marpa the Translator from Tibet
Met because of previous practice and the same aspiration.
I attended you for sixteen years and seven months.
I accompanied you; we were not separate for an instant.
Therefore it is impossible for me not to be in your mind.

At this glorious monastery of Ravishing Beautiful Flowers,
You completely empowered me by the river of the four
abhiṣekas.
You gave me the ultimate oral instructions of the
hearing lineage.
In the nondual truth of the supreme, unsurpassable vehicle,

I meditated one-pointedly
And grabbed the śūnyatā-mind.
For the northern Land of Snow,
You established me as regent and prophesied.
Therefore I, a novice, now go to Tibet.

As for me, a novice, going to Tibet:
There are three things I miss upon leaving.
There are three things that make me sad.
There are three things I fear on the road.
There are three things I am apprehensive of on the way.
There are three things ahead that make me proud.
There are three great wonders.
If I do not interpret this song,
The words and their meaning will not coincide.

As for the three things I miss upon leaving:
Headed by Lord Nāropa and Maitrīpa,
There are a hundred siddha gurus.
Leaving them behind, I miss them more than my mother.

Headed by Śrī Abhayakīrti,
There are a hundred dharma brothers and sisters.
Leaving them behind, I miss them more than my mother.

Headed by the place Phullahari,
There are a hundred holy places of siddhas.
Leaving them behind, I miss them more than my mother.

As for the three things that make me sad:
Divine Dharmabodhi Aśoka and others
Were my kind hosts and hostesses.
Not daring to separate from them, I feel sad.

The brahman youth Suvarṇamāla,
Dead or alive, will always be my friend.
Not daring to separate from him, I feel sad.

The dark-skinned daughter of the merchant
Was with me constantly as an authentic consort.
Not daring to separate from her, I feel sad.

As for the three things I fear on the road:
The foremost is the boiling poison lake,
But soon I have to cross the Ganges river in the East.
Even before I see this, I am afraid.

In the jungle of the Uśiri mountain,
Bandits and thieves lie in wait on the road.
Even before I see them, I am afraid.

At a city in Tirahuti,
Shameless custom taxes fall like rain.
Even before I see them, I am afraid.

As for the three things I am apprehensive of on the way:
Not only is there the dangerous defile of Palahati,
There are eighty-one dangerous bridges and passages.
Kye ma! I quake like quicksilver.

Not only is there the snow pass of Khala Chela,
There are eighty-one small and large passes.
Kye ma! I quake like quicksilver.

Not only is there the great plain Palmo Palthang,
There are eighty-one small and large plains.
Kye ma! I quake like quicksilver.

As for the three things ahead that make me proud:
Headed by the grammars of *Kalāpa* and *Candra*,

I know one hundred and eight different languages.
In the company of fellow translators, I will feel proud.

Headed by the *Catuḥpīṭha* and the *Hevajra,*
I know one hundred and eight commentaries on the
tantras.
In the company of fellow great teachers, I will feel proud.

Headed by the oral instructions of the four special
transmissions,
I know one hundred and eight hearing lineage teachings.
In the company of fellow meditators, I will feel proud.

As for the three great wonders:
Besides the mixing of mind and prāṇa, and the
ejecting of consciousness,
I know one hundred and eight special dharmas.
O how wondrous, how great indeed!

Besides the devī Vetālī,
I know one hundred and eight protectors of the teachings.
O how wondrous, how great indeed!

Besides the oral guidance in the five stages,
I know one hundred and eight sampannakramas.
O how wondrous, how great indeed!

All these are the kindness of the lord guru.
Even though I cannot repay his kindness,
Still the lord dwells inseparably as an ornament on the
top of my head.

Finally, I, a novice, going to Tibet,
Request from my dharma brothers and sisters
Good wishes that my journey be free from obstacles.

This is the last time we will ever meet.
Let us definitely meet in the next life
In the celestial realm of glorious Uḍḍiyāṇa.

Thus, the guru translator sang this song.

His elder friends, the brahman Sumatikīrti and the yoginī Sukhadhari, eight altogether, burst into tears. Lord Marpa received the four abhiṣekas of the body maṇḍala of the guru, prayed, and then departed. His dharma brothers and sisters escorted him away, carrying all his belongings and gear. Lord Marpa himself, walking backward and prostrating until he reached the bottom of the stone steps of Phullahari, prostrated to the guru at each step. At the bottom of the stone steps he prostrated many times with intense yearning. At that place, Lord Marpa left a footprint in the stone, which is still there now.

The ḍākinīs invited glorious Nāropa to the celestial realm in that very life. The guru and the vajra brothers and sisters blessed Lord Marpa so that he would be free from obstacles on his return to Lhotrak in Tibet, and would greatly benefit the teachings and sentient beings until the end of his life.

At that time, in accordance with the guru's command, Marpa went to stay with Master Maitrīpa. While he was once again receiving the abhiṣeka of Hevajra, a rain of divine flowers fell from the sky and scents of sandalwood, aloe wood, and others permeated the air. As a sign that he was accepted by the ḍākinīs, a cedar torch a finger's length in size quivered and remained blazing for a week, and various ravishing sounds of divine music were heard. While Marpa was receiving the Cakrasaṃvara abhiṣeka, the ḍākas and ḍākinīs of the three levels, though invisible, proclaimed mantras. Torma was offered to the kṣetrapāla ḍākinīs and Marpa witnessed seven red jackals, emanations of the kṣetrapāla ḍākinīs, actually receive the torma. Lord Marpa thought, "I have arrived in some other world, like Akaniṣṭha," and felt immeasurable joy and delight. Maitrīpa commanded him to keep these signs secret while he was in India. The conviction arose in Marpa that both Nāropa and Maitrīpa were even greater than the Buddha.

Marpa returns to Tibet.

Having offered farewell prostrations to Maitrīpa, Śrī Śāntibhadra, Jñānagarbha, and his other kind gurus, Marpa thought he would rest and stay in Nepal for the winter. He departed toward Tibet, and went to Phamthing in Nepal.

At that time, Chitherpa, who possessed the eye of dharma, had died there, and the many dharma brothers and sisters led by Paiṇḍapa held a gaṇacakra to welcome Marpa. During the gaṇacakra, Paiṇḍapa said, "You, the translator! From the very first, the compassion of the master and the devotion of the student were in harmony. Therefore I told you that you would certainly find Nāropa, and later I heard the wondrous news that you did.

"Besides where we previously searched together for the guru, where else did you look? And where did you meet the guru? What wondrous signs and great virtues of his did you see? Besides both Nāropa and Maitrīpa, how many gurus did you attend?

"We have given this small gaṇacakra as a celebration of your arrival here without obstacles. In return, please sing a song in answer to these questions."

In answer, Marpa sang in the melody of the whistling song of the dharmapālas, which removes the sadness of fervent longing. He offered this grand song of the eight wondrous signs of meeting his guru to the guru Paiṇḍapa and his dharma brothers and sisters:

Leader, glorious Kanakaśrī,
Brothers and sisters sitting here, listen to me!

If you ask who I am,
I am the famed Marpa the Translator.
My umbilical cord was cut in Ü in the land of Tibet.
I was educated in southern Nepal and India.

I traveled to India three times.
This last time, I truly made persistent request.
Touching their lotus feet to my head,
My gurus bestowed on me the amṛta of true speech.

Generally, I have many gurus with whom I have a dharmic connection.
Led by glorious Siṃhadvīpa,
They have completely mastered insight and the higher perceptions,

And thirteen of them can transform one's perception of
the world.

Amongst all of them, the most worthy of offering
Is the unrivaled Lord Nāropa,
Who is great Vajradhara in human form.
There is no way to repay this lord's kindness.

Though deeply missing the father nirmāṇakāya,
I could not find him anywhere.
Whatever face I saw, it was not his.
Finally, in the foothills of Dark Forest mountain,
I saw on a boulder of wondrous crystal,
Like a symbol carved in relief,
Footprints left by the father jetsün.
O how wondrous, how great indeed!

Above a medicinal sandalwood tree,
Through a miraculous display of Nāropa's compassion,
The nine emanation devīs of the Hevajra maṇḍala
appeared.
In the heart center of the coemergent consort,
The aṣṭamantra wheel
Appeared as if drawn with the tip of one hair,
With a variety of light rays streaming forth.
Thus, Nāropa granted me the permission-blessing.
O how wondrous, how great indeed!

Helplessly, I burst into tears.
Filled with yearning, I felt like crying forever.
Overwhelmed completely, I wailed aloud.
I supplicated him with one-pointed mind.

He looked on me with compassion, and came before me.
Joy arose in me, like on the path of seeing.
O how wondrous, how great indeed!

I offered rare and precious gold dust.
He said, "I do not want all that."
Again and again, I asked him to accept.
He said, "Offer it to the father gurus and the
three jewels,"
And casually tossed it into the forest.
I was stunned with loss.
Saying, "If you want it, here it is again,"
He opened his joined palms.
Not lost, unspoiled, it was there just as before.
O how wondrous, how great indeed!

Striking his big toe on the ground,
Rocks and pebbles became gold.
He said, "Everything is a land of gold."
O how wondrous, how great indeed!

He gazed into the sky,
And from the stomach of a white-bellied fish,
He set out the offerings of a gaṇacakra
With food of a hundred flavors.
O how wondrous, how great indeed!

As I bathed in a pool of eight qualities,
A crow snatched away my protection yantra.
Nāropa made the threatening yogic gaze and mudrā.
At that very moment, the crow was paralyzed and fell
to the earth.

Nāropa said, "You are victorious over the obstacles of
Māra!"
O how wondrous, how great indeed!

"You should not stay here, but go to Tibet.
In that northern Land of Snow
Is a disciple who is a worthy vessel."
Thus, he gave this prophecy to me.
O how wondrous, how great indeed!

These are the eight wonders I saw
Of the nirmāṇakāya, Mahāpaṇḍita Nāropa.
Besides you vajra brothers and sisters,
If I repeated this to anyone, they would not believe it.
In this dark age of the teaching,
People with perverted views and great envy
Will slander you if you speak of virtue.
Therefore, please keep this secret
And do not discuss these words with others besides
yourselves.
I present this song of offering to the lord guru.
May it gladden your minds, my heart friends.

Thus he sang and pleased the hearts of all.

That evening, at the memorial service for Chitherpa that coincided with the tenth day gaṇacakra, about twenty yogins and yoginīs led by the bhikṣu Abhayakīrti assembled together. The bhikṣu Abhayakīrti then said to Marpa, "In general, you are a Tibetan skilled in song. In particular, you, the translator, stayed in India for a long time and completely accomplished your studies without obstacle to your life. Therefore, we would like you to sing an auspicious song. Your guru Maitrīpa is said to emphasize the view in his teaching. Please tell us what his approach is."

In answer, Marpa sang this song of his realization of Maitrīpa's approach and expositions:

Blessed by the glorious and venerable Hermit
Who has completely mastered the ultimate wisdom, the essential truth,
The pith instructions of the dharma of mahāmudrā,
Great lord Master, I pay homage to you.

Vajra brothers and sisters, my heart friends,
We cannot be separated by any means.
Brothers and sisters, though our bodies are separate, our minds are one.
Are you not the glorious Abhayakīrti?

I, who came from the land of India,
And you, who dwell in central Nepal,
Since the conditions for our long lives have not waned in strength,
Now on this holy day
At this gaṇacakra of the ḍākinīs,
We meet together again.
It must be that there is no hypocrisy in our samaya.
I feel completely joyful.
Do you, who are sitting here, feel joyful too?

Though I am a stupid novice from Tibet,
You call me the famous translator.
You said, "Translator, sing a Tibetan song."
Though my voice is not good,
I cannot refuse your request, honorable ones.
Here is a song recalling the kindness

Of both Lord Nāropa and Maitrīpa.
There are various ways of seeing their wonders.
Listen carefully, brothers and sisters!

The realized Lord Maitrīpa
Is famed far and wide
As a nirmāṇakāya who lives in India.
In a city in the valley of Vaiśālī,
The king, the protector of the earth, attended the lord,
touching his crown
To the anthers of the lord's lotus feet.
Among the mahāpaṇḍitas of the five sciences,
Maitrīpa is known as the Master, the crest jewel.
The banner of his fame is renowned in the ten directions.
In the month of miracles of the Bird year,
Through his mastery in making offerings to the Sugata,
His name became universally renowned as the Master.
This lord buddha gave the transmission
Of the perfection of the yānas, the pith instructions,
The dharma of mahāmudrā:

"Outer grasping, the appearance of sense objects,
Continuously flows as great bliss.
Realize it as unborn dharmakāya.

"Inner fixation, the mind-consciousness
Is discursive, which cannot be grasped as real.
Therefore, see it as naked insight without foundation.

"Generally, all dharmas of apparent existence
Are primordially nonexistent and unborn.
Realize them as the essence of simplicity.

"Do not desire to abandon saṃsāra
And there is no nirvāṇa to attain.

Saṃsāra and nirvāṇa are the self-liberated innate state.
Realize this unity as great bliss.

"Even if you emptied out the minds of the buddhas of the three times,
There is nothing more ultimate than this," Maitrīpa sang.

I have cut all doubts with this.
This is the approach of the great Lord Maitrīpa.
If you express the view, do it this way.

I present this offering song to the three jewels.
May it gladden the hearts of you sitting here.

Thus he sang. Everyone there was struck with further wonder at Lord Marpa.

At Mejadvīpa, there was a guru named Atulyavajra who was one of the dharma brothers gathered around the Master Maitrīpa. He also was an ācārya who had once given teaching in kriyā yoga to Lord Marpa himself. One day, Marpa went to pay his respects to Atulyavajra. Atulyavajra and others were consecrating a maṇḍala of Śrī Guhyasamāja made by a friend, a Kashmiri artist. When Marpa arrived at this gaṇacakra, they said, "You, the translator, went to India and stayed a long time. Your guru Nāropa is extremely famous. How long did you stay with him? What teachings did you hear and how much confidence have you gained in your understanding of them? Please sing a song as a gift from India."

In answer, Marpa sang this song of how he met Nāropa:

I prostrate to the lord siddhas.
Grant your blessings to me, a fortunate one.
Guide me, your yearning son, on the path.

Though I have no skill in singing,
I cannot refuse your request, my honorable dharma
brothers and sisters.
Now I will sing this song of pride untouched even by
death.
You who are assembled here, take this to heart
And practice the dharma properly.

I, Marpa the Translator from Tibet,
And Mahāpaṇḍita Nāropa of India
Met in a city in a valley blooming with flowers,
At the mountain monastery of the Golden Land.
This seemed to be the result of pure aspiration
in former lives.

At this famous and blessed place,
I attended the renowned jetsün
For sixteen years and seven months.
I received the full four abhiṣekas seven times.
He granted me the blessing of Śrī Cakrasaṃvara.
He taught me the profound tantra of Hevajra.
He gave me the yidam, the coemergent consort.
Again and again, I requested oral instructions.
I grabbed the path of the nāḍīs and prāṇa,
And buddha was in the palm of my hand.

One day, when so-called death is revealed,
I will be freed from the trap of my inherited body,
I will have the confidence of the profound teachings on
the moment of death,
I will join the techniques of mixing and ejecting,
And I will be received by ḍākas and ḍākinīs.
Accompanied by victory banners and a symphony of music,
I will go to the celestial realm of great bliss.
There I am certain to meet glorious Nāropa.
Now, even if I die, I feel proud.

All you lords and tāntrikas sitting here,
If you do not receive the transmission of the hearing lineage,
Do not hope to attain enlightenment in one lifetime
Through the sophistry of the scholastic lineage.
However, if you intend to practice the holy dharma wholeheartedly,
Take hold of the lineage of Nāropa and Maitrīpa.
Later disciples will be even better than previous ones.
They go from bliss to bliss.

Did my song agree with you, you who are sitting here?
Please forgive me if the meaning is confused.

Thus Marpa sang.

Then they asked Marpa, "You, the translator! In general, how many gurus did you have beyond Nepal? Whom do you regard as your principal guru? When you stayed at the feet of the Master, what virtues of his greatness did you see? What principal oral instuctions did you request?"

In reply, the lord translator sang this song:

Successor of the Great Brahman,
He has realized the innate truth free from extremes,
And is therefore the yogin of space, beyond analogy.
His name is renowned as Maitrīpa.
I am a follower of the tradition of this father jetsün.
He is a yogin for whom meditation is inseparable from the path.

This Marpa the Translator
Was born in an inferior place, but the place he visited is supreme.

I went to India three times.
Without consideration for life and limb, I sought the holy dharma.
I met the lord nirmāṇakāya buddhas
Who accepted me with abhiṣekas along with their oral instructions.
Now I will repay their kindness.

You asked me, "How many gurus do you have?"
I am linked with thirteen gurus by dharmic aspiration.
In particular, there are five siddhas.
Among them, there are two lords unrivaled by anyone,
Chiefly, Mahāpaṇḍita Nāropa
And after him, Prince Maitrīpa.

The kindness of Maitrīpa is even greater than a mother's.
Missing him more and more,
I went to the Ganges river in the East.
At the monastery of Blazing Fire Mountain,
In the cool shade of a nyagrodha tree,
I saw the great lord Master sitting there.
Joy like that of the first bhūmi arose.
I presented an offering to please the ḍākinīs.
As a maṇḍala to please the guru,
I set out flowers of pure gold.
I joined my palms and offered a full prostration.
Longing with one-pointed mind, I supplicated him.

I requested the profound tantra *Mañjuśrī-nāma-saṅgīti,*
And the yidam Hevajra.
He gave me the ultimate mahāmudrā.
He is Śrī Advaya Avadhūti.

Thus, the father jetsün kindly accepted me.
He empowered me with the four profound inner sign
abhiṣekas.*
He blessed me, completely purifying my being.
The germ of motivation sprouted deep within.
Inwardly, the character of insight-mind
Is luminosity, free from arising and ceasing.
Thus he showed me the unfabricated, innate essence.
Momentary thoughts dissolved into space
And undefiled bliss arose within.
The stream of ālaya, primordially pure,
Was resolved as the ground of the trikāya.
I met mind as mother dharmatā, face to face.

At that time, there were wondrous signs:
A cedar torch the size of a finger's length
Burned for seven days.
A tree, though inanimate,
Became unbearably agitated and moved.
There emanated seven red jackals
Whom I actually saw receive torma.
Ḍākinīs dwelling at the three levels,
Though invisible, proclaimed the sounds of mantras.
Kṣetrapālas filled the sky,
And I heard the sounds of various musical instruments.
"After three births,
You will attain the supreme siddhi,"
Thus I heard from the great lord Master.

*According to Padma Karpo, the abhiṣekas of the four signs (T: brda-bzhi) are part of the formless ḍākinī teachings. The four signs are: (1) skull cup (T: thod-pa), (2) mālā or rosary (T: 'phreng-ba), (3) viśvavajra (two crossed vajras (T: sna-tshogs rdo-rje), and (4) head ornament (T: dbu-rgyan). See *Padma dkar-po'i gsung-'bum,* vol. 7, *Snyan-rgyud las zab-mo brda'i dbang gi cho-ga.*

Even though I am unworthy, my guru is good.
Thus, I solved the final point of the view of dharma
And have no fear of falling into inferior views.
This is the approach of the great Lord Maitrīpa.
Gladden your hearts and practice in this way.

This song was given as an arrival gift to the dharma brothers and sisters led by the guru Atulyavajra.

That winter, Lord Marpa rested in Nepal as he had planned. At the charnel ground of Ramadoli, the guru from Yerang was performing an abhiṣeka and gaṇacakra. He invited Marpa to take part in the assembly. Marpa came and the guru from Yerang asked him, "You, the translator, met the guru Nāropa many times. It is a great wonder that you have received so many ritual traditions and teachings. By practicing these, what kinds of experiences and realizations have arisen in you? What kind of wondrous virtues did you see in Nāropa? Please give a short account of how you first met with the dharma and so forth."

In answer to this request, Lord Marpa sang this song:

Blessed by the lord forefathers,
I am a translator from Tibet.
Born on the border of Mön and Tibet,
My karmic connection was reawakened in the place of
  Mangkhar.

From the translator Drogmi
I learned the colloquial and literary languages and
  grammars.
I sought the holy dharma in the land of India.

With a gait like a wheel of wind
I traveled from the land of Tibet.

The buddha, Mahāpaṇḍita Nāropa,
And I, Marpa the Translator of Tibet,
Met as buddha and sentient being.
I received the full abhiṣeka seven times.
Overall I have thirteen gurus.
Nāropa and Maitrīpa are like the sun and moon;
Mahāpaṇḍita Nāropa is the chief one.

I saw great wonders like these:
Above a medicinal sandalwood tree
I saw the nine emanation devīs of Hevajra.
In the heart center of the coemergent consort
I saw the aṣṭamantra wheel.
From the stomach of a white-bellied fish
I received food of a hundred flavors.

Thus I saw the self-born sambhogakāya.
I saw inner mind as dharmakāya.
I saw outer appearances as nirmāṇakāya.
Emanations of buddha Nāropa
I saw filling all space.
In a natural boulder of crystal
I saw the footprint left by Nāropa.
There is no greater wonder than this.

When the Master, Prince Maitrīpa,
Gave an abhiṣeka in the forest,
I saw jackals roaming in the cemetery
Actually receiving the torma.
I saw the ḍākinīs of the three levels

Actually performing their activities.
This illusory contrivance of outer appearance
Was locked in the house of still space.
Appearance, this dream of habitual patterns,
Dissolved and disappeared into luminosity.
A cedar torch a finger's length in size
Burned for seven days.
I touched the feet of the great Maitrīpa,
The yogin for whom meditation is inseparable from the
path.
I hold the lineage of the Great Brahman.
I saw great wonders like these.

If I explain all of my realization,
Some of you will not be able to contain it in your mind.
If I explain just a corner of it, it is like this:
Having confidence in luminosity
Is indeed the view free from bias or partiality.
Meditation is continuous, like the flowing of a wide river.
By not regarding meditation as limited to the four periods
And by abandoning hypocritical thoughts,
There is no distinction between meditation and
postmeditation.
By obtaining the power of both prāṇa and mind,
The fear of saṃsāra disappeared long ago.
These are my realizations.

Thus Marpa sang. All the assembly saw Lord Marpa as a guru.

In the charnel ground, the jackals howled and other noises resounded. Everyone assembled there became very afraid and said, "We should make sure to finish our gaṇacakra by evening. This charnel ground is very sensitive and there is the danger that obstacles from spirits will arise."

Lord Marpa thought, "If it were my gurus Nāropa and Maitrīpa, they would prefer to actually sit on a corpse and acquire human flesh in the charnel ground. If they could not acquire these, they would visualize them through samādhi, and so enjoy them. Even when rows of kṣetrapāla ḍākinīs lined up in person to receive torma, they would not be afraid. But tonight these people are afraid of the howls of the jackals in this empty valley and the natural sounds of the elements."

Suddenly he remembered the virtues of Nāropa and Maitrīpa. He regretted that he had come back from India and decided he would go back again. Then he sat down and cried and cried.

In the early hours before dawn, Marpa dreamt that a beautiful woman dressed in clothes made of leaves came and put her hand on top of his head. "Now, rather than going to India, if you return to Tibet it will be of greater benefit to beings. You will have many worthy disciples. On your return to Tibet there will be no obstacles." Thus she prophesied. Marpa awoke and decided that the kṣetrapāla ḍākinī was sent through the kindness of Nāropa and Maitrīpa. He felt very happy and decided to go on to Tibet.

Later, Lord Marpa was staying at the Rinchen Tsül vihāra in Nepal. There he received from guru Paiṇḍapa a few selected instructions on the abhisamaya of Ekajaṭī, on the *Amṛtaprabhasādhana,* and on sampannakrama.

One night, Marpa dreamt of the lord Master Maitrīpa traveling through the sky riding on a lion. Marpa cried and wailed, saying, "Father jetsün, kindly accept me!"

Maitrīpa arrived in the sky before him, and showed him a sign teaching. He uttered the dharma beyond analogy, and Marpa achieved realization free from extremes. Thus, in this dream, Marpa had a meditation experience that he had never had before. Then, awakening from his dream at daybreak, he remembered the guru and shed many tears.

The next evening, Marpa arranged an excellent gaṇacakra to thank guru Paiṇḍapa for the teaching he had received and to supplicate Maitrīpa. During the gaṇacakra, Paiṇḍapa said, "Tonight, at this gaṇacakra, we wish to hear whatever song arises from your heart."

Thus, Lord Marpa sang this grand song proclaiming the dream prophecy in the melody of sparkling water, which clears away slothfulness.

Lord who has realized the essential truth,
  the dharmakāya,
Your name is renowned as Maitrīpa.
When I think of you and your kindness,
I miss you greatly.
I continually yearn one-pointedly for you.
Father nirmāṇakāya, grant your blessings.
You, kind guru, are the guide.

Headed by Śrī Paiṇḍapa,
You yogins and yoginīs sitting here,
Listen a while to this song.
This song possesses the blessings of the ḍākinīs.

I, the teacher Marpa Chökyi Lodrö,
Spent one-third of my life in India.
For forty years, I have learned and studied.
Last year, the dangerous Snake year,
In the Hawk month of miracles,
I was on the road.
I crossed the terrifying river Ganges.
Two low-caste bandits, happy to die,
Dove into the water like fish,
And raced toward me like horses across a plain.

Thinking of past and future lives, I panicked.
I meditated on the father jetsün on the top of my head.
They looked at me again and again, stopped, and turned around.
Like rescuing a drowning man, his kindness saved my life.
Father, it is impossible to repay your kindness.

In the first part of last month,
On the tenth day of the waxing of the moon,
At the Ramadoli charnel ground,
I presented offerings to please the gurus.
I conducted a gaṇacakra to please the ḍākinīs.
When I saw the yogins assembled there,
I suddenly recalled Lord Nāropa and Maitrīpa.
Inseparable from their loving kindness, I am protected.
Therefore, I called to mind the actions of the father.
Overwhelmed with yearning, I burst into tears.

Then I thought, "Should I return to India again?"
In a dream at the break of day,
A woman dressed in clothes made of leaves
Stretched out her right hand
And touched my head with her fingers,
Saying, "You should not return to India,
But go to Ü in the land of Tibet.
You will arrive in the Land of Snow
Without any outer or inner obstacles arising.
There are students there who are worthy vessels."
She gave me this blessing and prophecy.
Surely, she was a kṣetrapāla ḍākinī.

Then, through the kindness of the jetsün,
Last night, after my dreams born from habitual patterns,
I saw the lord Master, Prince Maitrīpa,
Traveling through the sky riding on a lion.
He arrived in front of me
And showed three signs revealing the unborn.
He spoke the dharma without letter.
I realized an inexpressible truth.
An unprecedented experience dawned.

At daybreak, as soon as I woke up,
I remembered Lord Maitrīpa again and again.
I could not separate him from my mind.
I wailed and cried, covering my face with tears.
I could not breathe; my lungs were blocked.
Father, in my heart I long for you, like a thirsty man for water.
Do you know of my longing?
Father nirmāṇakāya, guide me on the path.
Although generally dreams are born from habitual patterns,
The father jetsün appeared; O how wondrous, how great indeed!
The greatest joy and deepest sorrow arose.
You who are sitting here, this is what I say to you.

Thus Marpa sang.

Then guru Paiṇḍapa inspired Lord Marpa to feel proud by singing this song to show how, from his point of view, the one essence of the guru in Marpa's dream manifested various virtues:

You, the translator, are a heart friend.
I have profound faith in you, my son,

I have great respect for your attainment of fundamental mastery,
And I have the greatest love and compassion for you.
We hold the vows which purify our being.
You are the noble son of an excellent family.
In your former lives, you did not despise the guru.
Therefore, you have now met real siddhas.
This was through the kindness of me, your friend.
Since you are grateful for this,
You also see me as a crest jewel.
Son, what a great wonder that you know what I have done!

You have the superior samaya,
The supreme path, the imperial mantrayāna,
Which is the foundation of all journeys.
The teachings granted by the devas and ḍākinīs
And the oral instructions of the guru have entered into your heart.
It is certain that you will obtain bliss in this life.

Of all the buddhas of the three times,
The lord guru is the root of all siddhis.
As for this supreme nirmāṇakāya, the jetsün:
If you recognize him as space,
You will realize the unborn truth.

If you recognize him as the sun,
All-pervading great compassion will arise.

If you recognize him as the moon,
You will dispel the anguish of the kleśas.

If you recognize him as the ocean,
You will acquire supreme, unwavering samādhi.

If you recognize him as a jewel,
Needs, desires, and hopes are spontaneously fulfilled.

If you recognize him as the captain of a ship,
He will convey you to the jewel island of liberation.

If you recognize him as a general,
He will quell the attack of the enemies, perverted views.

If you recognize him as a sword,
You will cut the bonds of fixation.

If you recognize him as a wheel,
You will realize the truth of not dwelling in extremes.

If you recognize him as a lion,
You will overpower the wild animals of grasping and fixation.

If you recognize him as an elephant,
You will be freed from dreadful māras.

If you recognize him as a steed,
He will carry you to the realm of nirvāṇa.

If you recognize him as a king,
All will honor you and make offering.

O you of noble family, however you see him,
You recognize him as the kind father.
Therefore, the kingdom of dharma is continuous.
My son, after your dreams born from habitual patterns,
The great lord Master appeared.
He showed a sign revealing the unborn
And spoke the dharma without letter.
Having realized the truth beyond extremes,
An experience dawned, never before arisen.
It would be good if you would speak about these truths.

Thus Paiṇḍapa sang.

Then Lord Marpa offered his realization of what he saw in his dreams and what he experienced in his mind to the dharma brothers and sisters headed by guru Paiṇḍapa:

Lord Paiṇḍapa, you who practice yogic discipline!
Your name has been prophesied by the devas; O how wondrous, how great indeed!

Under the hand of glorious Advayalalita
Are the vajra brothers and sisters, whose minds do not differ.
Headed by Śrī Guṇamati,
Ḍākas who are sitting in the right hand row, listen to me!

After them, the secret yoginīs,
Headed by the consort Sukhavajrī,
Ḍākinīs who are sitting in the left hand row, listen to me!

Generally, all dharmas are illusion.
Dreams are exalted as special illusion.
Early in the night, dreams arise born from habitual patterns.
There is nothing whatsoever to rely on there.
At midnight, the deceptions of Māra appear.
One should not trust in these.
At dawn, there are prophecies by the devas.
O how wondrous, how great indeed!

At the break of dawn this morning,
The great lord Master appeared
And taught the dharma which revealed the ultimate.
This is the unforgettable memory of what Maitrīpa said:

"In general, all dharmas are mind.
The guru arises from one's mind.
There is nothing other than mind.
Everything that appears is the nature of mind,
Which is primordially nonexistent.
The natural state, unborn and innate,
Cannot be abandoned by the effort of thought.
So rest at ease, naturally, without restriction.

"This can shown by signs:
A human corpse, an outcaste, a dog, a pig,
An infant, a madman, an elephant,
A precious jewel, a blue lotus,
Quicksilver, a deer, a lion,
A brahman, and a black antelope; did you see them?" Maitrīpa asked.

The realization of the truth was shown by these signs:
Not fixated on either saṃsāra or nirvāṇa,
Not holding acceptance or rejection in one's being,
Not hoping for fruition from others,
Mind free from occupation and complexity,
Not falling into the four extremes,
Nonmeditation and nonwandering,
Free from thought and speech,
Beyond any analogy whatsoever.

Through the kindness of the guru, I realized these.
Since the experience of these realizations has dawned,
Mind and mental events have ceased,
And space and insight are inseparable.
Faults and virtues neither increase nor decrease.
Bliss, emptiness, and luminosity are unceasing.
Therefore, luminosity dawns beyond coming or going.

This transmission of the innate, the pith of the view,
Through the sign meanings which reveal the unborn,
I heard from the great lord Master.
The reason why I sing these words
Is the insistent request of the honorable lord.
I could not refuse the dharma brothers and sisters.
Ḍākinīs, do not be jealous!

Thus this song was sung for the dharma brothers and sisters headed by Paiṇḍapa, at the Rinchen Tsül vihāra in Nepal to show the meaning of the signs of mahāmudrā as revealed by Maitrīpa's appearance in a dream.

Lord Marpa did not give this song to anyone in Tibet except Jetsün Mila and Marpa Golek. These two lord brothers gave it to

Changchup Gyalpo, the teacher of Ngen Dzong. For the benefit of all sentient beings, this song was then proclaimed to all.

Lord Marpa offered farewell prostrations to his Nepalese gurus and went back to Tibet.

At that time, the disciples at Lhotrak hoped with great yearning that the guru would soon return. They wondered whether they could meet him in Nepal; but even if they could not do this, they hoped to hear news of him and felt very impatient. Thus Marpa Golek decided to go to Nepal, and left. The master and disciple met when the guru arrived at the monastery known as Masangmam at Kyitrong. Marpa Golek served as Marpa's attendant and they left together. At Langpokhar in Mangyül, some disciples offered Marpa hospitality and requested teaching. While he stayed to rest for several days, the disciples offered many gifts of turquoise and other things.

Then Marpa and Marpa Golek went to Tsang and arrived at a monastery of Metön Tsönpo at Taktsal in upper Nyang. When a good welcoming feast offering had been arranged, Metön requested, "O guru, since you have arrived at this gaṇacakra tonight after a long journey, you must be weary. However, since you have great knowledge of the ways of the secret mantra, please perform a feast ritual and full sādhana so that future generations may benefit by this example."

Thus Lord Marpa performed the full ritual of a sādhana. Even though already devoted, Metön's outlook was transformed during the feast gathering. Afterward, he said, "O guru, though you have performed many gaṇacakras previously, tonight my mind was powerfully transformed. Precious lord, since you have seen and performed many gaṇacakras in India, please sing of the times when a gaṇacakra is necessary and of the great and wondrous sights you have seen." Thus he supplicated.

In answer, Lord Marpa sang this song of the times when feast offerings are necessary and of what he had seen:

As for that which is called a gaṇacakra:
When one performs the four abhiṣekas, the path that ripens,
A gaṇacakra is necessary.
When one performs a consecration,
A gaṇacakra is necessary.
When one requests the blessings of the ḍākinīs,
A gaṇacakra is necessary.
When there is teaching of and listening to the tantras,
A gaṇacakra is necessary.
When one requests profound oral instructions,
A gaṇacakra is necessary.

This Marpa the Translator
Has gone to India three times.
In general, gaṇacakras are inconceivable.
In particular, I have seen great wonders like these:

To the Mahāpaṇḍita Jetsün Nāropa,
A royal sovereign ruler
And Kuṇḍālī, the daughter of a tavern owner,
Made an offering of kārṣāpaṇa coins
Arranged on a maṇḍala of precious bell metal.
They had supplicated a year in advance
And great Lord Nāropa had accepted.

Then at a charnel ground in a teak forest,
Nāropa performed a gaṇacakra three times.
With immeasurable wealth and enjoyments,
Elaborate feast offerings and torma were arranged.
By the blessing of glorious Nāropa,
The divine assembly of Śrī Cakrasaṃvara,

An equal number of yogins and yoginīs of the
  secret mantra—
Altogether sixty-two men and women—
Conversed in profound code language.
Emanating from the heart center of the great Lord Nāropa,
The divine assembly of Cakrasaṃvara
Resided splendidly in the center of the maṇḍala.
Performing the full sādhana,
The great Jetsün Nāropa
Held the vajra and ghaṇṭā in his hands
And wore the six bone ornaments.
In space, a cubit above the ground,
He stood in the dance posture with his right leg extended.
The other yogins and yoginīs
Sounded ḍamarus with their right hands
And held cymbals in their left.
Thus I saw them enjoying and performing the dances.
I, Marpa the Translator,
Saw the coemergent dharmakāya,
The essence of the profound fourth abhiṣeka.

I met a lord like this.
I saw a gaṇacakra like this.
This is not for the ordinary, nor the way of the ordinary.
Isn't this a great wonder, teacher of Tsang?

Thus Marpa sang.

Further faith arose in Metön, and he said, "O guru, now I have witnessed the fruition of your journey. This time you certainly must have received special abhiṣekas and instructions you had not received previously. Please accept me with kindness." Thus Metön requested.

Because there was a command-seal of secrecy on the ḍākinī hearing lineage, Marpa did not give these teachings to Metön. But he did stay and give Metön many teachings he had not previously given to others.

At the time of Marpa's departure, since Marpa had returned from India for the third time, Metön made the first of three great offerings, a great and pleasing offering of wealth. He requested, "This gift, given in your presence, you have now returned by giving teachings. Precious lord, though you have grown old, you have returned from India safely and your disciples' wishes have been fulfilled. Please accept this celebration and thanksgiving gift and sing a song of praise to the guru forefathers."

In answer to this supplication, Lord Marpa sang this song in praise of the gurus:

Lord Akṣobhya, mahāsukhakāya,
United with Vajraḍākinī,
Chief of ḍākas,
Śrī Heruka, I praise you and prostrate.

Collector of all commands and secret mantras,
Possessor of the Secret,
Propagator of the holy dharma in the world of men,
Lord Nāgārjuna, father and son, I praise you.

You who bring down the overwhelming vajra thunderbolt,
The kind one who protects from fear,
Tilopa, lord of the three levels,
Who has attained supreme siddhi, I praise you.

Undergoing twelve trials attending the guru,
All the piṭakas and tantras

You realized in an instant;
Lord buddha in human form, I praise you.

Indestructible form of mahāmudrā,
Possessing the uncontrived primordial essence,
Realizing the truth of the bliss of simplicity,
Lord Prince Maitrīpa, I praise you.

Expounding the doctrine of the command lineage,
Attaining the siddhi of profound Guhyasamāja,
You are endowed with compassion and wisdom;
Venerable Jñānagarbha, I praise you.

Dwelling in charnel grounds, solitudes, and under trees,
A kusulu savoring potency,
Possessing the miracle of traveling in space,
Kukkurīpā, I praise you.

Having realized the truth of abundance,
Possessing the potency of moonbeams,
You satisfy and bring bliss to those who see you;
Yoginī, I praise you.

Resting in the shade of the excellent umbrella
Adorned with golden ribbons,
Seated in the sky, attaining mastery over the sun and moon,
Jetsüns of Nepal, I praise you.

Overcoming the worldly attachment of grasping and fixation,
Possessing the benefit of attending the guru,

Holding principally to the practice of enlightenment,
Preserving the learning of mahāyāna,
Clearing away obstructions as well as obstacles caused
by agents of perversion,
The friend who introduces one to the good guru,
Guiding masters, I praise you.

The merit of praising the guru
Is equal to that of offering to the buddhas of the
three times.
By this merit of praising the masters,
May all beings attend spiritual friends.

Thus Marpa sang. Metön and his disciples rejoiced with delight.

While Lord Marpa was giving teachings to Metön, Marpa Golek went ahead to Lhotrak to bring the good news. Arriving in Lhotrak, Golek then made welcoming preparations, using his own wealth. Many other disciples escorted Marpa from upper Nyang. When Marpa arrived safely in Lhotrak, Marpa Golek had arranged a good feast offering of thanksgiving.

Earlier, while they had been traveling together, Marpa had given a full and detailed account of his experiences to Marpa Golek. However, for the sake of the general gathering's understanding, Marpa Golek said to Lord Marpa, "O guru, you met Jetsün Nāropa and have returned here safely. There is no greater wonder than this. Please accept us further with your immeasurable kindness. After meeting the guru, what is the difference between the former oral instructions and those now? What kind of great wonders did you see? In order to bring joy to those of us gathered here, please sing to us."

In answer to this request, Lord Marpa sang of how he met with glorious, great Nāropa, how he was given the oral instructions without exception, and how he mastered them. In a melody that overpowers phenomena and transforms the outlooks of the ḍākas, Marpa sang this grand song of wondrous actions, miracles, and virtues:

Lord nirmāṇakāya who dwells in the land of India,
In the valley of Vaiśālī in Magadha,
You defeated the attacks of heretics
And were appointed the great guardian of the gate.
You are famed as Lord Nāropa.
Father nirmāṇakāya, I pay homage at your feet.

At the palace in a city of outlaws in the East,
While I was looking through the profound *Hevajra-tantra,*
My mind was uncomfortable and agitated.
Though I drew it like a bow, it flew away like an arrow.
Suddenly, I remembered Mahāpaṇḍita Nāropa
And overwhelming yearning filled my mind.

I was looking for Nāropa in a forest near the border
When, unknowingly, I was trapped in a town of barbarous people.
Through his tyranny, the king held me in prison.
In a palace heaped with glorious flowers,
I acted as the king's officiating priest for three days.
In the hearth of blazing fire offerings,
I saw whatever food and drink I desired miraculously arise.
I thought, "O how wondrous, how great indeed!"

I set out to search again.
I carried three dre of white rice for staple
And for meat a white-bellied fish.
Lord Paiṇḍapa who practices yogic discipline
Knew the land and so accompanied me as a guide.

For half a month I wandered in the four directions.
Roaming through forests and charnel grounds,
I could not find the jetsün anywhere.
Though I did not find Mahāpaṇḍita Nāropa,
I saw signs of great wonder:

Above a medicinal sandalwood tree,
The nine emanation devīs of Hevajra,
Almost touching the branches,
Appeared in the sphere of a rainbow.
A wondrous sign, how great indeed!

In the heart center of the coemergent consort,
The aṣṭamantra wheel,
Like a reflection in a mirror,
Clearly appeared, unobscured by her outer form.
A wondrous sign, how great indeed!

On a white crystal boulder,
A very hard and solid vajra rock,
I saw the footprint of great Lord Nāropa,
Complete in detail with even the imprint of his hair.
A wondrous sign, how great indeed!

I thought, "It won't be long now,"
And supplicated for a week.
Since the father clearly knows the minds of others,
The jetsün arrived before me in person.
I cried and wept with great joy.
Lowering myself, I placed the soles of his feet on
the top of my head.
Wailing, I said, "You have been so unkind."

My tears of longing flowed like blood.
A wondrous sign, how great indeed!

I embraced his body like a consort.
I touched my head to his heart.
At that time he bestowed the complete abhiṣeka on my mind,
Pouring the essence of mind into me, thus completing the teachings.
A wondrous sign, how great indeed!

Generally, both Mahāpaṇḍita Nāropa of India
And I, the teacher Lodrö, Marpa of Tibet,
Met as buddha and sentient being.
There is no doubt that I will become a siddha.
A wondrous sign, how great indeed!

You who keep samaya are like my heart son.
Basically, when I went to India,
Whenever I felt poor in wealth and possessions,
I filled a bowl with precious gold.
Such a story is worthy of fame; O how wondrous, how great indeed!

Since you are not stingy with your wealth,
You collected the last of your shoes and clothing,
And sent me away with all that I needed.
This was burying treasure, provisions for your next life.
Again I thought, "O how wondrous, how great indeed!"

The son's mind is more tender than the father's.
Isn't this you, Marpa Golek?

What need to speak of your generosity with illusory
wealth?
Your way is not to be concerned with this life.
A wonder greater than this is impossible.

How could I forget this long journey?
In the forest of Lhokha at the border of Tibet and Nepal,
Even in winter at the New Year, a ridge blooms with
flowers.
In that land where white salu rice is sown,
In that country of Mön where the language is different,
The heat makes it difficult to survive any sickness,
But I risked my life without fear of death.

Son, in order to keep the difficult samaya,
Keep this in mind; I, the father, won't forget this either.
At this time, it is certain that we will never be
separated.
It is impossible that we will not meet in the next life.
In the presence of yidams and ḍākinīs,
Let us, father and son, aspire together.

In order to express my gratitude for what you have done
I have sung this song for your benefit.
Please do not proclaim this to others; keep it secret.
Now I have given you these teachings to repay your
kindness.
Keep this confidential; we will speak of it privately.
We have met before and are the best of friends.
From now until we die, let us be together.

Thus Marpa sang.

This song of the wondrous appearance of visions of the five qualities of body, speech, and mind was sung to repay the kindness of Marpa Golek, a chief son-disciple.

Marpa gave to Marpa Golek great Lord Nāropa's practice mālā of one hundred and eight rubies, as well as a pair of vajra rings from Master Maitrīpa. He said, "Son, you have done great deeds for me. You should stay with me until I die. We have aspired together; so it is impossible that we will not meet in the next life. Because we have been brought together by the essence of samaya, we, father and son, will be born and live in the same place." Never leaving him for even one day, Marpa Golek served as his attendant until the guru died.

This song of the wondrous signs of how Marpa met Nāropa was sung three times in different words, but with one meaning. One should know that this song has one meaning, but was sung in reply to the requests of three different people.*

*The sequence of events about which Marpa later sang on three different occasions is originally described on pp. 81-87. Marpa sings the first song recounting these events to guru Paiṇḍapa, where he describes the eight wondrous signs he saw before and upon meeting Nāropa. This song accords very well with the previous narrative description. However, in Marpa's second song, which occurs on pp. 119-121, he gives a very abbreviated version of the events and does not keep them in strictly chronological order (i.e., he mentions seeing Nāropa's footprint after the vision of Hevajra and the gaṇacakra of a hundred flavors). However here he is relating these events to the perspective of the three kāyas, so chronological order does not seem to be emphasized.

The third and final song concerning how Marpa met with Nāropa is found on pp. 137-140. This song has several differences from the prose narrative. If we removed the line on p. 137, "At the palace in the city of outlaws in the East," and moved the rest of this verse to after the verse ending "Knew the land and so accompanied me as a guide," we would then have the same sequence as laid out in the prose narrative.

Moreover, on p.138, the two stanzas (i.e., beginning with "Above a medicinal sandalwood tree. . . ." and ending with "Clearly appeared, unobscured by her outer form. / A wondrous sign, how great indeed!") should be placed after the lines "I thought, 'It won't be long now,' / And supplicated for a week." According to the prose narrative Marpa's vision of Hevajra happens after he supplicates Nāropa and just before he meets Nāropa in person.

It seems clear from Tsang Nyön's comment here that he was aware of the contradictions in Marpa's songs. The fact that Marpa sang these songs in reply to the requests of three different people can partially explain their differences. But since these songs were spontaneous, Marpa sang of these events as they came up in his mind. Therefore, he would not always recount all of the events nor would he stick to strictly chronological order.

Then guru Ngokpa, Tsurtön, and many son-disciples gathered together. They offered a thanksgiving feast to the guru, who had returned safely and with great fame. They came to request teachings and, during the feast, two of them gave offerings and made this request, "O guru, now that the lord has arrived here safely, the many wishes of the disciples and attendants have been fulfilled and the sun of happiness has risen. Precious lord, we heard it said that you endured many hardships and illnesses and much fatigue and we felt anxious. Today, please sing us a song explaining how you endured your hardships and illnesses."

Marpa said, "Now listen and I will sing a song about the hardships I endured searching for Lord Nāropa, and tell the story from when I first entered the dharma until now." In the melody that gathers wild, scattered, and discursive thoughts in meditation, the iron hook of insight, the ḍākinīs' wail, Marpa sang this grand song of the hardships he endured for the sake of the dharma:

Lord Vajradhara whose essence is Akṣobhya,
Please dwell as the crest ornament on the crown of
 my head.
Once I relate the examples of my difficult labors,
You lords, great teachers staying here,
Should practice the dharma properly, not regarding
 it as easy.

This Marpa the Translator
Was born in the center of Lhotrak.
My karmic connection to the white dharma was
 reawakened.
At the glorious monastery in Nyugu valley,
Under the translator Drogmi Lotsāwa,

I learned the colloquial and literary languages and
grammars.
His kindness certainly is great, not small.

I sought the holy dharma in the land of India.
While traveling the path in Nepal
I crossed over endless precipices and rivers,
Went through endless thick forests,
And traveled a long, endless road.
I was alone, like a solitary tree or a human corpse.
Enduring all the suffering on this path,
Even the wings of a soaring bird would tremble.
Nevertheless, it was worth the price of such fatigue.

I saw Nepal, heaven descended on earth.
Seeing such sense pleasures, one could never get enough.
I thought, "This is a land of demigods in the desire realm.
This must be the golden age."
Though the way was difficult to travel, it was best to
keep going.
While going from there to India,
In the barbarous regions I encountered bandits, happy
to die.
There seemed no hope that my life would be saved.
When I heard the roars of the beasts of prey,
Little did I think that this body would reach a
comfortable place.
When I saw the breath of a giant serpent,
Though my mind was steady, my steps faltered.
All these dangerous things, I saw upon the path.
Even remembering them now, my heart and
lungs tremble.

Finally, I crossed the famous Ganges river.
Nevertheless, it was worth the price of such hardship.

I saw the magnificent sights of Magadha.
Beginning with glorious Vajrāsana,
I made offerings to wondrous shrines.
I thought, "I have arrived too late."
Anxiously I searched for the dharma with all my heart.
Like a river, I wandered East and West through the land of India.
On a plain so vast it was difficult to cross,
I thought, "I have arrived on a plain of fire."
Though I thought of the dharma, my heart swelled with depression.
I was overcome by the heat and a fever, which made it difficult to survive.
I came near to death thirteen times.
There was no one with whom to leave a will of three words.
Three times I passed into a coma.
Seeing all the suffering of that time,
Even hateful enemies would shed tears.
Nevertheless, it was worth the price of risking my life.

Headed by the lord, Mahāpaṇḍita Nāropa,
There were five siddha gurus that I met.
In general, I studied the four orders of tantra.
In particular, I learned the complete mother tantra
As well as the *Guhyasamāja* of the father tantra.

I went to the bank of the river Ganges in the East.
By the blessings of Lord Maitrīpa,

I attained the realization of the ground, unborn dharmatā,
Grabbed the śūnyatā-mind,
Saw the innate essence, the truth of simplicity,
Met mother trikāya in person,
And resolved my own complexity at that time.

When I returned again to Ü in the land of Tibet,
I thought, "I have the greatest oral instructions."
I thought, "Some disciples will become siddhas."
I thought, "Many benefits for beings have been
accomplished."
These are my profound confidences.
This is the way I endured hardship.
Think of how difficult it is to obtain the dharma;
Please do not be lazy, but practice!

Thus Marpa sang. Many shed tears at this feast led by the great sons.

This was the last time that Marpa went to India.

CHAPTER III

The practice of the oral instructions is born in Marpa's heart.

In general, Marpa practiced according to the oral instructions that he received, and excellent experiences and realizations were born in his heart. He then sang various songs of realization. In particular, Marpa attained confidence through practicing the transference of consciousness.

ONCE some disciples, headed by Gyang-ro Shangtön, and many benefactors were offering an excellent thanksgiving gaṇacakra. At that time, a young pigeon from a nest near the house was flying behind its mother pursued by a hawk. Though the young pigeon escaped to its nest, it died from being out of breath.

Seeing this corpse, Marpa said, "Should I show you a demonstration of the transference of consciousness today?" Everyone offered prostrations and supplicated for this. Marpa tied a string to the pigeon's leg and then transferred his consciousness. The pigeon arose, staggered, and as it was about to fly up, it reunited affectionately with its mother.

Gyang-ro Shangtön looked at the guru's body. It had the appearance of a corpse and he became terrified. Weeping before the body, he requested, "Precious guru, please do not do this." As this had no effect, he became even more frightened. Then he went before the young pigeon and supplicated.

The young pigeon fell over; immediately the guru arose and said:

Having abandoned my body like an empty house,
I entered another body, a young pigeon.

Extending its wings and about to fly in the sky,
The mother and son birds met affectionately.
Everyone witnessed this; what a great wonder!

Thus Marpa said and he laughed. All of those assembled there acquired great confidence in the transference of consciousness and were struck with wonder.

When Marpa's older brother, Chowo, heard the story of this transference of consciousness, he said, "Is this just a rumor or is it true? If it is true, there is no greater wonder than this." He thought over and over, "I must see for myself whether the transference of consciousness is true or false."

One day while Chowo's weaver-lady was working, a white lamb died from being overfed with milk. Chowo said to Lord Marpa, "Perform the transference of consciousness here as you did with the pigeon."

Marpa replied, "From India I received the rasāyana of the consort Vajravārāhī, the oral instructions that are a remedy for death, the only medicinal compound of wisdom; therefore I will perform the transference." Lord Marpa said to Chowo, the son-disciples, and the many benefactors assembled there, "I will stay here and transfer my consciousness to the lamb. Watch what the lamb will do."

Accordingly, Chowo and all the others started walking over to the lamb's corpse. When the guru entered into samādhi, the lamb suddenly got up and leaped about.

The weaver-lady was astonished and trembled, saying, "Look at this! It was completely dead; but now it gets up and jumps about."

She was about to hit the lamb with a broom when the witnesses finally arrived there and said, "Don't hit it! This is guru Marpa who is performing the transference of consciousness."

The weaver-lady said, "I have heard of this before, but today I see this with my own eyes. How wondrous!" She loosened the tension in her loom and then prostrated to the lamb and in the direction of Lord Marpa.

Chowo said to his employees, "Bring the revived lamb to the place where the guru is." Chowo himself went near the guru, who appeared to be dead.

The disciples supplicated the lamb, "Please go to where your body is." The lamb walked over to the guru's body, and again jumped about, and then fell over.

Marpa got up and said:

> The deathless wisdom,
> The rasāyana of the mother of the buddhas of the three times,
> The medicinal compound of the amṛta of the transference of consciousness,
> Revives the dead lamb and so he dances.

An overflowing faith arose in Chowo. He requested teachings and abhiṣeka and became Marpa's disciple and attendant.

At that time Marpa Cha-se, a relative of Lord Marpa who really disliked and even hated him, said, "Chowo is very gullible. Marpa talked a lot about his travels to India. He learned some magical tricks and deceived Chowo with one of them. On the other hand, if the so-called transference or whatever is genuine, Marpa will claim that he has arrived at buddhahood splendidly without breaking or damaging even a corner of his kleśas, but keeping them intact. His breath has a rotten stench. His crotch stinks. He lives by devouring gifts from his devotees. Now that he has attained buddhahood, we will never see any dharma from him." Thus he slandered Marpa.

When Lord Marpa heard about this, he said, "The transference of consciousness is genuine. Therefore I have actually done it. If you do not abandon sense pleasures or do not bring them to the path, the vast and profound buddhahood attained through the many methods and fewer hardships of the secret mantra will not come about. According to the profound knowledge of the secret mantra, if you do not bring sense pleasures to the path, but instead abandon them, it is a disservice to oneself."

Then Marpa sang this song of the greatness of the secret mantra path:

I, Marpa Lotsāwa,
Know the king of tantras, the *Hevajra.*
I have the oral instructions of Mahāpaṇḍita Nāropa.
If I do not remain in solitude, it is a disservice to
myself.

I know the king of tantras, the *Catuḥpīṭha.*
I have the oral instructions of the ejection and
transference of consciousness.
If I die in the ordinary way, it is a disservice to
myself.

I know how to mix dhyāna and sleep.
I have the oral instructions of the luminosity of
dreams.
If I sleep in the ordinary way, it is a disservice to
myself.

I know the caṇḍālī, the regal way of holding the mind.
I have the oral instructions that pierce to the pith
of mind.
If I do not practice their meaning, it is a disservice
to myself.

I know the seventy qualities of prāṇa.
I have the oral instructions of utilizing illness.
If I summon a doctor, it is a disservice to myself.

I know my body to be the maṇḍala of the victorious ones.
If I do not expand nāḍī, prāṇa, and bindu
Through enjoying meat and liquor, it is a disservice
to myself.

In order to bring another person on the path,
I have the oral instructions of karmamudrā.
If I do not enjoy the mudrā, it is a disservice
to myself.

Thus Marpa sang.

All the son-disciples attained conviction in the wisdom of the profound orders of tantra and felt great devotion.

Marpa Cha-se said, "He has to bring up dharmic words in order to justify his actions." Hearing this, others believed in what Marpa Cha-se said. Some disciples were displeased.

Guru Ngokpa and many other son-disciples were gathered at a feast offering when one disciple told guru Marpa what Marpa Cha-se had said. The guru replied, "Ngokpa and others who understand the dharma should not be afraid of this. Beings with perverted thoughts have committed innumerable actions that accumulate evil. Among them, those who are extremely partial to their own opinion and beings who profane sacred outlook are extremely slanderous, even toward the Buddha himself. Many of these even curse their own shadow. Not following their conceptualizations, let go naturally in the state of compassion and illusion. When you arrive at self-purity, you will not accumulate evil. That is how it is." Then Marpa sang this song:

Bhagavat, great Vajradhara,
In this dark age of five thousand years,
When you ripen and free those of good karma
You appear in the form of the great Lord Nāropa.
This unresourceful Marpa the Translator—
Do you hear, see, or think of him?
O father nirmāṇakāya, please accept me with kindness.

In the avadhūti, the main path of enlightenment,
Prāṇa and mind, bliss and warmth are united,
Becoming unconditioned great bliss.
The wisdom of unobscured insight dawns.
"This is unsurpassable," the guru has said.

The darkness of ignorance is purified in space.
One is free from the two obscurations of grasping
and fixation.
Therefore bliss and luminosity dawn in simplicity.

This appearance of collective coincidence
Is a reflection without self-nature.
All appearances are realized like that,
And just like appearances in a dream,
All dharmas arise as illusions.
Gods, asuras, humans,
Hell beings, pretas, animals—
These various ways of fixating on appearance
Are realized as nonexistent, like an illusion.

When conceptions of the world and its inhabitants
And the gate through which these arise are controlled
by the technique of prāṇa,
There appears whatever is desired.
Therefore the mixing and ejecting of consciousness arise
free from stain.

When thoughts arise, rest naturally.
When dreaming, be mindful without corrupting it.
When in the pardo, don't control, but be aware.
When there is fruition, let it arise without
obscuration.

You followers of Nāropa,
Practice the profound oral instructions.
As you have insight, certainty will arise.
Narrow-minded people with perverse realization
Slander even the Buddha.
Cursing even their own shadow,
They chase after deception
And cannot distinguish truth from falsity.
When the fool runs and cries out,
The wise do not follow.

The dharma is empty of sophistry.
This body is a maṇḍala of deities.
This speech is the nature of dharma.
This mind is the essence of wisdom.
Sons, practice free from boredom.
Undoubtedly, you will attain enlightenment.

Thus Marpa sang and everyone gained certainty.

Another time, Marpa and his attendants went to take a walk along the river bank. Some hunters' dogs appeared chasing a deer, and the deer ran into the river and drowned.

Marpa said, "I will perform the transference of consciousness. Some of you go after the deer and protect it from the dogs. Some of you stay here by my body." Marpa then transferred his consciousness into the deer and brought the corpse of the deer up to the courtyard outside his house, leaving a trail of wet prints. Then the guru stood up and went there.

While the guru, some disciples, relatives, and many others were looking at the corpse of the deer, the hunters arrived and prepared to butcher it. The guru said jokingly, "I found the corpse of this deer in the river. I don't want you to take it." The disciples and many people told the story of how the guru performed the transference of consciousness.

Some of the hunters said, "Well then, we ask you to perform the transference of consciousness where we can see it and then we will offer you the body of the deer." Some others said, "If you do this and we see it, we will offer other things in addition to the deer."

So Lord Marpa transferred his consciousness into the deer and brought it through the gate into the courtyard. Then the guru stood up and said:

> Through the transference of consciousness kindly
> given by the guru,
> A requisite for the feast, a samaya substance
> That fulfills all needs and desires,
> Is found in this wish-fulfilling gem, the deer.

And he said, "While my consciousness inhabited the body of an animal, my mind appeared to be dull."

After Marpa had done this, everyone there was filled with wonder and amazement. The hunters rejoiced and offered the corpse of the deer as well as other gifts. Many others entered the gate of dharma. In particular, Marpa Cha-se was present there and faith was born in him. He regretted his previous perverted views and deeds and made confession. He requested, "You said that if one does not enjoy meat, liquor, and women, it is a disservice to oneself. It appears to us that this is no different than what we do. Now, since you seem to possess some confidence, please tell us how this is."

Marpa replied, "You do not understand. Therefore, even if you were to see deities in union, you would say this is the same as what you do. Though I enjoy sense pleasures, I have these confidences that I am not fettered by them."

Then Marpa sang this song of fathoming realization and of the confidence that has totally mastered the dharma:

> I prostrate to the father gurus.
> By the kindness of the lord forefathers,

When in solitude and at leisure, I meditate on
nāḍī and prāṇa.
Exerting body and mind again and again, I meditate.
Even when my elements are in turmoil, I have no anxiety.
I have confidence in knowing this will heighten my
practice.

While asleep, I meditate on luminosity.
Focusing appearances again and again, I meditate.
Even when experiencing delusion, I have no anxiety.
I have confidence in knowing this as unity.

At the time of dream, I meditate on the illusory body.
Expanding on appearances again and again, I meditate.
Even when the dreams become discursive, I have no
anxiety.
I have confidence in knowing them as illusory.

While enjoying sense pleasures, I meditate on the
deity.
Experiencing their taste again and again, I meditate.
Even when seeing ordinary food and drink, I have no
anxiety.
I have confidence in knowing these as a feast offering.

On the occasion of upāyamarga, I meditate on another's
body.
Arousing bliss again and again, I meditate.
Even when it appears to be mundane, I have no anxiety.
I have confidence in knowing this as coemergent.

At the time of death, I meditate on the ejection of
consciousness.
Practicing the ejection of consciousness again and again,
I meditate.

Even when the signs of death appear, I have no anxiety.
I have confidence in knowing them as sampannakrama.

At the time of death, I enter the pardo.
The pardo is like a cloud or mist.
Even when passion and aggression arise, I have no anxiety.
I have confidence in knowing them as self-liberated.

Thus Marpa sang.

Unwavering faith was born in Marpa Cha-se and he requested teachings and abhiṣeka. Later he became a patron who rendered perfect service.

At another time, a yak had died near the site of a feast where many people had gathered. When the workers were preparing to take the corpse away, Marpa said, "My share of the work will be to carry away the corpse of the yak." He then transferred his consciousness into the yak and brought the yak's corpse up to the courtyard. Then Marpa stood up and said:

The essence of the ḍākinī's body, speech, and mind
Is the horse of nāḍī, prāṇa, and bodhicitta.
Urged by the whip of equal taste,
The old yak crosses the dangerous passage.

Because he achieved certainty in the transference of consciousness, Marpa became completely renowned as a siddha, undisputed by anyone. In the same way, he gave the supreme single transmission lineage of the profound instructions on the transference of consciousness to his son Tarma Dode.*

*The transference of consciousness (T: grong-'jug) is a special practice connected with the practice of ejection (T: 'pho-ba; see note p. 94). Due to Tarma Dode's untimely death, it is said that the lineage of this teaching and practice was broken and did not continue. However, though this is true and transference is not practiced, according to H. H. Dingo Khyentse, Rinpoche, the reading transmission of this practice has continued to the present day.

CHAPTER IV

Through manifesting his realization, Marpa benefits sentient beings and the teachings.

In general, guru Ngokpa and the other worthy disciples assembled there are ripened and freed through abhiṣekas and oral instructions. In particular, by means of sadness and renunciation at the death of his son, Marpa strengthens everyone's practice.

HAVING offered thanksgiving feasts upon the guru's return from India, most of the disciples and attendants departed to their own homes. The guru, the father and all his sons, dwelt in strict retreat according to the command-prophecy of Nāropa. The guru dwelt in the upper part of the castle. Below him dwelt his son Tarma Dode. Below him dwelt some of the great son-disciples. The other son-disciples also practiced sādhana in strict retreat. Marpa's wife, Marpa Golek, and Bawachen of Parang served them.

The father gave the oral instructions of the ejection and transference of consciousness to his son Tarma Dode. Tarma Dode totally mastered these oral instructions and attained confidence.

One day as a dog barked, someone knocked on the door of the castle. From his window, the son saw a tall man dressed in white carrying a bow and some arrows. Tarma Dode's mother went out to meet him and the man said, "The annual Ngamo-chushül fair is the day after tomorrow. Your older brother is sponsoring it. Earlier, Marpa was offered the fame and honor of presiding over both the fair and the feast. I have come to invite

the guru, the father or the son, whoever is free to come. One of them must come no matter what." Thus he spoke insistently.

Dagmema gave him good food and chang, and while he was eating she said, "It is very wonderful that you people are giving both a fair and a feast. But, as I told you before, our guru Marpa says that he must fulfill the command-prophecy of Lord Nāropa. So the father and sons must all live in strict retreat for three years. Since only one year has passed, it is quite unlikely that the father or son will go. We might send one of the great son-disciples below them, an important one." The mother also spoke with insistence.

The man said drunkenly, "It must be the father or the son. No one else shall preside. If the guru was going, I would go along as his attendant. However, since he is not going, I will leave, but I have delivered the message anyway. Don't say I didn't deliver it!" He abruptly dusted off the bottom of his chuba and left.

The son thought, "Now, from society's point of view, I have the most prominent parents. Because of my family, relatives, and attendants, I have no sorrow or burdens and I am learned in the dharma. Therefore I am well suited to go to this year's fair. But if I ask my father and mother, they will not give their permission. I will have to sneak out."

Two days later, everyone from the upper valley came by on their way to the fair, wearing elegant clothing and jewelry. Thinking, "I must leave in such a way that my father and mother don't hear," the son got out of bed and prepared to leave. Then he thought, "It is said, 'The higher the mountain, the deeper the abyss. The greater the gain, the greater the risk. The more profound the dharma, the more profound the māra.' My father will chastise me. When the obstacles of Māra arise, there is great danger." Thus, he stayed in his bed.

Just then there came three old women, their mouths toothless and their heads as white as conches. They said, "We have seen the great Ngamo-chushül fair of Lhotrak again and again and still it is not enough. The time of death comes without warning, so we don't know if we shall see it again.''

Tarma Dode watched them go by swinging their staffs, their knees wobbling. Not realizing that the three old women were a magical creation of Māra, the son thought, ''If even old ladies like these are going, why shouldn't I go, since I am young and the favorite child, loved by my father and mother?''

Throwing a white cloak over his shoulders, he suddenly left his retreat. His mother happened to be bringing him some hot refreshment and met him. She said, ''Son, you are not permitted to leave your retreat so suddenly. Where do you think you're going? Go back up and keep to your practice.''

The son was afraid that his mother would grab him, so he ran down the stairs. Since his mother had food in her hands, she could not grab or stop him, and the son ran by. The son thought, ''Well, if my mother gives me advice, I must listen. But if she tells me to stay, I should go.'' At the threshold of the gate, he mounted a horse and turned around.

The mother thought, ''If my son obeys me and stops, I must keep him here. If he won't obey and won't stop, I should give him some advice.'' Then she said, ''O son, listen to your mother and come back up.''

The son replied, ''O mother, as it is said, 'When the moon is bright, it is in its first phase. When the parents are alive, the child is in his first phase.' I also have neither illness nor suffering. Therefore I am well suited to go to the fair. Please let me go there just this time.''

The mother said, ''Have you asked your father?''

''I didn't, but since I have asked you, my mother, that will do.''

As he was about to leave, the mother said, ''Son, since you are going without listening to me at all, let us, mother and son, make a vow. Keep these in the center of your heart. Today don't sit at the head of the row. Don't accept offerings as the guest of honor. Don't give the dedication speech. Don't give a discourse on the dharma. Don't drink chang. Don't ride horses. Come back no later than noon. These are the seven vows between the two of us, mother and son. You must keep them in mind.''

The son said hurriedly, ''It will be done,'' and rode off.

Then Dagmema sent a party of four trustworthy students, led by Jetsün Mila and Marpa Golek, to attend Tarma Dode, and insisted that they make sure the seven vows were kept. When the mother was alone, her heart was troubled as never before and she shed many tears. She thought, ''Before, even if my son went away for a month for the benefit of others, I wasn't upset like this. If I am so upset now when he is going away only for one day, isn't some terrible accident going to happen?''

When the young master and his attendants arrived at Ngamochushül, the people were assembled in many rows. The master and attendants took a place at the end of the spiritual teachers, but at the head of the laymen. The wise old lamas who were at the head of the rows were perplexed and said, ''Isn't that the son Tarma Dode?'' They sent someone to check whether it was the son. When they knew that it was the son, they invited him to take the seat of honor, but Tarma Dode did not want to go.

The lamas at the head of the rows said, ''It is not right, no matter how you look at it, for us to sit ahead of Jetsün Marpa's son.'' The lamas at the head of the rows carried their cushions and went below the son's seat, changing their seats like the flight of a flock of birds. Thus it came about that the son was at the head of the rows.

Therefore Tarma Dode had to take the position of honored guest, accept the gifts, and give the dedication speech. He also had to give a discourse on the dharma in answer to the questions of the spiritual teachers, and it became obvious that he was learned. Then, one by one, the noblemen offered him chang very insistently, so that he had to drink a little each time.

By then it was past noon and Jetsün Mila said, ''Precious guru, it is said, 'The feast and fair should end before it becomes too good, otherwise the gathering will conclude in a fight.' Most of your mother's commands have been violated. Now that it is past noon, we should definitely go."

The son replied, "Older brother, Great Magician, you are quite right!"

As Tarma Dode was getting ready to leave, his uncle, who was the wealthiest man in Lhotrak, but had no children, came up leading a horse named White-Shouldered Raven. This horse was the swiftest in Lhotrak and had splendid saddlery. His uncle said, "Nephew, stand up! In the dedication speech and the rest you excelled in your knowledge of dharma. Now excel in horsemanship! Ride this horse." And he put the reins into Tarma Dode's hand.

The son said, "Later I'll do what you say in any way I can, but don't ask me to ride this horse now. As I was coming here, my mother gave several instructions and I have already violated most of them. If I ride now, I shall have violated all of them."

His uncle replied, "Your mother Dagmema is very powerful, but she is my sister. However insignificant I may be, I am still her older brother. Since you obey your mother, why not me? The proverb says, 'If the river carries your uncle away, don't grab him by the hair.'* That is very true, so by all means you must ride this horse. After you ride I will give him to you, along with the saddlery." His uncle pulled him by the hand and forced him to mount the horse. Thus Tarma Dode was unable to avoid riding. As he galloped the horse, Tarma Dode's composure was magnificent and his skill was great. Thus, he was the very best in both spiritual and temporal ability, and many offerings were repeatedly pressed on him. For a while he felt satisfied with himself.

*The meaning here is that to grab one's uncle by the hair would be very disrespectful, even in trying to rescue him from drowning. Hence, the proverb points out the eminent position of an uncle who deserves great respect in all situations.

Then Jetsün Mila earnestly requested the son, "Sir, you have now violated all the vows you made to your mother this morning. It is said, 'Before you win over the crowd, rein in your horse.' We should definitely go before the crowd leaves."

Thus the master and disciples departed, with Tarma Dode riding the horse his uncle had given him and Jetsün Mila holding the halter. Tarma Dode said, "I am neither old, decrepit, sick, nor incapable of controlling this horse. You don't have to hold the halter. Go on ahead."

The disciples had gone a good distance ahead when they descended into Shen valley. On one side of the path were rapids, making it a dangerous passage. On the other side, among the rocks and boulders, was an abundance of bushes. Among the bushes was a partridge nest. As Tarma Dode was passing by, the sound of the horse's hooves startled the mother partridge and six little ones and they took flight. At the sound of their wings and their shrieking, the horse was startled and jumped. The son fell from his horse, and one of his feet caught in a stirrup. The horse dragged the son among the rocks the distance of an arrow's flight, and his skull was broken. From his head burst forth brains and a great deal of blood.

When the horse bolted, Jetsün Mila looked back and saw the riderless horse running off in the distance. He thought, "The son has been thrown from his horse." Holding his prāṇa, Mila ran and caught the horse, and tied it to a tree. He released Tarma Dode's foot from the stirrup. Seeing that Tarma Dode was unconscious, Mila placed his head on his lap and examined it. It was broken into eight fragments and there was a great deal of brains and blood. Since there was nothing to be done, Mila sat there, crying.

Then the other great son-disciples arrived. Holding Tarma Dode's hands and feet, they called his name and wept a great deal. Finally, they conferred, decided that Tarma Dode was unable to ride a horse, and so planned to carry him on a stretcher. They took a length of silk that had been offered to Tarma Dode and bound it around his head.

While the disciples were making a stretcher, a fresh breeze was blowing and the son regained consciousness. His eyes opened, and seeing Jetsün Mila, he said, "Brother, Great Magician, it is good that you have come. I've been thrown from my horse and it seems I have hurt my head. What are you all doing?"

They answered, "The guru is unable to ride the horse and can't walk, so we are preparing a stretcher."

Tarma Dode said, "As is said, 'Even though a gentleman is hungry, he must keep his garuḍa's horns.'* I will try to ride the horse. Take this sash off and rip it in half." They took it off and ripped it as he said. With half they bound his head, and with the other half they refastened his chuba. "Now put me on the horse," he said. After they put him on the horse, he said, "Uncle Golek, you are the oldest, so lead my horse. You other two, support me on the left and right. Elder brother, Great Magician, you go ahead and tell my father and mother the story of how I became a little injured." They did as he said, and then the master and students went forward slowly.

Jetsün Mila went ahead and came before the guru on the top floor of the castle. After prostrating, he said, "Precious guru, I have something to tell of which I don't dare to say even three words."

The guru said, "Whenever you arrived before, I felt joyful. This time my heart is unhappy. What has happened? Tell me!" Jetsün Mila was unable to speak and wept. After a while Mila told the guru the whole story.

"My son went to the fair this morning?" Marpa asked.

"Yes sir, he went."

*A garuḍa is a celestial bird of Indian mythology, somewhat like an eagle. Its two horns are its dignity, like a crown. Therefore Tarma Dode is saying that even though injured, he must try to keep his strength and dignity.

"Where did he break his head?"

"It was broken in Shen valley."*

"This valley called Shen has lived up to its name. He is not dead yet, is he?" Marpa asked.

"He has not died and is coming."

"How did you bandage him?"

"We ripped his sash in two lengthwise. We bound his head with half, and refastened his chuba with the other half," Mila replied.

"Then this is a sign that the father and son must be separated. Last night I dreamt that a black man came to me and said, 'Nāropa commands you to tear out your heart and give it to me to take to him.' I thought, 'I must obey this command of the guru.' Tearing out my heart, I gave it to him. He was delighted and put it in a skull cup. Covering it with a hooked knife, he went away. Also, I dreamt that a hole developed in the center of a maṇḍala, that the sun and moon simultaneously decayed in the midst of the sky, and that a lake of rakta dried up.

"Even if I go out to meet him, it will have no effect. However, there is still the samaya bond between father and son. Therefore, I must go out of compassion," Marpa said. He then went out and met his son as he arrived in the courtyard.

The son said, "I went to the fair this morning. I hurt my head. Please see if it's serious or not." Tarma Dode put his head on his father's lap. His father loosened the sash binding his head and examined it. Marpa saw that the skull was broken into eight fragments, that the cranial membrane was torn and the brains were spilling out. He thought, "My son will not live for long."

Again the son became unconscious and fell into a coma. The father laid his son's head in his lap, and turning him on his right side, he sang into his ear this song which clarifies the ejection of consciousness:

*shen (T:zhan) literally means "weak, feeble, inferior, or bad."

Listen son, Prince Dodebum.
I, Marpa the Translator,
Went to the land of India three times.
I attended with devotion the authentic gurus,
Lords Nāropa and Maitrīpa,
And received many tantras, commentaries, and oral instructions.
They granted transmissions of the pith of the four abhiṣekas.
In particular, I received the ejection and transference of consciousness.
Not keeping anything secret, I taught this fully to you, my son.
Do you remember these tantras, commentaries, and oral instructions, Dodebum?

In general, composite things
Are impermanent and perishable.
Son, this illusory body does not last forever.
Suddenly, the obstacles of Māra have arisen.
The white conch of your skull is broken.
The white silk curtain of your cranial membrane is torn.
Your brain, the divine assembly of the buddhas, has spilled out.
Son, it's quite true that your illusory body is perishable.

Your venerable father is a maṇḍala of deities.
Draw forth your consciousness through the aperture of Brahmā.

Now eject your consciousness into the heart center
of your venerable father.

Thus Marpa sang.

Tarma Dode's mother overheard all this from inside and thought, "The guru was practicing on the top floor of the castle, but now in the courtyard, he is singing a song which clarifies the ejection of consciousness. Has some obstacle befallen my son?" She hurried to the courtyard and saw her son, with his bloody head resting on his father's lap. She fainted and was unconscious for a while.

Regaining consciousness, she said to the father, "You are learned in the eightfold way of medical practice. Will our son live or die?"

The guru replied, "Though I am expert in the eightfold way of medical practice, there is no way to cure a body without a head. As is said, 'When the karma of sentient beings in the three realms comes due, the buddhas of the three times are powerless.' I have no means of curing him. If you know how, you cure him." He rested the son's head in the mother's lap and said, "You have spilt on the wall the one precious drop of oil in the cauldron of water.* Who else but you would have sent him to the fair while he was in the middle of his retreat? In general, as is said, 'A woman leading a meeting, a goat leading the way, a prairie dog acting as sentry, a heap of ashes as a cairn, or a lump of butter in the hot sun—there is nothing cheerful in any of these analogies.' " Covering his head, Marpa remained sitting there.

The mother thought, "I am not to blame, but now is not the time to argue because it might be harmful to my son's practice. Tarma Dode did not eject his consciousness into his father, venerable Marpa, who is also his guru who gave him mind transmission. However, because I am his mother who gave birth

*The precious drop of oil refers, of course, to Tarma Dode.

to his body and mind, he may, out of love, eject his consciousness into me.'' Bringing her mouth close to her son's ear and weeping, Dagmema sang this song which clarifies the ejection of consciousness:

Precious, supreme, and authentic nirmāṇakāya
Of all the lord buddhas of the three times,
Marpa the Translator,
I respectfully prostrate at your feet.

Listen son, Prince Dodebum.
Because you are going beyond this world,
You might be a little concerned
About the destruction of this composite body.

The venerable father, Marpa the Translator,
Went to the land of India three times.
Without regard for his life, he sought the dharma
And attended many authentic gurus.
In particular, from Mahāpaṇḍita Nāropa,
He learned all the oral instructions of the hearing
  lineage without exception.

Keeping nothing secret, the venerable father taught them
  to you, son.
Are they clear in your mind now or not?
In the oral instructions of Mahāpaṇḍita Nāropa,
Do you have confidence now or not?
In the oral instructions of the special teachings of
  mixing and ejecting consciousness,
Have you attained certainty now or not?
In the unborn mahāmudrā,
Is your meditation steady now or not?

In the oral instructions of the ejection and transference
of consciousness,
Do you have confidence now or not?

This composite body of flesh and blood
Is impermanent, like a rainbow in the sky.
This illusory body is never eternal.
I am your mother, Nairātmyā Devī,
The mother who gave birth to the buddhas of the
three times.
On the eight-petaled lotus of my heart, on a lion
throne
Is a sun- and moon-disk seat.
There sits the most excellent of beings, Marpa the
Translator.
He is Hevajra with nine emanation devīs.
Son, draw forth your consciousness through the aperture
of Brahmā.
Now eject your consciousness into the heart center
of your mother.

Thus his mother sang this song.

Because his consciousness was still impaired, she thought that he did not hear even a word and she shed tears the size of peas. Because these tears fell into the son's ear, and also due to the close relationship between mother and son, Tarma Dode regained consciousness and opened his eyes. He had understood the song, sung by his mother, which clarifies the ejection of consciousness.

The son said, "Older brother, Great Magician, help me stand up." He stood up and bandaged his own head, which had been broken into eight fragments, and said, "Older brother, Great Magician, my face does not feel well. Wipe it off." While the jetsün was wiping the son's face with his cloth, the son said, "I thought that in this life I would be able to repay my parents' kindness. But now, not only have I not repaid their kindness, I have made my parents upset. Since this has happened, I want to offer a few meaningful words asking my parents not to be upset. Accompany me as I sing."

The jetsün said, "Please don't talk like that. It might bring obstacles to your life."

"Older brother, Great Magician, what obstacles to life do you mean? Isn't this an obstacle? Now the time has come to go upon the great universal path of sentient beings known as the pardo of becoming, the long and dangerous passage, which is like a narrow tunnel. Most beings must undergo terrifying sufferings there. But, by the kindness of my father, Lord Marpa, I have the power of going directly to my next place of birth, and so do not have to undergo the sufferings of the pardo of becoming.

"In general, though they obtain a human birth, people do not practice the dharma. I feel compassion for all of them, but there is nothing I can do. Therefore, my parents, please do not be upset. Older brother, accompany me as I sing."

Then Tarma Dode offered this song of entreaty:

Precious lord guru, endowed with the three qualities,
Inseparable from glorious Vajradhara,
Father Hevajra with his nine emanation devīs
And mother Nairātmyā who gave birth to the buddhas,
I respectfully prostrate to both father and mother.
Father and mother, grant your blessings and abhiṣeka.

When I go beyond this world,
I have no fear or anxiety.
Dying without repaying your kindness,
I am a little sad,

But this death cannot be helped.
Father and mother, please do not be upset.

The tantras and commentaries taught by my lord father
Are now clear in my mind.
In the path of upāya, the six yogas of Nāropa,
I now have confidence.
In the oral instructions of the special teachings of
mixing and ejecting consciousness,
I now have attained certainty.
In unborn mahāmudrā,
My meditation is now steady.
In the special teachings of the ejection and transference
of consciousness,
I now have confidence.
Father and mother, please do not cry.

In unborn simplicity, mahāmudrā,
The skandhas, dhātus, and āyatanas
Are seen clearly as the nature of devas and devīs.
In general, what is ejected and the one who ejects
are free from any basis.
Therefore, I will eject my consciousness into unborn
dharmadhātu.
I will not direct my consciousness into the
heart centers of my father and mother.
I will not direct my consciousness upward.

Please give the tantras and commentaries of gurus
Nāropa and Maitrīpa
To Ngoktön, Great Magician,
And the other great son-disciples.
Please propagate the teachings of the Buddha.

Even if I were to live, I could do no more than this.
Even as I die, I have no other request than this.
I don't think that we—father, mother, and son—
Shall meet again in this life.
In Uḍḍiyāṇa or the celestial realm,
Please let us definitely meet again.

Thus Tarma Dode sang his reply.

The father said, "My son, if you had remained here, in every direction there would always be excellent harvests and animals. Rain would fall in the right season. Epidemic diseases of humans and animals would cease. In particular, the oral instructions of the ejection and transference of consciousness that bring enlightenment without effort in meditation would have flourished in Tibet. Sentient beings would have benefited by attaining abundant bliss and happiness. However, suddenly, obstacles of Māra have arisen."

Then they carried the son inside. The father, mother, and son-disciples all circled around him. Lady Palmo and some others endowed with faith requested him to perform the transference of consciousness for the sake of sentient beings.

The son said, "If you want these oral instructions of the ejection and transference of consciousness that bring enlightenment without effort in meditation to flourish in Tibet, find me the corpse of a pure youth that is without any wounds."

The son-disciples dispersed to the four directions and searched. However, since the oral instructions of the ejection and transference of consciousness that bring enlightenment without effort in meditation were not destined to spread in Tibet, they could not find even one male corpse without a wound. One tantric student brought the corpse of an old woman who had died of a goiter and requested Tarma Dode to eject his consciousness into it.

Tarma Dode said, "This cannot benefit sentient beings. I will not perform the ejection of consciousness."

Another disciple, a shepherd, found the corpse of a pigeon amongst the ruins of a temple. It had died from exhaustion after being chased by a hawk. He brought it to Tarma Dode and requested him to eject his consciousness into it.

Tarma Dode said, "Performing the ejection of consciousness into an animal will not benefit beings. Do you want me to be sent to such an inferior birth? I will not eject my consciousness into a pigeon."

Because Tarma Dode did not want to perform the ejection of consciousness, disbelief arose in some of the disciples and in the shepherd. They said, "The great being, Marpa Lotsāwa, claims that he has oral instructions that will bring enlightenment in one lifetime, but it does not seem to be true. The things that the guru performed before were just trickery."

The son replied, "In general, how is it possible that all the teachings translated in India are not true? In particular, how is it possible that the teachings spoken by my lord father are not true? Do not disbelieve in the guru. Disbelieving in the guru is a cause of wandering in the lower realms.

"Now, in order to spread the Buddha's teachings and to confirm the powerful teachings spoken by my lord father and also so that you, the shepherd and the others, will not fall into the lower realms, I will perform the ejection of consciousness into the pigeon.

"Now I am in the utpattikrama. When I dissolve that into sampannakrama, I will eject my consciousness. If one ejects his consciousness while in utpattikrama, one would commit the root downfall of killing the yidam deity. So now I will dissolve into sampannakrama. Put the pigeon on my pillow and prepare an offering."

They prepared an offering as he requested. When the son strengthened his utpattikrama visualization, everyone, even the common people, saw Hevajra with his nine emanation devīs bright and vivid. When Tarma Dode dissolved that into sampannakrama and ejected his consciousness, his body paled and the pigeon shook his feathers a little. Once the son had left his body completely, the pigeon suddenly stood up and ruffled his feathers. The pigeon appeared to prostrate to both the father and mother. Then he circumambulated them three times and flew toward the upper part of Trowo valley.

The father said, "Son, come back." At that moment the son came back and flew around the castle. Then he landed on his father's right shoulder and remained there. The father said, "Dagmema, such is the occasion that we have to treat this pigeon as our son. Let us bring him into the shrine room and make offerings to him."

They brought him up to the top story of the castle, made offerings to him, and let him settle there. They decided to perform a cremation and farewell ceremony together. First, they built a hearth for the cremation. As the father and the great son-disciples performed the fire offering, from the four cardinal and four intermediate directions, eight different rays of light entered the hearth. Music of the gods and demigods and other varieties of music were heard, and rains of different varieties of flowers fell, which everyone witnessed.

Then the pigeon, into whom the ejection of consciousness had been performed, was led to the cremation hearth on a path of silk. The father said, "Son, circumambulate the cremation hearth." Accordingly, the pigeon circumambulated the cremation hearth. Everyone there was amazed and saw the father guru and his son as buddhas in person.

At that time, Dagmema came in unexpectedly. She was about to jump into the cremation hearth when the disciples held her back. She said, "I am not allowed to jump into the fire, but please allow me to circumambulate my son's cremation hearth." She wept and uttered many heartfelt words of grief as she circumambulated the hearth, supported by the great son-disciples. Seeing this, everyone from Lhotrak could not help but shed tears.

Lord Marpa also showed signs of grief. Previously there had been an old man and woman whose only son had died. At that time, the guru thought that he could lessen the parents' grief and so explained many general teachings to them. In particular, he told them, "If you dreamt that you had a son who died, you would feel grief. You would feel suffering for the death of someone who had not been born. Your suffering for your present son is not different from this. Think of all this as a dream, as an illusion, and don't be upset."

Now the old man and woman to whom he had said this came to him and said, "Guru sir, when our only child died, you said, 'It is a dream, it is an illusion; don't be upset.' The guru still has six sons headed by Tarma Samten. Although Tarma Dode has died, it is nothing more than a dream, nothing more than an illusion. Please do not be upset."

The guru said, "I explained the dharma according to your situation at that time. It is true, yet I do not suffer from clinging to something as real. If your son had lived, he would first have robbed you of your vitality and taken the food from your mouths. Next, he would have robbed the wealth from your hands, as well as your estate. Finally, he would have cast you into the three lower realms. This is not like my son. If my son had not died, he would have benefited the teachings of the Buddha and sentient beings. Among dreams, this would have been a super dream; among illusions, this would have been a super illusion."

When they had finished making the offerings, Lord Marpa remained in meditation. Contemplating where his son would benefit sentient beings, he realized that it would be in India. He made offerings to the pigeon and gave him advice. Then, as witnessed by the whole crowd, he let him fly to India.

Marpa remained in meditation for a while, and then said, "Dagmema, gather the old offerings and arrange new ones. My son has lost his way." He clapped his hands, covered his head, and remained in meditation.

That evening, the exhausted pigeon returned and nestled in the father's lap. Marpa said, "Tonight, bring the pigeon into the shrine room and make offerings." They did as he said.

In the morning, the pigeon was brought to the place where many people were assembled.

The father said, "Son, the path you took yesterday was wrong. If you again follow the mountain on the left that looks like a poisonous snake sliding down, you will come to a land of heretics. Don't go there. To the right is a mountain like an elephant lying on its side. Follow the range of those mountains and go that way. At the end of the mountain range, you will find the yidam's light, which will guide you. Follow that light. At the Cool Grove charnel ground, you will find the fresh corpse of a thirteen-year-old brahman boy that has been brought there. Transfer your consciousness into him and work for the benefit of sentient beings."

The pigeon circumambulated the father and mother three times, and as a parting gesture, he bowed his head three times. Then he flew off in accordance with his father's command. Everyone shed tears, and felt certainty in the transference of consciousness. All saw Jetsün Marpa as the buddha in person.

Since the pigeon flew according to his father's command, he arrived without obstacle in the Cool Grove charnel ground, where the brahman parents had brought the corpse of their only son. The pigeon found it there just as the pallbearers were performing the funeral rituals. Immediately, Tarma Dode transferred his consciousness and the brahman boy stood up. The pallbearers were terrified.

Earlier, by the kindness of his father, Tarma Dode had learned enough of the Indian language to communicate. He said, "I'm not one of the walking dead. I have come back to life. Let's go home."

Astonished and amazed, the pallbearers cried out with joy. They all left together. The children who had been his playmates ran to him, saying to each other, "He isn't dead." His neighbors said, "The best healing ceremony was going to the charnel ground."

Upon meeting him, his mother and father embraced him, and then fainted. After recovering, they were overjoyed, as anyone would be upon having his son recover from death. They asked the pallbearers how he had come back to life.

The pallbearers said, "A pigeon came up to your son's body. It bowed its head and then died, and then your son came back to life."

The mother and father cared for him as lovingly as before, and were very close to him. As he possessed more gentleness in spirit, virtue in the dharma, kindness toward the poor, devotion to his parents and the three jewels, and exertion in virtuous actions than their former son, they realized that he was not their previous son. They asked him how this came about. Tarma Dode told the full story of how he had transferred his consciousness from the pigeon. In the language of that part of India, a pigeon is called tiphu, and because of this miracle, he was called Tiphupa.

Thus, the parents did not think of him as their son, but called him their guru. Both old parents served him, and throughout his life he cared for them as their son. Finally, he became a śramaṇera and studied, contemplated, and meditated. He was a great being who was learned and accomplished, known as Tiphu, the tree of the secret mantra. Later these stories were told by Tiphupa to Rechungpa in India.*

*Tiphupa, the tree of the secret mantra (T: gsang-sngags kyi sdong-po), became renowned in India as a teacher of the nine teachings of the formless ḍākinī hearing lineage (T: lus-med mkha'-'gro snyan-brgyud chos-skor dgu). Tilopa was the first to obtain these teachings. Having traveled to Uḍḍiyāṇa, he received them directly from the formless wisdom ḍākinī in a song. Basically, this song was comprised of these nine instructions: (1) Loose the seal knot of mind as ripening and freeing (T: smin-grol sems kyi rgya-mdud shig), (2) Look at the mirror of mind as samaya (T: dam-tshig rang-sems me-long ltos), (3) Slash water with a sword as activity (T: spyod-pa chu la ral-gri rgyob), (4) Sun yourself in realization as samaya substance (T: dam rdzas rtogs-pa'i nyi-ma 'des), (5) Look at the torch of wisdom as insight (T: rig-pa ye-shes sgron-me ltos), (6) Turn the wheel of the web of nāḍī and prāṇa (T: rtsa rlung dra-mig 'khor-lo skor), (7) Look at the outer mirror as equal taste (T: ro-snyoms phyi yi me-long ltos), (8) Meditate on self-liberated mahāmudrā (T: rang-grol phyag-rgya chen-po sgoms), and (9) Hold the jewel of the great bliss teachings (T: bde-chen gsung gi rin-chen zungs).

Tilopa later gave these pith teachings to his main disciple, Nāropa. In accordance with a prophecy from Tilopa, Nāropa in turn gave these teachings to Marpa, but placed a command-seal of secrecy on them. This meant that Marpa

When Marpa and the disciples opened Tarma Dode's cremation hearth, they discovered that the five devatās of Cakrasaṃvara had appeared on a piece of his skull. They also found many other representations of body, speech, and mind and many śarīra. Some people felt indifferent and said, "Guru Marpa still has six more sons who will be heirs to his family lineage. As for a dharma lineage holder, he has many excellent great son-disciples. If we think of this wondrous proof of the transference of consciousness, as well as the wonderful representations and śarīra, it is of greater benefit to sentient beings that the son Tarma Dode died than if he had lived."

From every direction there came the other great son-disciples, who had not yet arrived. Although they offered their condolences and gifts, Dagmema was still extremely upset. When the great son-disciples assembled for the memorial service for Tarma Dode, the guru said, "Dagmema, if you continue to grieve, these disciples who have come from all directions will be

---

had to be very restrictive about whom he gave these teachings to. Later, Nāropa apparently gave these teachings to Tiphupa as well.

In Tibet, Marpa gave only the first four of these nine teachings to Milarepa and then prophesied that Milarepa or some other lineage disciple would journey to India to obtain the remaining five teachings. Milarepa himself was satisfied with the teachings that he had received and was also too busy practicing to go to India. Therefore, at one point, when his disciple, Rechungpa, became restless to travel to India to study, Milarepa sent him to obtain the remaining five teachings.

In Nepal, on his way to India, Rechungpa met Bharima, a disciple of Tiphupa, and in India, he met with Tiphupa himself. Tiphupa gave Rechungpa all the teachings of the formless ḍākinī hearing lineage, and also presented him with an akaru staff as a gift for Milarepa. Rechungpa then returned to Tibet and thereafter the lineage of these teachings continued in Tibet.

Different aspects of this story are found in *The Life of Milarepa,* pp. 91-92, and in *The Hundred Thousand Songs of Milarepa,* vol. 2, "Rechungpa's Third Journey to India," pp. 397-401. Moreover, in vol. 5 of the *Gdams-ngag mdzod,* there are three texts that comment on the lineage and nature of these teachings. They are found on pp. 485-505, 506-510, and 735-743, listed under the general heading—Lus-med mkha'-'gro'i chos-skor dgu Zur-mang snyan-brgyud.

further distressed. In general, death is characteristic of all composite things. This isn't a mishap particular to us alone. Moreover, Tarma Dode's death is in accord with the guru's prophecy. Finally, grieving cannot bring our son any benefit and only causes you pain. This makes it difficult to expound the dharma to others, as in the case of the old man and woman. Now, don't grieve."

Then Marpa sang this song to clear away her grief:

I prostrate to the lord gurus.

To the prajñā consort who expounds and understands
  the dharma,
To Dagmema I give this advice.
Steady your mind, not mixing it with the mundane.
Arouse certainty and abandon your grief.
Our son Dodebum, whom we cherished so dearly,
Has passed into the realm of luminosity.
Thus his kindness is equal to the lord guru's.
I will clarify this with these seven reminders of
  illusion.
There is no one to grieve for.
With impartiality toward sentient beings,
Cherish all beings with kindness, Dagmema.
Dagmema, clear away your grief for our son.

Many sūtras and other texts written in gold
And sacred representations of body, speech, and mind
Were produced for the sake of our son Dode.
But Dode has passed into the realm of luminosity.
These sacred representations are ownerless, like a
  rainbow in the sky.
With the realization that appearances are empty,
One cannot find anyone to care for.

However, make offerings to all worthy ones,
Dagmema.
O Dagmema, clear away your grief for our son.

The tantras and commentaries obtained through hardship,
The pith oral instructions of the concentrated heart
essence,
The quintessence of this gathering of all that is
profound,
As well as translation of the literary and colloquial
languages
Were all studied for the sake of our son Dode.
But Dode has passed into the realm of luminosity.
Dharma is ownerless, like possessing merely a list of
treasures.
With the realization of dharmas as equanimity,
O Dagmema, give to all.
O Dagmema, clear away your grief for our son.

Food and wealth gathered through frugality
And cattle and sheep offered by disciples
Were all accumulated for the sake of our son Dode.
But Dode has passed into the realm of luminosity.
Wealth is ownerless, like undiscovered riches
underground.
Cattle are ownerless, like wild animals in a meadow.
With the realization of possessions as mahāmudrā,
There is no need to tend them.
O Dagmema, give everything away.
O Dagmema, clear away your grief for our son.

Castles and fields in the fatherland of Pesar
And the tower built by Mila

Were all for the sake of our son Dode.
But the castles are ownerless, like a city of gandharvas.
With the realization of this land as illusory appearance-emptiness,
Grasping and clinging to it are futile.
O Dagmema, cast off grasping and clinging to castles.
O Dagmema, clear away your grief for our son.

Being polite to relatives of the Mar clan,
But turning our backs to enemies and annoying people
Were done for the sake of our son Dode.
But Dode has passed into the realm of luminosity.
With the realization that appearance is mind,
There is no difference between friends and enemies.
O Dagmema, meditate on everything as dharmakāya.
O Dagmema, clear away your grief for our son.

In general, it is characteristic of all composite things
That ultimately they are never permanent.
In particular, the connection and relationship
Between ourselves and Tarma Dode have ended.
This is our karma about which nothing can be done.
O Dagmema, do not grieve.
O Dagmema, clear away your grief for our son.

There is nothing other than dharma for us.
Be kind to those who are impoverished.
We have six sons who remain,
But there is no hope that they will be holders of the teachings.
Nonetheless, cherish them with kindness, as you did Tarma Dode.

O Dagmema, do not grieve.
O Dagmema, clear away your grief for our son.

In accordance with the prophecy of Mahāpaṇḍita Nāropa,
The lineages of my son-disciples,
Like the waxing moon,
Will grow and spread further and further.
The Kagyü teachings will flourish and expand.
Great benefit for the teachings and beings will be accomplished.
O Dagmema, rejoice and be happy.
O Dagmema, clear away your grief for our son.

Thus Marpa sang.

The grief of Dagmema and all the others there was cleared away, and their realization was heightened.

Marpa prophesies the spreading and flourishing of the teachings and grants oral instruction, sacred representations carrying blessings, as well as advice.

When all the students and son-disciples gathered at a memorial service for Tarma Dode, the disciples and the great son-disciples requested, "Precious guru, your son was like the buddhas of the three times, but the merit of ourselves and sentient beings was insufficient. Since you are now getting old, please prophesy how the precious teachings of the Kagyü will spread and how further disciples and actions will arise."

The guru said, "As a descendant of the lineage of Mahāpaṇḍita Nāropa, I have mastered recognizing auspicious coincidence. Mahāpaṇḍita Nāropa also gave excellent prophecies for the teachings of the Kagyü. Therefore, you great son-disciples should await your dreams."

After practicing dream yoga, the great son-disciples related their dreams. Most of the dreams were rather good, but they were not prophetic. However, Jetsün Mila had a dream of four great pillars, which he offered to the guru as follows:

In accordance with the command of Lord Vajradhara,
Last night's dream
I will offer to the guru just as it occurred.
Please listen to me for a little while.

In this vast northern region of Jambudvīpa,
I dreamt that there was a massive snow mountain.
I dreamt that the snowy summit touched the skies.
I dreamt that the sun and moon circled around the peak.
I dreamt that their light rays filled the sky.
I dreamt that the base covered the vast ground.
I dreamt that rivers descended in the four directions.
I dreamt that their water satisfied all beings.
I dreamt that the rivers flowed into the ocean.
I dreamt that various flowers bloomed.
In general, I dreamt a dream like this.
Thus I relate it to you, guru, the buddha of the three times.

In particular, next to this massive, high snow mountain:
I dreamt that a great pillar was established in the East.
I dreamt that on top of the pillar a great lion was poised.
I dreamt that the lion was fully displaying his thick turquoise mane.
I dreamt that his four paws clawed at the snow.
I dreamt that his eyes gazed upward.
I dreamt that the lion leapt to a white snow mountain range.
Thus I relate it to you, guru, the buddha of the three times.

I dreamt that a great pillar was established in the
South.
I dreamt that on top of the pillar a tigress roared.
I dreamt that the tigress was fully displaying her
well-striped coat.
I dreamt that she puffed out her chest three times.
I dreamt that her four paws clawed at the jungle.
I dreamt that her eyes gazed upward.
I dreamt that the tigress leapt into a jungle.
I dreamt that she strode among the trees.
Thus I relate it to you, guru, the buddha of the
three times.

I dreamt that a great pillar was established in the West.
I dreamt that above the pillar there soared a great garuḍa.
I dreamt that the garuḍa's wings were fully extended.
I dreamt that the horns of the garuḍa pointed to the
sky.
I dreamt that his eyes gazed upward.
I dreamt that the garuḍa soared through the expanse
of space.
Thus I relate it to you, guru, the buddha of the
three times.

I dreamt that a great pillar was established in the
North.
I dreamt that above the pillar there soared a great
vulture.
I dreamt that the vulture's wings were fully extended.
I dreamt that the vulture made her nest among the rocks.
I dreamt that this vulture gave birth to a young one.
I dreamt that from this one the sky was filled with
a flock of birds.

I dreamt that the vulture's eyes gazed upward.
I dreamt that the vulture soared through the expanse
of space.
Thus I relate it to you, guru, the buddha of the
three times.

Because of the auspicious coincidence of a dream like
this,
I thought these might be good and virtuous signs.
I rejoiced and felt inspired.
Please interpret this and grant us a prophecy.

Thus Mila sang.

The guru was very pleased and said, "This is an excellent dream." He told his wife Dagmema to prepare a good gaṇacakra.

When his wife had gathered the requisites together and the great son-disciples had assembled, they performed a splendid gaṇacakra. The guru said, "Mila Dorje Gyaltsen* has had an excellent dream. O how wondrous, how great indeed!"

The great sons asked him to interpret the signs of the dream and tell what they prophesied. In the melody of the regal voice of transmitting the signs, the most excellent of beings, the great translator, sang to the son-disciples this grand song that prophesies the future spreading and flourishing of the teachings and that interprets the signs of the four pillars in Mila's dream:

*Mila's name, Dorje Gyaltsen (Vajra Victory Banner), was revealed to Marpa in a dream that he had the night before Mila's arrival in Lhotrak. In that dream, Nāropa gave him a "slightly tarnished, five-pronged vajra made of lapis lazuli," as well as a golden vase of amṛta. He told Marpa to clean the vajra with the amṛta from the vase and then to mount the vajra on top of a victory banner. Marpa did so and the vajra radiated a great brilliance that dispelled the sufferings of all beings. Filled with happiness, everyone then prostrated and paid reverence to Marpa and this victory banner. See *The Life of Milarepa*, p. 43.

Lord, buddha of the three times and refuge of beings,
Mahāpaṇḍita Nāropa, I pay homage at your feet.
All you son-disciples seated here,
These signs that arose in the dream
Prophesy a wondrous future.
I, your old father, will explain them; now listen!

The land in the northern region of Jambudvīpa
Means that Śākyamuni's teaching will spread in Tibet.
The snow mountain rising above it
Is the old father, Marpa the Translator,
And the teachings of all the Kagyü.
The snowy peak touching the sky
Is the unrivaled view.
The sun and moon circling the peak
Are meditation containing luminosity, wisdom, and
compassion.
The light rays filling the sky
Are kindness clearing away the darkness of ignorance.
The base covering the vast ground
Is buddha activity covering the earth.
The rivers descending in the four directions
Are the oral instructions of the four abhiṣekas that
ripen and free.
Their water satisfying all sentient beings
Is the ripening and freeing of disciples.
The rivers flowing into the ocean
Are the meeting of the mother and son luminosities.
The various flowers blooming
Are the experiences of fruition free from any faults.
All you son-disciples assembled here,
In general, this dream is not bad, but an excellent dream.

In particular, next to the massive, high snow mountain:
The great pillar established in the East
Is Tsurtön Wang-nge of Tölpo.
That great lion poised on top of the pillar
Is his lion-like character.
The lion displaying his thick turquoise mane
Means that he has received the oral instructions of
the hearing lineage.
His four paws clawing at the snow
Is the sign that he is endowed with the four immeasurables.
His eyes gazing upward
Is the sign that he will bid farewell to saṃsāra.
The lion leaping to a white snow mountain range
Is the sign that he will go to the realm of liberation.
All you son-disciples assembled here,
This dream of the East is not bad, but an excellent
dream.

The great pillar established in the South
Is Ngoktön Chödor of Shung.
That tigress roaring on top of the pillar
Is his tiger-like character.
The tigress fully displaying her well-striped coat
Means that he has received the oral instructions of the
hearing lineage.
The puffing out of her chest three times
Is the sign that he has realized the trikāya.
Her four paws clawing at the jungle
Is the sign that he has accomplished the four karmas.
Her eyes gazing upward
Is the sign that he will bid farewell to saṃsāra.
The tigress leaping into the jungle
Is the sign that he will go to the realm of liberation.

That she strode among the trees
Is the sign that his sons and nephews will be lineage holders.
All you son-disciples assembled here,
This dream of the South is not bad, but an excellent dream.

The great pillar established in the West
Is Metön Tsönpo of Tsangrong.
That great garuḍa soaring above the pillar
Is his garuḍa-like character.
The garuḍa fully displaying his feathers
Means that he has received the oral instructions of the hearing lineage.
That the garuḍa's horns point to the sky
Is the sign that he will overcome straying from the view and practice.
His eyes gazing upward
Is the sign that he will bid farewell to saṃsāra.
The garuḍa soaring through the expanse of space
Is the sign that he will go to the realm of liberation.
All you son-disciples assembled here,
This dream of the West is not bad, but an excellent dream.

The great pillar established in the North
Is Milarepa of Kungthang.
That vulture soaring above the pillar
Is his vulture-like character.
The vulture fully displaying her feathers
Means that he has received the oral instructions of the hearing lineage.
The vulture making a nest among the rocks

Is the sign that his life-force will be harder than
 rock.
The vulture giving birth to a young one
Is the sign that one without equal will come.*
The flock of birds filling the sky
Is the sign that the Kagyü teachings will spread.
Her eyes gazing upward
Is the sign that he will bid farewell to saṃsāra.
The vulture soaring through the expanse of space
Is the sign that he will go to the realm of liberation.
This dream of the North is not bad, but an excellent
 dream.
Thus I have explained this to you assembled here.

Now the deeds of this old father have been accomplished.
The time is now ripe for you son-disciples.
If you trust the words of this old man,
Later, the teachings of the Practice Lineage will spread.

Thus Marpa sang. Everyone assembled there felt immeasurable joy.

Then the guru opened the treasury of teachings and oral instructions for his great son-disciples. During the day he taught and at night he let them practice. Everyone gained success in their practice. From time to time, the son-disciples gave feasts and gifts.

At one time, Metön came and arranged a feast. At this feast, Metön offered his second gift. He said, "O guru, your son was like the Buddha, but our merit was insufficient. You yourself are like the sun and moon, and the great heart sons headed by guru Ngokpa encircle you like constellations. You make the teachings of the secret mantra shine as the sun. How wondrous! O

*This "one without equal" prophesies Milarepa's main disciple, Gampopa. He is often referred to as incomparable or without equal (T: mnyam-med).

guru, this evening at the feast, please think of us kindly and sing a song of your deeds so that we can benefit from your example."

Lord Marpa knew that Metön had been too restrictive in giving dharma instruction, and so he sang this song of his thoughts to him:

Lord guru, inseparable from Akṣobhya,
Please remain as the crest ornament on the top of my
 head.
Today, in order to explain the tantras at this feast,
I, the teacher Marpa Chökyi Lodrö,
Will sing this useful story.

Hearing of Tsang, I went there.
At the glorious monastery of Nyugu valley,
Starving for the teachings of the secret mantra,
I waited three years, my mind a hungry ghost.
In general, I thought I wasted my time there.
I thought I would go to Nepal in the South.
Desiring the dharma, I suffered like a man thirsting
 for precious water.
I thought if it ever came about that I knew the dharma,
I would give it to anyone who desired it.
This dharma was obtained through hardship, even at
 the risk of my life.
I would feel devastated if these profound oral instructions
 were to disappear.

Although I have not explained the textual commentaries
To anyone other than Metön and Ngoktön,
I told them to explain the dharma to whomever desires it.
When disciples offered their wealth,
As their guru, I did not restrict my teaching.

And to Great Magician who had no wealth
And to Ngoktön who rendered service,
I was neither strict nor loose with the oral instructions.
Therefore, practice the holy dharma properly.

I obtained these oral instructions through great
hardship.
Not wasting my wealth,
I took a hundred and ten *sang* of gold with me to India.
I made offerings to special shrines.
I made offerings to gurus.
I offered feasts and torma in special places.
The kind service that you sons have rendered
I repay by giving the immeasurable holy dharma.
With the sustenance of dharma, practice.
Benefit sentient beings as much as you can.

Thus Marpa sang. Metön was led to certainty and great aspiration arose in him.

One night while giving the profound abhiṣeka of Nairātmyā, Lord Marpa thought, "I have to give each son-disciple the appropriate special transmission and activity. Therefore, in the morning, at dawn, I will look for auspicious signs."

At dawn, within luminosity, Marpa saw the great son-disciples. Ngoktön Chödor of Shung was studying some commentaries on the *Hevajra-tantra.* Tsurtön Wang-nge of Töl was practicing the ejection of consciousness. Metön Tsönpo of Tsangrong was practicing luminosity. Jetsün Mila was practicing caṇḍālī. Thus Marpa knew the appropriate special transmission and activity for each of them.

To guru Ngokpa he gave oral instructions on the method of explaining the tantras by means of the six views and four methods, which are like pearls on a string. He also gave him Nāropa's six ornaments and ruby practice mālā, a pātrī and śruva, and a Sanskrit commentary. Marpa said, "Benefit beings by expounding the teachings."

To Tsurtön Wang-nge of Töl he gave the teaching of the ejection of consciousness, which is like a bird flying through an open skylight. He also gave him Nāropa's hair, nails, amṛta pills, and crown of the five buddha families. He said, "Practice the ejection of consciousness."

To Metön Tsönpo of Tsangrong he gave the teaching of luminosity, which is like a lamp blazing in the darkness. He also gave him Nāropa's vajra and ghaṇṭā, ḍamaru, and a kapāla made out of mother-of-pearl. He said, "Cross the pardo."

To Jetsün Mila he gave the special teaching of caṇḍālī, which is like a blazing fire of kindling. He also gave him Maitrīpa's hat and Nāropa's clothing. He said, "Wander in slate and snow mountains and practice the view and meditation."

At a gaṇacakra where all the students had gathered, Marpa said, "Just as I have given you oral instructions in accord with auspicious signs, you should give these special oral instructions to your lineage disciples. Thus, great and vast benefits and buddha activity will arise. Dodebum is no longer here. I have given you the lineage of blessings and oral instructions of my excellent Kagyü fathers. Practice them earnestly. Then benefit for sentient beings will increase."

Later, at the feast, Metön made his third gift and said, "O guru, today please think of me with kindness. In accordance with the aspiration of Mahāpaṇḍita Nāropa and with whatever meditation experience has arisen in your mind, please sing a song that puts the view into proper perspective."

Because guru Marpa had always thought that Metön had been too restrictive in giving teachings, he said, "I will sing a song as you wish. Not only am I pleased that you have offered abundant wealth to me, but I am also pleased that you have assimilated the vast variety of our ritual traditions, since we place great emphasis on practicing these. Do not hold back the oral instructions too strictly. Enter those who are endowed with faith and who will not waste the dharma into the abhiṣekas and oral instructions.''

In accordance with Metön's desire and request, Marpa sang this song, emphasizing the complete removal of restrictions:

Lord, master of bliss, refuge of beings,
Nirmāṇakāya, heruka in union with consort,
Possessing the nine moods, within bliss and emptiness
You join in union; coemergent being, I pay homage to you.

By merely witnessing a sign, the meaning is realized.
Whoever truly hears even a corner of this will be liberated.
Not shown by conventional words,
The wisdom of unconditioned truth is bestowed.
At the very moment when movement is blissful,
One is free from suffering.
In this way, since conditioned mind can never be convinced,
In the stream of bliss-emptiness samādhi,
Rest your mind free from thought.
The guru who is like the Buddha has taught this.
Other lineages also say this.

Through an authentic consort,
One's ability becomes developed.
Like a person shooting a bird with an arrow,
One always depends on one's ability.

Even when habitual patterns of desire arise,
This primordially pure mind
Is not corrupted by temporary conditions.

It remains unconditioned, like space.
This is the unperverted natural state.

Free from even a speck of mind's activity,
There is not even a speck to cling to.
Thoroughly trained in the oral instructions,
At the time one leaves this body behind,
One dissolves into the space of pāramitā.
Thus, mind is unborn.
Mind is like the sky.
Don't corrupt it with a mist of conceptualizations.

The lord Mahāpaṇḍita Nāropa spoke these words:
"In order to practice the dharma properly,
Like a snake placed in a bamboo tube,
Don't make any effort to move.
Those who suffer from desire
Are like one hit on a sore point.
Don't let your mind of nonaction wander.
The innate nature of mind is primordially empty.
Like smashing things with a hammer,
It liberates through seeing, touching, and thinking."

Please understand this completely.
This is a meditation song of mahāmudrā.
Since the holy dharma benefits others,
Don't clutch it in a death grip, Metönpa.
For those who are worthy
Don't keep it secret, but give them instructions.

Thus Marpa sang.

Then the great son-disciples went to their respective residences. Marpa asked Jetsün Mila to stay on for awhile.*

Although Lord Marpa had many heart sons who were worthy disciples, he did not give them the oral instructions of the hearing lineage. In accord with the prophecy of Nāropa, Marpa gave Jetsün Mila the abhiṣeka, oral instructions, and auxiliary teachings of the ḍākinī hearing lineage of Cakrasaṃvara, and finally completed these with the further secret command-seal teachings. Moreover, having given him these many instructions, Marpa sang this song extolling the greatness of the hearing lineage:

*We have amended the text slightly here. Marpa's biography literally says "a few days" (T: zhag-shas), whereas Milarepa's biography says "a few years" (T: lo-shas). While it is unclear exactly how long Mila stayed with Marpa after this point, it is clear that he stayed longer than a few days.

The events following this point are described in more detail in Milarepa's biography. First, Marpa sent Mila into retreat to consolidate his experience of the oral instructions he had received. While in retreat Mila had a vivid dream wherein he saw his mother and relatives dead, his sister a beggar, his farm overgrown, and so on. A great yearning to return to his homeland and see if these visions were true arose in Mila, and he left his retreat to ask Marpa's permission to leave. Marpa gave his permission and subsequently gave the secret oral instructions of the ḍākinī hearing lineage, which were to be restricted to a single lineage holder for thirteen generations. He also told Mila of the five teachings of the formless ḍākinī hearing lineage that he had not received and that a lineage disciple must go to India to obtain.

At a farewell gaṇacakra for Mila (which is described very briefly in our text on p. 196) Marpa displayed various miracles, manifesting the forms of Hevajra, Cakrasaṃvara, and others. (Our text describes these miracles differently here.) At that point, Marpa said, "that is it" and "you can go now," as Mila had received all his teachings completely and was convinced of their truth. Marpa prophesied the places of mountain solitude where Mila and his later disciples were to meditate, and gave him a small scroll sealed in wax, containing oral instructions for a time when obstacles would arise in Mila's practice. The next day, Marpa and Dagmema sadly saw Mila off and sang songs of instruction and farewell. Mila departed for his homeland and soon after for the mountain solitudes where he was to spend his life in solitary meditation. See *The Life of Milarepa,* pp. 89-100.

Although everyone has a lineage,
If one has the ḍākinī's lineage, that is it.
Although everyone has forefathers,
If one has Tilopa, that is it.
Although everyone has a guru,
If one has Nāropa, that is it.
Although everyone has oral instructions,
If one has the hearing lineage, that is it.
Although everyone attains enlightenment by meditating,
If one becomes enlightened without effort in meditation,
that is it.

Thus Marpa sang.

Jetsün Mila said, "Our lineage and oral instructions are greatly renowned in all of India and Tibet. Therefore, precious guru, your fame in Tibet is no different than that of the lineage forefathers. Lord, because of your powerful longing and devotion for the gurus and your buddha activity, you yourself must also be renowned as a precious guru in India."

The guru replied, "There's no need to speak of the great fame of my lineage and oral instructions in India, and as you have said, I am renowned for my great devotion to the guru."

Because he could not help but proclaim these essential truths, Marpa sang this song:

Why shouldn't my lineage be famed,
Since we possess the dharma eye of the ḍākinīs.
Why shouldn't the forefathers be famed,
Since Tilopa is no one other than the buddha.
Why shouldn't my guru be famed,
Since Nāropa is a torch of dharma.
Why shouldn't I be famed,

Since I am the only heart son of Nāropa.
Why shouldn't the oral instructions be famed,
Since this wish-fulfilling jewel of the hearing lineage
Is the special dharma that no one else possesses.

Thus Marpa sang.

Jetsün Mila received this hearing lineage, the special dharma that no one else possesses. Like a vase that is filled from another, Mila received Jetsün Marpa's oral instructions and so his mind was satisfied. As a result of all this, the sun of the Buddha's teachings rose in the snowy mountain ranges of Tibet. The dark ignorance of all sentient beings was dispelled as the light of wisdom illumined the day.

Marpa manifests miracles in order to uplift all sentient beings.

Once when Jetsün Mila went before the guru, Marpa displayed various miracles—multiplying his own body, appearing as the four elements, disappearing, appearing as a rainbow, appearing as light, and so on. Then he asked Mila, "Did you see? Are you convinced by these?"

Mila replied, "I saw them, sir, and I cannot help but be convinced. I also will meditate so that I can do this."

"Son, that is it. If you want to go, go now," Marpa said. Thus Jetsün Mila returned to the land where he was born.

Later, several son-disciples, Marpa Golek and others, as well as some other people saw the guru as Hevajra, Cakrasaṃvara, Guhyasamāja, Vajravārāhī, and other deities. This happened many times, and they asked Marpa, "Why is this?"

Marpa replied, "That is how it is."

They asked him again, "Please tell us what this is," and supplicated him.

Marpa said, "Because the vividness of my utpattikrama of the yidam and your sacred outlook coincided, this occurred."

Many did not see Jetsün Marpa in his bed or elsewhere, but instead some saw a dazzling golden box, some clear swirling water, some a blazing fire, some a rainbow, some nothing whatsoever, some swirling light, and so on. Thus the guru appeared in many ways, and so they asked him, "Why is this?"

Marpa said, "If you had a dream of me, to whom would you be talking?"

"Even there, we would be asking you. Please tell us."

"Well, the nāḍī, bindu, and prāṇa of my five elements have become refined. My being firmly established in this and your sacred outlook coincided and brought forth these visions."

Marpa then sang this song:

> In the stable nāḍīs, prāṇa moves.
> There, the horse of bodhicitta is placed
> And is urged on by the whip of equal taste.
> Luminosity gallops free from coming or going.
> Thus, worthy people see a variety of things.

Thus Marpa sang.

"Moreover, I remember riding a tiger in a previous life and roaming through jungles and charnel grounds. Because I could now leave this body and enter another through the practice of the transference of consciousness, death need never occur for me. However, glorious Nāropa commanded me to come to the celestial realm of Uḍḍiyāṇa since there will be greater benefit for sentient beings, and so I must go there."

Marpa knew the past and future without difficulty, and whenever he went outside his house or returned inside, he had no need of stairs or a door. He simply entered wherever he wished, without difficulty. His son Pal Ö said, "Our father cannot be impeded by a wall or a door. If someone had to guard him, they could not do it." In this way, Marpa completely actualized the practice of overpowering the elements and so was unhindered by any phenomena. After he had displayed signs and miracles beyond measure, his wife Dagmema melted into light and dissolved into Lord Marpa's heart.*

*This description of Dagmema's death seems to be symbolic of her role as Nairātmyā (T: Bdag-med-ma), the consort of Hevajra, Marpa's personal yidam.

CHAPTER V

After teaching the view and working for the benefit of sentient beings, Marpa dissolves into dharmadhātu.

AFTER teaching and working solely for the benefit of beings his entire life, on the fifteenth day of the Horse month in the Bird year,* as the sun dawned over the mountain peaks, Marpa, eighty-eight years old, was free from sickness in body and joyful in mind. A rainbow appeared in the sky and various flowers rained down. There arose sounds of various kinds of music ravishing to the mind and immeasurable kinds of delightful scents. Smiling, Marpa shed tears, joined his palms together, closed his eyes, bowed his head again and again, and performed the sevenfold service. At that time Marpa Golek asked him, "What is happening?"

*If Marpa did in fact die in a Bird year, it probably was the Water Female Bird year, 1093. In order to see some of the problems in determining Marpa's dates, it would be helpful to review the chronology of his life, from the facts in this biography as well as other sources.

According to this biography, Marpa was 12 years old when he began his dharma training. Some time after this, he studied with guru Drogmi for 3 years. He then journeyed to Nepal and stayed at Svayambhūnāth for 3 years. Going on to India, Marpa spent 9 years studying with Nāropa and others, and then returned to Tibet.

In Tibet, Marpa met his students Ngoktön, Marpa Golek, Tsurtön, and Bawachen of Parang. He also married Dagmema and his sons were born. The biography does not specify how long Marpa remained in Tibet before returning to India.

On his second journey, Marpa spent 6 years in India. After returning to Tibet he taught more disciples, including Metön Tsönpo and Milarepa. Again the biography does not specify how long Marpa stayed in Tibet before making his final journey to India. We do know, however, that Marpa's wife and

Marpa replied, "Prepare excellent offerings. Glorious Nāropa surrounded by immeasurable hosts of ḍākas and ḍākinīs has arrived to escort me as he promised. Now I must go to the celestial realm as his attendant." Then he remained in meditation. While Marpa Golek and other disciples arranged and offered immeasurable offerings, a rain of flowers and the sounds of music occurred even greater than before, and Marpa passed away.

In general, Marpa was the sun of the Buddha's teaching, and in particular, he dispelled the darkness in the Land of Snow and was the life tree of the teachings of the secret mantra. Jetsün

---

disciples discouraged him from making a third journey to India because of his age.

On his last journey, Marpa spent 3 years in India. In a song to Paiṇḍapa, during his final return to Tibet, Marpa states that he spent one third of his life in India. Since Marpa spent approximately 18 years in India, this would make him around 54. He also states in the same song that he learned and studied the dharma for 40 years. Since Marpa began his dharma training at the age of 12, this would make him 52. Finally, in the same song, Marpa mentions that the previous year was a Snake year. This could have been the Wood Female Snake year, 1065, which would make Marpa 53 (assuming Marpa was born in 1012, as stated in *The Blue Annals* [*BA*]).

Hence there is good evidence that Marpa was in his early fifties after his last journey to India. Finally, the biography states that Marpa died when he was 88.

The years of Marpa's birth and death can also be found in *BA* (pp. 88, 404). According to this work, Marpa was born in the Water Male Mouse year, 1012, and died in the Fire Female Ox year, 1097. Hence Marpa lived to be 85 (or perhaps 86, as stated in *BA*, p. 404), as opposed to 88 years as given in the biography. (It is traditional for Tibetans to reckon their ages to include one year in the womb.)

In addition, there are many other discrepancies between the biographical information in *BA* and in this biography. For example, *BA* states that Marpa only met Nāropa on his first two visits to India, and that he first met Maitrīpa on his third visit to India. Leaving these points aside, we learn from *BA* that Marpa was 15 when he met guru Drogmi, that he was 31 when Atīśa traveled to Tibet, and that he was 42 when he married Dagmema.

Marpa Lotsāwa was an emanation of a bodhisattva mahāsattva in a previous life. Through the kindness of the authentic holy gurus, he received abhiṣekas and oral instructions of the secret mantra from the wisdom ḍākinīs. He achieved inner luminosity and mastered prāṇa and mind. Even though he had completely realized the immeasurable virtues of the transference of consciousness, miracles, higher perceptions, and the like, he lived in a hidden manner. Appearing to share the outlook of ordinary people, he enjoyed the five qualities that please the senses and the eight worldly dharmas. Thus he benefited many worthy vessels.

In the expanded *Mother of the Victorious Ones,** it is said, "Some bodhisattvas need a father and mother, but do not need a wife. Some bodhisattvas need a father, mother, and a wife, but do not need any sons or daughters. Some bodhisattvas need a father, mother, wife, sons, daughters, servants, and all desirable things." It is said that Marpa was like this last example. He worked for the benefit of sentient beings in the same way as the noble bodhisattvas Dharmodgata and Sadāprarudita.

In the seventh chapter of the *Buddha-samāyoga-tantra,* it is said:

Many Tibetan scholars (i.e., Helmut Hoffmann, Hugh Richardson, David Snellgrove, R. A. Stein, and Giuseppe Tucci) agree on Marpa's dates as being 1012-1096. Their sources are generally not given. In his introduction to *The Life and Teaching of Nāropa,* Herbert Guenther states that Tilopa lived from 988-1069 and Nāropa from 1016-1100. Nāropa is said to have first met Tilopa in 1057, and left him in 1069. This yields further contradictions if we are to assume 1012 as the year of Marpa's birth. According to Marpa's biography, Marpa met Nāropa after Nāropa began his studies with Tilopa. This would make Marpa at least 45 when he first met Nāropa,which is highly unlikely.

Thus, we can see the difficulties in ascertaining the exact dates of Marpa's birth, journeys, and death, especially when the traditional dates of Nāropa and Tilopa are taken into account. Much more research needs to be done in this area before these difficulties can be resolved further.

**Rgyal-ba'i yum rgyas-pa*—this text is the *Śatasāhasrikā-prajñāpāramitāsūtra.*

Beautifully adorned daughters,
As well as beautiful wives,
Are offered as the ransom
For the supreme enlightenment of the Buddha.

Again paying that ransom
By reoffering these precious substances he has received,
That vajra holder
Gives the supreme gift.

In accordance with this, by means of receiving gifts and then giving them to his gurus, Marpa benefited sentient beings, and so the realization of the teachings of the Practice Lineage became as limitless as space.

Lord Marpa had thirteen highly renowned and supremely kind gurus: learned and accomplished Mahāpaṇḍita Nāropa, Prince Maitrīpa, glorious Śāntibhadra, Jñānagarbha, Yoginī Adorned with Bone Ornaments, Kasoripa and Riripa (the brothers from Siṃhadvīpa), Jetaripa, the great Kusulu, Prajñārakṣita, Chitherpa and Paiṇḍapa (the brothers from Nepal), and Lord Atīśa.

Marpa's seven sons of his own blood were Tarma Dode, Tarma Samten, Chöpal, Marlep, Pal Ö, Trak Ö, and Charik Khorlo. His four great son-disciples, born from his heart and highly renowned, are mentioned in his song interpreting the dream of the four pillars. His four worthy disciples were the great prince of Lokya of Kyerphu in Tsang, the lady practitioner Palmo of the region of Phen, Marpa Golek of Nyingtrung in Dam, and Bawachen of Parang in Layak in the South.

After the great lord translator dissolved into dharmadhātu, everyone was convinced that he was the buddha. They offered many large gifts to receive pieces of his hair, fingernails, clothing, and the like. His body was like a wish-fulfilling gem and so was not burned, but was wrapped in silk and remained for the benefit of beings. His son Pal Ö and others gave away Marpa's flesh and accepted gifts in return. Thus, the skin of his face was taken to a monastery in the region of Phen.

When guru Ngokpa heard of this, he could not bear it. He made a great offering to the sons and said, "You must give me Marpa's body."

They replied, "Well, the principal offering we would need is the ruby mālā given to the lord father by Nāropa."

Accordingly, Ngokpa offered them the ruby mālā and immeasurable wealth and took the body to Shung. He put Marpa's body inside a stūpa and there it remained as the main shrine object.

Author's Colophon

THUS ENDS *Seeing Accomplishes All,* the biography of the jetsün, the teacher Marpa Chökyi Lodrö. Originally, it was given orally and in full detail by Jetsün Mila and Marpa Golek to the teacher of Ngen Dzong. Jetsün Mila also gave it to Rechungpa. Then, Rechungpa and Changchup Gyalpo, the teacher of Ngen Dzong, discussed it and compiled a biography, which remains here as the main text. To this was added many biographical anecdotes recounted by guru Ngokpa, Tsurtön, and Metön.

This biography is the supreme example for sincere beings. This garland of precious vaiḍūrya, which fulfills all needs and desires of saṃsāra and nirvāṇa, joins together in elegant fashion direct quotations and prose passages through the higher intention of the eye of kindness. It is the garland of precious ornaments that ravishes the mind of those who desire to attain the ornament of omniscient buddhahood.

Thus, I, Trakthung Gyalpo, a yogin who wanders through charnel grounds, dictated this to the glorious lotsāwa-paṇḍita Jampal Chölha at Chuwar, the nirmāṇakāya palace, the supreme place where Lord Milarepa attained perfect, complete buddhahood.

Translator's Colophon

Like a sword slashing through water
One sees mahāmudrā
And attains the teachings of the formless ḍākinīs.
This indeed is your kindness, Marpa the Translator.

Though enveloped by the darkness of māras,
One sees the luminosity of the Great Eastern Sun
And discovers the sun of insight transcending mind.
This indeed is your kindness, Marpa the Translator.

The view arises free from bias,
Meditation arises free from grasping,
Action arises free from hesitation—
This indeed is your kindness, Marpa the Translator.

If we did not have you, Marpa the Translator,
The hearing lineage could not pervade everywhere.
Whenever your life example is heard,
Darkness in the mind of this little one, Chökyi Gyatso,
Is always dispelled.

By the power of propagating your life example,
This kalpa of plague, war, and famine is pacified.
In the great bliss of That
May all beings without exception

Enjoy this feast offering
Together with you, Vajrācārya Marpa,
And may all attain enlightenment.

This was written on 10 May 1982 by Chökyi Gyatso, the Eleventh Trungpa at the Kalapa Court within the dharmic sphere of Karma Dzong.

PRONUNCIATION GUIDE

SANSKRIT

Vowels

Vowels are pronounced as in Italian or Spanish, but there is a distinction between long and short vowels; a line over a vowel makes it long:

short *a* as in siest*a*, but long *ā* as in c*a*r.
short *i* as in s*i*t, but long *ī* as in f*ee*t.
short *u* as in p*u*t, but long *ū* as in l*oo*t.

The following vowels are always long:

e as in d*ay*.
ai as in p*ie*.
o as in g*o*.
au as in h*ow*.

ṛ is also a vowel (short), pronounced as a rolled r, rather like *ri*. Accent is usually placed on the penultimate syllable when this contains a long vowel; otherwise it is placed on the antepenultimate. Other syllables containing long vowels may be somewhat stressed; e.g., yoginī is pronounced *yo*-gi-*nī,* not yo-*gi*-nī.

Consonants

Most consonants are pronounced as in English. The aspirated consonants *kh, gh, ch, jh, th, dh, ph, bh,* are considered single consonants in the Sanskrit syllabary. For example, the aspirated consonants *th* and *ph* must never be pronounced as in the words *things* and *photo,* but as in po*th*ole and she*ph*erd. The other aspirated consonants are pronounced similarly. Note also the following:

c is always pronounced *ch*.
g is always pronounced as in *g*o, never as in *g*em.
ṅ is pronounced in the throat as in ha*n*ger.
ñ is pronounced as in lu*n*ch, or, before a vowel as in ca*ny*on.
ṭ, ḍ, ṇ are pronounced approximately as in English, but the tongue turns back along the palate.
t, d, n are pronounced with the tongue at the teeth, as in Italian or Spanish.

v may be pronounced *w* when it follows a consonant.

ś is pronounced as in *sh*ape.

ṣ is pronounced as in *sh*ould or *s*ugar.

ḥ is a breathing sound, generally at the end of a word.

ṃ is a nasal sound at the end of a word; if it comes before a consonant it is assimilated to it, becoming either *ṅ, ñ, ṇ, n,* or *m*. In principle, it nasalizes the preceding vowel.

TIBETAN

We have utilized a system of Tibetan transcription based on an approximation of pronunciation. Our aim has been to transcribe Tibetan for the non-specialist.

In general, vowels and consonants are pronounced as outlined above. There are the additional vowel sounds of *ö* and *ü*. The aspirated consonants *kh, ch, th,* and *ph* are pronounced as in Sanskrit. The consonant *ts* is pronounced as in ha*ts; dz* is pronounced as in wor*ds;* and *lh* is pronounced as *hl.*

We have included a proper orthographic transliteration of all Tibetan words in the Glossary and/or Index. The rules for the pronunciation of this transliteration are too complex to be dealt with here, and such transcription is meant only for those knowledgeable in the Tibetan language.

LIST OF TRANSLATIONS BY MARPA LOTSĀWA

IN THE BKA'-'GYUR:

Śrī-sarvatathāgata-guhyatantra-yoga-mahārāja-advayasamatā-vijaya-nāma-vajra-śrī-paramamahākalpa-ādi (Peking Tripitaka No. 88; translated with Jñānagarbha)

IN THE BSTAN-'GYUR:

Śrī-saṃvaropadeśa-mukhakarṇa-paraṃpara-cintāmaṇi-nāma (P. T. No. 2238; written by and translated with Nāropa)
Gaṇacakra-vidhi-nāma (P.T. No. 2360; written by Ḍombī Heruka, translated with Jñānakara)
Śrī-ḍākinī-vajrapañjara-maṇḍala-saṃharaṇa-nāma-anusaraṇa-sādhana (P. T. No. 2454; written by Devạvrata)
Daśatattva (= Ḍākinī-vajrapañjara-upadeśa) (P. T. No. 2455; written by Vimalakīrti)
Mahāmudrā-kanakamālā-nāma (P. T. No. 3282; written by and translated with Maitrīpa)
Bhagavac-chrī-cakrasaṃvara-sādhana-nāma (P. T. No. 4614; written by Abhayakīrti of Kaśmīr, translated with Nāropa)
Śrī-guhya-ratna-cintāmaṇi-nāma (P. T. No. 4623; written by and translated with Nāropa)
Śrī-cakraśambara-vikurvaṇa, Caturviṃśati-deśa-pramāṇa-śāsana (P. T. No. 4628; written by Nāropa)
Ṣaḍdharmopadeśa-nāma (P. T. No. 4630; written by and translated with Nāropa)
Karṇatantra-vajrapada-nāma (P. T. No. 4632; written by and translated with Nāropa)
Dharmacaryāparādha-svayaṃmukti-nāma (P. T. No. 4636; written by and translated with Rāhula)
Vajrayoginī-sādhana (P. T. No. 4673; written by Nāropa)
Śrī-guhyasamājopadeśa-pañcakrama-nāma (P. T. No. 4789; written by and translated with Nāropa)

Pañcakrama-saṃgraha-prabhāva (P. T. No. 4790: written by and translated with Nāropa)
Śrīmatī-devīmahākālī-guhya-sādhana-nāma (P. T. No. 4929; written by Nāropa)

There are two collections of texts compiled by Jamgön Kongtrül Lodrö Thaye that concern the lineage of teachings that Marpa received and passed on. The first of these is entitled *Bka'-brgyud sngags-mdzod,* being one of the five "treasuries" (T: mdzod) that Jamgön Kongtrül compiled. It primarily contains many teachings, liturgies, and ritual texts based on the major tantras that Marpa received (e.g., Hevajra, Cakrasaṃvara, Guhyasamāja, Mahāmāyā, etc.). These teachings were mainly passed down through Ngoktön Chödor, who was the one of the four main disciples to specialize in the exposition of Marpa's teachings. However, the majority of the actual texts found in the *Bka'-brgyud sngags-mdzod* were written by Jamgön Kongtrül himself.

The second collection of texts is found within the twelve volume treasury entitled *Gdams-ngag mdzod* (*A Treasury of Instructions and Techniques for Spiritual Realization,* reproduced from a xylographic print from the Dpal-spuṅs blocks, Delhi: N. Lungtok and N. Gyaltsan, 1971). Three volumes (5, 6, and 7) of the *Gdams-ngag mdzod* are devoted to Marpa's lineage of teachings. Of particular interest is volume 5, since it contains the earliest texts.

GLOSSARY

This Glossary contains most of the technical terminology and many names of people and deities appearing in *The Life of Marpa the Translator,* whether in Sanskrit, Tibetan, or English. Most points covered in the Introduction are not included here. Please note that the definitions given here are often particular to the usage of the term in this text and should not be construed as the single or even most common meaning of a specific term.

abhisamaya (T: mngon-par rtogs-pa; clear realization) An abhisamaya is a text that describes the iconographical details of a certain visualization practice. It is often a brief liturgy containing the visualization and mantra practice of a sādhana, without any elaborate praises or offerings.

abhiṣeka (T: dbang-skur; a sprinkling, anointment, empowerment, or initiation) A ceremony in which a student is ritually entered into a maṇḍala of a particular tantric deity by his vajra master. He is thus empowered to practice the sādhana of that deity. In anuttarayogayāna there are four principal abhiṣekas: (1) vase abhiṣeka (kalaśābhiṣeka), which includes the abhiṣekas of the five buddha families: water (vajra), crown (ratna), vajra (padma), bell (karma), and name (buddha); (2) secret abhiṣeka (guhyābhiṣeka); (3) prajñājñāna-abhiṣeka; and (4) fourth abhiṣeka (caturthābhiṣeka).

An abhiṣeka is usually accompanied by a reading transmission (T: lung) and instructions (T: khrid). The lung authorizes the student to read and practice the text. The tri is the master's oral instructions on how to practice. *See also* reading transmission.

ācārya (T: slob-dpon) An accomplished master of meditation practice and study. An official position in a monastery.

accumulations, two The accumulation of merit (S: puṇya-sambhāra; T: bsod-nams kyi tshogs) is creating favorable conditions for following the path, by means of surrendering ego-oriented approaches and exerting oneself toward dharma practice. The accumulation of wisdom (S: jñāna-sambhāra; T: ye-shes kyi tshogs) is the resulting realization. Merit is accumulated by making offering and performing service to the guru and the three jewels. Wisdom is accumulated by performing these in the threefold purity—free from the subject who offers, the object offered to, and the act of offering.

activities of postmeditation, four (T: spyod-lam bzhi'i mnyam-rjes) In the sūtras, the Buddha speaks of continuing one's mindfulness practice whether standing, walking, sitting, or lying down. These are the four activities of postmeditation.

Ākarasiddhi Most sources indicate that he was the Kashmiri Jñānakara. Jñānakara worked with Naktso Lotsāwa (see entry) on translating several texts. The Bstan-'gyur attributes authorship of three texts to Jñānakara, two of which he translated with Naktso. There are seven other texts that he translated, one of them with Naktso and one of them, the *Gaṇacakra-vidhi-nāma* by Ḍombī Heruka, with Marpa. The *Guhyasamāja-tantra,* which he received from Nāropa, apparently became his principal practice and teaching. Moreover, the most significant text that he helped translate into Tibetan is the *Pradīpoddyotana,* the famous commentary on the *Guhyasamāja-tantra* written by Candrakīrti.

Akṣobhya (T: mi-bskyod-pa; immovable) The sambhogakāya buddha of the vajra family. *See also* buddha family.

ālaya-vijñāna (T: kun-gzhi rnam-par shes-pa; store-house consciousness) The root of dualistic consciousness, and hence of saṃsāra. It is the eighth consciousness according to the Yogācāra abhidharma exposition of mind. From a vajrayāna perspective, this term is also used as a synonym for dharmatā, the absolute, primordial basis of both saṃsāra and nirvāṇa. Ālaya-vijñāna is often abbreviated to ālaya.

amṛta (T: bdud-rtsi; deathless) Blessed liquor, used in vajrayāna meditation practices. More generally, spiritual intoxication.

aperture of Brahmā (S: brahmarandhra; T: tshangs-bug) A minute opening at the crown of the head. The central psychic channel, the avadhūti, leads to the brahmarandhra.

āryan riches, seven (T: 'phags-pa'i nor bdun) The seven riches of a bodhisattva: faith, discipline, generosity, learning, decorum, modesty,and knowledge.

aṣṭamantra wheel A mantra circle of eight syllables.

Atīśa Born of royal parentage in 982 in Bengal, at an early age he received training in vajrayāna from such illustrious teachers as Rāhulagupta, Maitrīpa, and Virūpa. Later, he became ordained as a monk and studied the three piṭakas for several years. He then traveled to Suvarṇadvīpa (Sumatra) where he studied mahāyāna philosophy and logic for twelve years under the master Dharmakīrti. Returning to India, Atīśa was appointed the head of discipline at Vikramaśīla (or Nālandā ?). This is when he was forced to acquiesce in the expulsion of Maitrīpa to preserve the monastic discipline, though he had personal doubts about the propriety of doing so. It was also during this time that Atīśa was first invited to Tibet to teach, and after much discussion, he left India for Tibet in 1040, arriving in western Tibet two years later. After spending three years teaching in Ngari, Atīśa met with Dromtön (1004-64), who invited him to teach in Central Tibet. Thus Atīśa traveled and taught in Central Tibet for a while, and finally settled down in Nyethang, south of Lhasa, where he died in 1054. His main disciple, Dromtön, continued his teaching and was responsible for establishing the Kadampa school, which based itself on Atīśa's teachings.

In general, Atīśa is credited with firmly reestablishing the basic precepts of Buddhism in Tibetan Buddhism and with reforming the excesses due to misunderstandings of tantric principles. He authored over one hundred works (many of them quite short) included in the Bstan-'gyur, and helped to translate most of his works as well as over 75 other Indian works into Tibetan.

Atīśa is said to have also been a student of Nāropa. While it is not unlikely that Marpa met Atīśa in Tibet, it is uncertain that he met him when the story says. All indications point to Marpa being around fifty when he traveled to India for the third time, and by this time, seemingly, Atīśa would no longer have been alive. *See also* note on page 199.

atsara Probably a corruption of the Sanskrit term ācārya, which means master, and classically designates a teacher of high status. In *The Life of Marpa,* atsara has become a Tibetan term for a relatively low-level teacher. In the songs of Milarepa, it has sunk even lower and designates a particular type of shape-shifting demon who imitates Buddhist practitioners. This may be confused with the Sanskrit apsara, a type of demon.

Atulyavajra (T: mi-mnyam rdo-rje) Atulyavajra was a famous Nepalese teacher who was one of the seven middle disciples of Maitrīpa. He himself had several Tibetan disciples, one of the more noted ones being Khyungpo Naljor. Atulyavajra is also noted for teaching Cakrasaṃvara according to the system of Nāropa and is credited in the Bstan-'gyur for translating a commentary on Cakrasaṃvara.

auspicious coincidence (T: rten-'brel; S: pratītya-samutpāda; dependent coorigination) The coming together of factors to form a situation. The Tibetan word often has an additional connotation of auspiciousness. From the view of sacred outlook, coincidence gives rise to fitting, proper situations.

avadhūti (T: kun-'dar-ma, dbu-ma) The central nāḍī of the illusory body. *See also* nāḍī, prāṇa, and bindu.

Avalokiteśvara (T: spyan-ras-gzigs dbang-phyug) The bodhisattva of compassion. The Gyalwa Karmapa is said to be an incarnation of this bodhisattva; so also is the Dalai Lama.

āyatana (T: skye-mched; sense-field) A category articulated in the abhidharma, including the six sense organs (eye, ear, etc.) and their objects.

benefits, two (T: don gnyis) Benefit for oneself and for others; in particular, attaining enlightenment oneself and liberating others.

Śrī Bhadra (T: dpal bzang-po) Śrī Bhadra is the Kashmiri paṇḍita otherwise known as Bodhibhadra. He was a disciple of Nāropa and Maitrīpa, and according to Tāranātha in *History of Buddhism in India,* he succeeded Nāropa as the northern gatekeeper. He was also a teacher of Atīśa and was noted as a translator. The

Bstan-'gyur attributes three translations to him, two of which concern Kālacakra.

Bhagavat (T: bcom-ldan-'das) The blessed one—referring to the Buddha. Can also refer to a peaceful male yidam.

bhagavatī (T: bcom-ldan-'das-ma) A general term for a peaceful female yidam.

bhikṣu (T: dge-slong) A fully ordained monk.

bhūmi (T: sa; earth, stage, level) The bhūmis are the stages of realization on the bodhisattva path, usually enumerated as ten. It may take years or even lifetimes of practicing the six pāramitās to achieve the first bhūmi (S: pramuditā; T: rab-tu dga'-ba; very joyful), which is considered a tremendous breakthrough into the stabilized experience of egolessness.

bindu (T: thig-le; drop, dot, point) *See* nāḍī, prāṇa, and bindu.

blessings (S: adhiṣṭhāna; standing over, resting upon; T: byin-rlabs; splendor wave—conveying the sense of atmosphere descending or coming toward the practitioner) One's root guru and lineage gurus are said to be the source of blessings. When the student can open himself with uncontrived devotion, the grace of the lineage manifests as blessings, which dissolve into him and awaken him to a sense of greater reality.

bodhicitta (T: byang-chub kyi sems; heart of awakened mind) Absolute bodhicitta, according to Gampopa, is emptiness indivisible from compassion—radiant, unshakable, and impossible to formulate by concepts. Relative bodhicitta arises from a glimpse of ultimate bodhicitta, and is the inspiration to practice the pāramitās and, through one's compassion, to deliver all sentient beings from saṃsāra.

bodhisattva (T: byang-chub sems-dpa') One who has committed himself to the mahāyāna path of compassion and the practice of the six pāramitās. The bodhisattva vow, taken in the presence of one's spiritual friend (S: kalyāṇamitra; T: dge-ba'i bshes-gnyen, dge-bshes), is to relinquish one's personal enlightenment and to work for all sentient beings. The vow is continually renewed in order to mix one's being with the mahāyāna mind of bodhicitta.

Bodhisattva deities represent qualities of enlightened mind active in our life.

Brahmā (T: tshangs-pa) According to Hindu tradition, Brahmā is the creator of the universe and the father of living beings. In Buddhist cosmology, he is the chief of the gods of the lower levels of the realm of form (S: rūpadhātu).

brahman *See* castes, four

buddha (T: sangs-rgyas; awakened, enlightened) May refer either to the principle of enlightenment or to any enlightened being, in particular to Śākyamuni Buddha, the historical Buddha.

buddha families (S: buddhakula; T: sangs-rgyas kyi rigs) The maṇḍala of the five tathāgatas, or jinas (victorious ones). They embody the five wisdoms, but in saṃsāra, these energies arise as the five confused emotions. Everything in the world is said to possess a predominant characteristic of one of these five. Thus, they are called families. The five families, tathāgatas, wisdoms, confused emotions, directions, and colors, respectively, are as follows: (1) buddha, Vairocana, dharmadhātu wisdom, ignorance, center, white; (2) vajra, Akṣobhya, mirror-like wisdom, aggression, East, blue; (3) ratna (jewel), Ratnasambhava, wisdom of equanimity, pride, South, yellow; (4) padma (lotus), Amitābha, discriminating-awareness wisdom, passion, West, red; (5) karma (action), Amoghasiddhi, wisdom that accomplishes all actions, envy, North, green. Some of these qualities vary in different tantras, especially those of buddha and vajra.

Buddhakapāla (T: sangs-rgyas thod-pa; skull cup of enlightenment) A mother tantra of the anuttara yoga, its central deity is associated with the vajra family and is depicted as blue, four-armed, and in union with his consort, Citrasena.

cakras, four (T: 'khor-lo; wheel) The four primary centers in the body, located along the avadhūti, or central channel, at the head, throat, heart, and navel.

Cakrasaṃvara (T: 'khor-lo sdom-pa, bde-mchog; binding or union of the cakras) A mother tantra of the anuttara yoga, its central deity is a heruka associated with the padma family and with the transformation of passionate energy. He is a particularly important yidam in the Kagyü lineage.

cakravartin (T: 'khor-los sgyur-ba; one who turns the wheel) A universal monarch; in ancient Buddhist and Vedic literature, a king who rules the entire world by his wisdom and virtue. The wheel symbolizes dominion. When Prince Gautama was born, it was foretold that he would become either a buddha or a universal monarch. The cakravartin can thus be seen as the secular equivalent of a buddha, for his reign ushers in a golden age of civilization and religious values.

caṇḍālī (T: gtum-mo; fierce, wrathful) A vajrayāna term for a kind of psychic heat generated and experienced through certain meditative practices. This heat serves to burn up all types of obstacles and confusion. One of the six yogas of Nāropa.

castes, four (T: rigs bzhi) The four castes of Hindu society: brahman (S: brāhmaṇa, T: bram-ze), the priestly caste; kṣatriya (T: rgyal-rigs), the warrior or royal caste; vaiśya (T: rje'u-rigs), the merchant or tradesman caste; and śūdra (T: dmangs-rigs), the servant or laborer caste. In addition, there are the so-called "outcaste," the lowest rung of society. All these divisions have numerous subdivisions.

Catuḥpīṭha (T: gdan-bzhi; four seats) A mother tantra of the anuttara yoga, its central deity is associated with the vajra family.

celestial realm (S: khecara; T: mkha'-spyod; moving in the air) A realm of the ḍākinīs. *See also* levels, three.

chang (T: chang) Tibetan barley beer. This term is also used in a general sense, referring to any liquor.

charnel ground ornaments, six (S: ṣaṇ-mudrā; T: phyag-rgya drug; the six symbolic ornaments) Elements of iconographical costume associated with cemeteries and thus representing the transformation of negative forces into positive ones. Certain deities and yogins are described as wearing these six symbols, which are made of bone: necklace (S: kaṇṭhī; T: nor-bu), bracelets (S: haste rucaka; T: lag-gdub), earrings (S: kuṇḍala; T: rna-cha), skirt (S: mekhalā; T: ska-rags), a circlet or crown worn on the head (S:

cakrī, T: 'khor-lo), and the cemetery ointment made from ashes, which is smeared on the body (S: bhasma; T: thal-ba). The ashes are sometimes accompanied by the brahman's thread (S: yajñopavīta; T: tshangs-skud), symbolic of noble birth. These ornaments represent the six pāramitās, respectively: generosity, discipline, patience, exertion, meditation, and prajñā.

chuba (T: chu-pa) The Tibetan national dress: a long robe worn by men and women alike. The robe hangs nearly to the floor and is gathered at the waist by a sash, producing a pouch where things can be carried. The sleeves are longer than the arms and are usually rolled back around six inches, to expose the hands.

code language (T: brda-skad) Some portions of tantric teachings are so secret that they are actually written in a code language. This term, however, has a broader meaning when it is applied to the use of symbolism in an esoteric manner, in order to communicate spiritual messages indirectly.

coemergent wisdom (S: sahajajñāna; T: lhan-cig-skyes-pa'i ye-shes) A key term in vajrayāna referring to the simultaneous arising of saṃsāra and nirvāṇa, naturally giving birth to wisdom.

command-seal (T: bka'-rgya) Just as a letter may be sealed with wax, not to be opened until the seal is broken, just so a teaching may be sealed by the command of the guru so that it is not revealed until a certain moment in time. Sometimes such teachings are passed on to a single disciple, along with such a command-seal. Thus a "single lineage" (T: gcig-brgyud) develops, where a certain body of teachings are passed from one teacher to only one student. An example of this is mentioned in the note on p. 90.

compassion (S: karuṇā; T: snying-rje) A key principle of mahāyāna Buddhism, describing the motivation and action of a bodhisattva, i.e., the practice of the pāramitās. Compassion is said to arise from experiencing the suffering of sentient beings, including ourselves; insight into the four noble truths; seeing the suffering inherent in bewilderment about cause and effect and in clinging to solid and permanent existence; and spontaneously, from śūnyatā.

ḍāka (T: dpa'-bo; S: one who goes in the sky, T: hero, warrior) Specifically, a masculine semiwrathful yidam. More generally, it can refer to a type of messenger or protector. *See also* yidam.

ḍākinī (T: mkha'-'gro-ma; one who goes in the sky) A wrathful or semiwrathful female yidam, signifying compassion, emptiness, and prajñā. The ḍākinīs are tricky and playful, representing the basic space of fertility out of which the play of saṃsāra and nirvāṇa arises. They inspire the union of skillful means and prajñā. More generally, a ḍākinī can be a type of messenger or protector. *See also* yidam.

ḍamaru A type of hand drum, usually two-headed, made of either skulls or wood, and used frequently in vajrayāna practice.

dark age (S: kaliyuga; T: snyigs-ma'i-dus) The present world age marked by the degeneration of all discipline, morality, and wisdom.

devatās of Cakrasaṃvara, five (T: bde-mchog lha lnga) There are several systems of visualizing Cakrasaṃvara—one with two arms, others with four or twelve. There are also different numbers of retinue devatās (deities) in each system. This particular style of Cakrasaṃvara visualization with five retinue devatās is the two-armed version.

devī (T: lha-mo; goddess) A general term for any type of female deity.

dharma (T: chos; truth, law) Specifically, the Buddha's teaching. Lower dharma is how things work on the mundane level, e.g., how water boils. Higher dharma is the subtle understanding of the world—how mind works, how saṃsāra perpetuates itself and how it is transcended, and so on. More technically, in the abhidharma it refers to the most simple, basic elements of existence, which were enumerated in differing numbers by various schools.

dharmacakra (T: chos kyi 'khor-lo; wheel of dharma) Generally, this term is used as in dharmacakra-pravartana ("turning the wheel of dharma"), which refers to teaching the dharma. More technically, it can refer to the heart cakra.

dharmadhātu (T: chos kyi dbyings; space, realm, or sphere of dharma) All-encompassing space, unconditional totality—unoriginated and unchanging—in which all phenomena arise, dwell, and cease.

dharmakāya *See* kāya.

dharmapāla (T: chos-skyong; protector of the dharma) A type of deity whose function is to protect the practitioner from deceptions and sidetracks. Oath-bound to the dharma, not bound to the six realms, the dharmapālas fulfill the four karmas, or enlightened actions, of pacifying, enriching, magnetizing, and destroying, thus serving and protecting the integrity of the teachings and practice.

dharmas, eight worldly (S: aṣṭau lokadharmāḥ; T: 'jig-rten gyi chos brgyad) Gain (S: lābha; T: rnyed-pa) and loss (S: alābha; T: ma-rnyed-pa), fame (S: yaśas; T: snyan-grags) and disgrace (S: ayaśas, T: ma-grags), praise (S: praśaṃsā; T: bstod-pa) and blame (S: nindā; T: smad-pa), pleasure (S: sukha; T: bde-ba) and pain (S: duḥkha; T: sdug-bsngal).

dharmatā (T: chos-nyid; dharma-ness) The essence of reality, completely pure nature.

Dharmodgata *See* Sadāprarudita.

dhātu (1) The three realms of saṃsāra: realm of desire (S: kāmadhātu; T: 'dod-pa'i khams), realm of form (S: rūpadhātu; T: gzugs kyi khams), and formless realm (S: ārūpyadhātu; T: gzugs-med khams). (2) The eighteen elements classified in the abhidharma: the six sense organs, sense objects, and their corresponding consciousnesses.

dohā A type of verse or song spontaneously composed by vajrayāna practitioners as an expression of their realization.

Ḍombī Heruka (or Ḍombipa) was one of the eighty-four mahāsiddhas. He was a king in Magadha who received teaching on the *Hevajra-tantra* from Virūpa. For twelve years, he practiced secretly while ruling his kingdom until he attained siddhi. After this, he secretly took a low-caste musician, a ḍombī, as his consort. He again practiced for twelve years. He was then discovered by his subjects who were outraged at the king's violation of the caste restrictions, whereupon he abdicated the kingdom in favor of his son. Thus, Ḍombī Heruka and his consort went to the forest for twelve years.

When famine overwhelmed the kingdom, the subjects searched for their former king to request him to rule again. Ḍombipa emerged from the forest, riding with his consort on a tigress and holding a poisonous snake in his right hand. He displayed several wondrous signs of his mastery over phenomena, and finally, refusing to rule the kingdom, went to the celestial realm.

According to some sources, Ḍombipa was a disciple of Nāropa as well as a teacher of Atīśa and Phadampa Sanggye. He authored seventeen texts found in the Bstan-'gyur. He is included in the lineage of the *Hevajra-tantra,* and Tāranātha's *Bka'-babs bdun-ldan* places him in the lineage of caṇḍālī.

doorways, nine (T: sgo dgu) According to Gampopa (as quoted in *The Life and Teaching of Nāropa,* p. 198, n. 1), the nine possible doorways for the ejection of consciousness are, of superior quality: (1) the navel, (2) the space between the eyebrows, and (3) the crown of the head (the brahmarandhra); of intermediate quality: (4) the nose, (5) the ears, and (6) the eyes; and of inferior quality: (7) the mouth, (8) the anus, and (9) the urinary passage. However, generally, as is stated in Marpa's biography (p. 96), the very best doorway for the ejection of consciousness is the crown of the head, the brahmarandhra.

dre (T: bre) A Tibetan measure for dry substances as well as fluids. It was common for a dre to vary throughout Tibet, and so it may be equivalent to two to four pints.

dri (T: 'bri-mo) A female yak.

dzo (T: mdzo) A cross between a yak bull and a common cow.

dzoki Probably a corruption of the Sanskrit word "yogī." For example, the mahāsiddha Āyogipāda is also known as Ajokipada or Adzokipada (the Tibetan letter "dz" is used to transliterate the Sanskrit letter "j").

Ekajaṭī (T: ral-gcig-ma; one topknot) This protector is described as a wrathful mamo or ḍākinī, who has one topknot, one eye, one fang, and one breast. She holds a heart in her right hand, emanates wolves from her left, and has a tigerskin around her waist. She has come to be primarily an important protector of the ati teachings of the Nyingma lineage.

elements (S: mahābhūta; T: 'byung-ba chen-po) According to the abhidharma, all materiality can be seen as having the aspects of earth (solidity, tangibility), water (cohesion), fire (radiation, sustaining), air (movement), and space (accommodation).

emanation devīs (of Hevajra), nine (T: kye'i rdo-rje lha dgu) The maṇḍala of the deity Hevajra includes Hevajra himself as the central deity plus nine goddesses who are considered complementary manifestations of the same principle. The first of these is Nairātmyā, who appears in the center of the maṇḍala as consort to Hevajra. Then there are eight other devīs in the cardinal and intermediate directions: Gaurī, Caurī, Vetālī, Ghasmarī, Pukkasī, Śavarī, Caṇḍālī, and Ḍombinī. Marpa's principal yidam was Hevajra, and it was said that his household represented the maṇḍala of Hevajra. Thus, for example, his wife was named Dagmema (T: bdag-med-ma), which is Tibetan for Nairātmyā.

emptiness *See* śūnyatā.

enlightenment (S: bodhi; T: byang-chub) According to the buddhadharma, theistic and mystical experiences of all kinds still fall within saṃsāra, as long as they confirm the experiencer or solidify his experience, even in the most subtle way. Buddhist norms of experience are: universal impermanence, existence as suffering, egolessness, and peace as absence of struggle to attain or maintain anything.

According to the hīnayāna tradition, enlightenment (also S: nirvāṇa; extinguished) means the cessation of ignorance and of conflicting emotions, and therefore freedom from the compulsive rebirth in saṃsāra. Its degrees of attainment were enumerated as four levels: stream enterer (S: srotāpanna), oncereturner (S: sakṛdāgāmin), nonreturner (S: anāgāmin), and arhat.

According to mahāyāna tradition, hīnayāna nirvāṇa is a way station, like an illusory city in the desert created by the Buddha to encourage travelers. Enlightenment requires not only cessation of ignorance but also compassion and skillful means to work with the bewilderment of all sentient beings. The arhat does not attain complete enlightenment because of his underdeveloped compassion.

According to vajrayāna tradition, hīnayāna and mahāyāna attainment are necessary, but they contain dogma. It is necessary for the yogin to develop complete partnership with the phenomenal world and to experience a more penetrating unmasking of the root of ego. In presenting the final fruition, the vajrayāna teaches either four or six tantric yānas.

The term nirvāṇa can have the utmost positive sense when referring to enlightenment; or it can have a limiting or pejorative sense when referring to a limited goal of cessation.

enter the action (T: spyod-pa la gshegs-pa) A technical term in vajrayāna referring to the stage of practice where one abandons all concepts of meditation and nonmeditation and directly encounters the phenomenal world. *See also* Introduction, p. xlvi.

equal taste (S: samarasa; T: ro-mnyam) The yogic practices and visualization exercises of Buddhist tantra are extremely complex, but underlying them is a single experience of things as they are. This realization or state of mind is sometimes called equal taste, meaning that all extremes of good and bad, awake and asleep, and so on have the same fundamental nature of emptiness and mind itself.

equalizing the elements (T: 'byung-ba ro-snyoms) Another term for the practice of "one taste," one of the four yogas of mahāmudrā. *See also* equal taste.

extremes, four (S: catuṣkoṭi; T: mtha' bzhi) The tetralemma of Buddhist argumentation: a form of argument used by Buddhist logicians, particularly in Madhyamaka texts. Any meaningful proposition is held to be either true or false or both or neither. Usually this occurs in the form of assertions of existence: something either exists, does not exist, both does and does not exist, or neither exists nor does not exist. It can also be applied to predications: "x is either red, not red, both, or neither." These four legs of the argument are regarded as extremes, none of which can be held as true, because reality is beyond the extremes of existence and nonexistence.

free and well-favored (S: kṣaṇa-sampad; T: dal-'byor) A technical term describing the very special situation of a human birth that allows one to hear and practice the dharma. By "free" is meant that one has the time and opportunity to practice the dharma. There are eight aspects of this state: freedom from being a hell being, preta (hungry ghost), animal, barbarian (unable to hear or understand the dharma), long-living deva, person holding perverted views, being born in a time when there is no buddha, and an ignorant one—deaf and dumb to the dharma. "Well-favored" is divided into five favorable circumstances that arise from ourselves and five through the agency of others: obtaining a human body, born in a land where the dharma is taught, possessing all one's senses, entering the path and not acting contrary to the dharma, having confidence in the three jewels; and, the appearance of a buddha, the teaching of the dharma, the dharma endures, it is practiced by many, and having compassion for others.

gaṇacakra (T: tshogs kyi 'khor-lo) A feast offering; a practice in which desire and sense perceptions are made part of the path. By celebrating the phenomenal world, the practitioner simultaneously extends his understanding of sacredness and further surrenders ego.

gandharva (T: dri-za) A class of deities said to live off of odors. They are celestial musicians.

garuḍa (T: khyung) A bird of Indian mythology said to hatch fully grown and hence symbolizes the awakened state of mind.

gates, three (T: sgo gsum) Body, speech, and mind. The three gates, or modes, through which one relates to the phenomenal world.

ghaṇṭā (T: dril-bu) A bell, used in vajrayāna ritual, often in combination with a vajra. The ghaṇṭā is always held in the left hand, thus symbolizing prajñā (feminine principle); the vajra is always held in the right hand, thus symbolizing upāya (masculine principle).

grasping and fixation (S: grāhya-grāhaka; T: gzung-ba dang 'dzin-pa) The two processes that constitute the ego of self and the ego of dharmas. Objects are fixated on (T: gzung-ba'i yul) as solid independent existences, and the mind then grasps them (T: 'dzin-pa'i sems).

great bliss (S: mahāsukha; T: bde-ba chen-po) A term for the quality of the experience of egolessness in mahāmudrā tantra. Ultimate nondualistic wisdom (S: jñāna) is beyond ego and so there is no entity to experience the freedom of this state. Nevertheless, one can speak of the quality of this experience without an experiencer because it is not a blank state of mind. According to the teachings of mahāmudrā, ego is actually a sort of filter or obstruction that stands between the mind and the world. When this filter is removed, experience becomes so rich that it is as if ego has been intoxicated beyond its ordinary limitations and experiences the greater bliss, which is of another order and is beyond pleasure and pain. Thus, in a sense, great bliss is the unrecognized quality of all consciousness, whether dualistic or freed.

Great Eastern Sun (T: shar-chen nyi-ma) An important image in the Shambhala tradition, representing indestructible wakefulness. Being spontaneously present, it radiates peace and confidence. Being brilliant, it illuminates the way of discipline. Since it shines over all, heaven, earth, and man find their proper place.

Guhyasamāja (T: gsang-ba 'dus-pa; secret assembly) A father tantra of the anuttara yoga, its central deity belongs to the vajra family and exemplifies the penetrating quality of transmuted anger. Usually he is blue in color, sitting in vajrāsana with six arms and four faces.

guru (T: bla-ma; master, teacher) The term guru is applied so generally to Tibetan teachers that in English it has come to mean almost any monk or teacher. Nevertheless, technically the word lama ("high one") or guru ("heavy, weighty one") only refers to enlightened masters.

habitual patterns (S: vāsanā; T: bag-chags) Patterns of conditioned response that exist as traces or tendencies stored in the unconscious mind. This mind is known as the ālaya-vijñāna, "storehouse consciousness," because it is a repository of all karmically conditioned patterns. All dualistic or ego-oriented experience leaves a residue, which is stored in the ālaya-vijñāna until a later time when some conscious occurrence activates the habitual pattern. The pattern then generates a response in the form of a perception or an action. This response leaves its own karmic residue, stored again in the unconscious repository, and the cycle continues. The explanation of this system is a central teaching of the Yogācāra tradition of mahāyāna Buddhism.

hearing lineage (S: karṇa-tantra; T: snyan-brgyud) A lineage of instruction passing orally from teacher to disciple. Teachings of a hearing lineage are usually very secret, since they can only be received by direct, personal communication with the guru. "Hearing lineage" is also a common epithet for the Kagyü lineage.

heruka (T: khrag-'thung) A wrathful male yidam, the masculine principle of energy and skillful means that makes situations powerful and creative. The Tibetan word means "blooddrinker," that which drinks the blood of ego-clinging, doubt, and dualistic confusion. In the tantras, Śrī Heruka (an epithet, usually of Cakrasaṃvara) is explained as follows: "*Śrī* (glorious) is nondual wisdom; *he* means cause and effect are śūnyatā; *ru* means free from accumulation; *ka* is not dwelling anywhere."

Hevajra (T: kye'i rdo-rje) A mother tantra of the anuttara yoga. "He" is said to be an exclamation of joy. Hevajra transforms sense pleasures and form into joy through the realization of the identity of form and emptiness. He is depicted in two, four, six, twelve, and sixteen-armed forms, dancing in union with his consort, who is usually Nairātmyā.

higher perception (S: abhijñā; T: mngon-shes) Certain abilities that the Buddha possessed and which may be attained through meditation practice. There are several lists of abhijñās, which include the ability to hear and see for great distances, reading others' minds, and so on. These are more mundane compared to the final abhijñā, the wisdom of the termination of defilements (S: āsravakṣayajñāna), marking the attainment of the arhat.

hīnayāna (T: theg-pa dman-pa or theg-chung; lesser vehicle) The first of the three yānas, which is subdivided into the śrāvakayāna and pratyekabuddhayāna. *See also* śrāvaka and pratyekabuddha.

illusions, three *See* note on p. 55.

immeasurables, four (S: apramāṇa; T: tshad-med-pa) Maitrī (friendliness), karuṇā (compassion), muditā (joy), and upekṣā (impartiality). These are a catalyst to the bodhisattva's attitude. When these have a conditional reference point, they are also referred to as the "dwelling places of Brahmā" (S: brahmavihāra). The bodhisattva sees these as indivisible with śūnyatā, and in this case, they are called "immeasurables."

individual liberation (S: prātimokṣa; T: so-sor thar-pa) A term that refers to the monastic discipline of the vinaya, which supports the individual liberation of the monk or nun. More generally, the nontheistic attitude of taking responsibility for one's own liberation from saṃsāra.

infant death (S: mṛtavatsā; T: sri'u) A disease or condition that causes the death of an infant at, or soon after, birth.

Jambudvīpa (T: 'dzam-bu-gling) The southern continent or island of the Indian world-system named after the jambu (rose-apple) tree. The entire known world was regarded as Jambudvīpa. Since the buddhadharma is taught there, it is an auspicious place. *See also* Mount Meru.

jetsün (T: rje-btsun) An honorific Tibetan term applied to revered teachers.

jewels, three (S: triratna; T: dkon-mchog gsum) Buddha, dharma, and saṅgha—the three objects of refuge. Buddha is an example of a human being who transcended confusion, and also refers to enlightenment itself. Dharma includes the teachings that are spoken and written, as well as their realization—the dharma that is experienced. Saṅgha is the community of practitioners and also the assembly of realized ones.

jñāna (T: ye-shes; wisdom) The wisdom-activity of enlightenment, transcending all dualistic conceptualization. One's being is spontaneously wise, without needing to seek for wisdom. The Tibetan term means "primordial knowing."

jñānaḍākinī (T: ye-shes mkha'-'gro-ma; wisdom or ultimate ḍākinī) This term may imply the actual feminine principle instead of the anthropomorphized deity that symbolizes it. It may mean the central deity in a maṇḍala instead of its many possible emanations. Sometimes jñānaḍākinī refers to the yidam Vajrayoginī, because she represents ultimate wisdom. Sometimes Marpa uses the term to refer to the great teacher Niguma, the disciple and consort of Nāropa.

Kalāpa and **Candra** *Kalāpa-sūtra* (Peking Tripitaka No. 5775) and *Candra-vyākaraṇa-sūtra-nāma* (P. T. No. 5767) are the names of Indian grammatical texts.

kalpa An extremely long aeon, sometimes reckoned at 4,320 million years.

kapāla (T: thod-pa; skull cup) Used in vajrayāna rituals; usually contains amṛta.

karma (S: karman; T: las; action) According to the doctrine of cause and effect, action and result, one's present experience is a product of previous actions and volitions, and future conditions depend on what we think, say, and do in the present. Actions may be classified in three ways: (1) wholesome—tending toward higher realms of saṃsāra or, in the presence of an enlightened attitude, toward liberation; (2) unwholesome—tending to perpetuate confusion and pain; and (3) neutral.

Karma originates from the false belief in an ego, which prompts a chain reaction of seeking to protect territory and maintain security. Virtuous action can lead to better states, but the chain reaction process itself can only be cut and transcended by insight and discipline. Karma is precise down to the minute details of body, mind, and environment. There is a "group karma" of families and nations, as well as individual karma.

karmamudrā *See* mudrā.

karmas, four (T: 'phrin-las bzhi) The four kinds of buddha activity that express skillful means: pacifying (S: śāntika; T: zhi-ba), enriching (S : puṣṭika; T: rgyas-pa), magnetizing (S: vaśī-karaṇa; T: dbang), and destroying (S: abhicāraka; T: drag-po).

kārṣāpaṇa coin ("weighing a karṣa") A coin of differing values—if gold, it equals between 176-280 grains troy; if silver, it equals roughly twenty times that of the gold; if copper, it equals about 176 grains.

kāya (T: sku; body) Historically, the use of the term kāya originated with attempts to describe the nature of Śākyamuni Buddha. Some schools maintained that the Buddha existed in two forms when he taught in the fifth century B.C.—as rūpakaya (T: gzugs kyi sku; form body), or physically manifesting being; and as dharmakāya (T: chos kyi sku; body of truth, dharma), his ultimate form.

The Buddha was later conceived of as having three kāyas, or modes of existence, relating to body, speech, and mind. The dharmakāya is the mind of the Buddha, enlightenment itself—unoriginated, primordial mind, devoid of concept. The sambhogakāya (T: longs-spyod-rdzogs kyi sku; body of complete enjoyment) is the speech of the Buddha, the environment of compassion and communication. Iconographically, its splendor is represented by the five buddhas, the yidams, and the dharmapālas. The nirmāṇakāya (T: sprul-pa'i sku; emanation body) is the physical form of the Buddha. These latter two comprise the rūpakaya, described above.

People who attain enlightenment are said to have attained the trikāya (T: sku gsum; three bodies), becoming divine like the Buddha. In vajrayāna, the root guru's body, speech, and mind are regarded as the trikāya. Sometimes a fourth and fifth kāya are elaborated: the svabhāvikakāya (T: ngo-bo-nyid kyi sku; self-nature or essence body), which is the essence or unity of the first three kāyas; and the mahāsukhakāya (T: bde-ba chen-po'i sku; body of great bliss), which is the inseparability of the first four.

kleśa (T: nyon-mongs) *See* poison.

kriyā tantra (T: bya-ba'i rgyud; action tantra) The first of the tantric yānas. The emphasis in the kriyā yāna is on personal purity and the understanding that all phenomena are inherently pure—in the sense that they are beyond grasping and fixation and all extremes of saṃsāra and nirvāṇa. The practices of kriyā are principally "outer practices." That is, they are mainly composed of certain ritual actions. In particular, kriyā yoga involves a great number of gestures that dramatize purification—dietary practices, styles of clothing, and so on. *See also* sacred outlook.

kṣatriya *See* castes, four.

kṣetrapāla (T: zhing-skyong; protector of the land, field) A kind of local deity often associated with charnel grounds.

kusulu (= S or kusali ?) Indian tradition gives several meanings, for instance, a simple yogin who has no interests or occupations beyond the practice of meditation or a man who has literally or figuratively come back from the dead. In Tibet, only the first meaning was in broad use. A kusulupa was said to have, in addition to meditation practice, only three occupations: eating and drinking, defecating and urinating, and sleeping.

lama *See* guru.

learning, contemplating, and meditating (T: thos bsam sgom) Three aspects of developing prajñā, which describe how the practitioner comes to a true understanding of the teachings. *See also* prajñā, three kinds of.

levels, three (S: tribhuvana; T: sa gsum) A partitioning of the phenomenal world into three habitats of various worldly and supramundane beings. In a physical sense the highest is the celestial realm (S: khecara; T: mkha'-spyod), which is primarily the abode of ḍākinīs and enlightened deities. Then there is the terrestrial realm (S: bhūcara; T: sa-spyod), encompassing humans, animals, and various earth-bound spirits. Lastly, there is the subterrestrial realm (S: nāgaloka; T: sa-'og-spyod) of those who live underground, such as the nāga (T: klu) "serpent spirits."

lotsāwa (translator; said to be a corruption from Sanskrit) Usually an epithet of Marpa.

luminosity, mother and son (T: 'od-gsal ma bu) Mother luminosity refers to primordial, self-existing luminosity, whereas son luminosity refers to the meditator's various levels of experience of luminosity. Therefore, when it is said that mother and son luminosities are united, it means that the meditator has attained full realization of the nature of luminosity.

Madhyamaka (T: dbu-ma) A mahāyāna school, founded by Nāgārjuna, which emphasizes the doctrine of śūnyatā. Vajrayāna has many of its philosophical roots in Madhyamaka. Some of the principal texts of this tradition are the *Mūlamādhyamikakārikā* and *Vigrahavyāvartanī* by Nāgārjuna, the *Bodhicaryāvatāra* by Śāntideva, and the *Prasannapadā* and *Madhyamakāvatāra* by Candrakīrti. *See also* svatantra-madhyamaka.

Mahāmāyā (T: sgyu-ma chen-mo; great illusion) A mother tantra of the anuttara tantra, its central deity is associated with the vajra family, and may be depicted as blue, four-armed, and in union with his consort, Buddhaḍākinī.

mahāmudrā (T: phyag-rgya chen-po; great seal, symbol, or gesture) The meditative transmission handed down especially by the Kagyü school, from Vajradhara Buddha to Tilopa up to the present lineage holders. *See also* Introduction, pp. xxxviii-xliii.

mahāpaṇḍita (great scholar, teacher) *See* paṇḍita.

mahāsattva (T: sems-dpa' chen-po; great being) A term that refers to great bodhisattvas often at the level of the seventh bhūmi or higher.

mahāsiddha *See* siddha.

mahāyāna (T: theg-pa chen-po; greater vehicle) The mahāyāna schools appeared in literary form several hundred years after the Buddha's death, although traditionally the transmission lineage goes back to Śākyamuni himself, who is said to have first presented mahāyāna teachings on Vulture Peak mountain near Rājagṛha to a celestial assembly. Going beyond the somewhat nihilistic emptiness of the hīnayāna schools and the preoccupation with individual liberation, the greater vehicle presents greater vision based on śūnyatā, compassion, and the acknowledgment of universal buddha nature. It introduced the ideal of the bodhisattva, who lives in the world to deliver sentient beings, while dwelling neither in the struggle of saṃsāra nor in a quietistic nirvāṇa. Socially, the mahāyāna expanded the buddhadharma beyond the monastic communities to the lay population.

mālā (T: 'phreng-ba) A rosary, usually strung with 108 beads.

mamo (= T) Wrathful goddesses, usually pictured as furious, ugly women. They are bringers of disease and catastrophe and inflict their fierce attacks upon violators of the tantric precepts, as well as those who threaten the teachings. On the other hand, mamos can act as worldly protectors of the dharma, bringing further prosperity if the practitioners do not violate their vows.

Mamos as a class of deities are quite numerous and are usually emanations of some more exalted feminine principle. In addition, some very important female protectors (S: dharmapālī), such as Palden Lhamo, are considered to be mamos.

maṇḍala (T: dkyil-'khor; circle, sphere, group, society) The Tibetan word dkyil-'khor means "center and periphery." It is the unification of many vast elements into one, through the experience of meditation. Seeming complexity and chaos are simplified into a pattern and a natural hierarchy.

A maṇḍala is usually represented by a diagram with a central deity, a personification of the basic sanity of buddha nature. The outer world, one's body and state of mind, and the totality can all be seen as maṇḍala. The constructed form of a maṇḍala has as its basic structure a palace with a center and four gates in the cardinal directions. It may be painted, made of colored sand, heaps of rice, or represented by three-dimensional models.

mantra (T: sngags) Mantra is explained in the tantras as that which protects the cohesiveness of the vajra mind. It is a means of transforming energy through sound, expressed by speech, breathing, and movement. Mantra is usually done in conjunction with visualization and mudrā, according to the prescriptions of a sādhana transmitted by one's guru. Mantras are Sanskrit words or syllables. They express the quintessence of various energies, whether or not the mantra has conceptual content.

From the view of fruition, the practitioner should recognize all sound as mantra, all appearance as the deity's presence, and all thoughts as wisdom.

mantrayāna (T: sngags kyi theg-pa; vehicle of mantra) Another term for vajrayāna, whose meditation practices make extensive use of mantra.

Māra (T: bdud; death) The tempter of Śākyamuni Buddha, who appeared just prior to his attaining enlightenment. More generally, māras are difficulties that the practitioner may encounter, often classified as: skandha-māra, misunderstanding the five skandhas as a self; kleśa-māra, being overpowered by the kleśas; mṛtyu-māra, death or the fear of death, which interrupts one's practice unless the yogin knows how to make it part of the path; and devaputra-māra, seduction by the bliss of meditation—still dwelling in the god realms of saṃsāra.

meats, five (S: pañca-māṃsa; T: sha lnga) Symbolizing the five buddhas (Vairocana, Akṣobhya, Ratnasambhava, Amitābha, Amoghasiddhi), the five meats are the flesh of a human, cow, dog, elephant, and horse. These are linked with the five amṛtas—urine, excrement, blood, semen, and brains—which symbolize the five female buddhas, their consorts.

medical practice, eightfold way of The eight limbs of medical practice that are presented in the *Gyü Shi* (T: *Rgyud bzhi* is short for *Bdud-rtsi snying-po yan-lag brgyad-pa gsang-ba man-ngag gi rgyud;* S: *Aṣṭāṅgahṛdayasaṃhitā; The Tantra on the Secret Oral Instructions of the Eight-Limbed Essence of Amṛta)* and which every Tibetan doctor must know: (1) diseases of the adult body, (2) childhood diseases, (3) female diseases, (4) nervous diseases, (5) surgery, (6) poisoning, (7) diseases of senility, and (8) aphrodisiacs.

methods, four (T: tshul bzhi) Four methods by which the dharma is expressed or taught: in words (T: tshig gi tshul), through the general or outer method (T: phyi yi tshul), in a hidden way (T:

sbas-pa'i tshul), and through the ultimate method (T: mthar-thug gi tshul). *See also* views, six.

moods of a heruka, nine (S: rasa; T: gar-stabs dgu) Nine aspects of the symbolism of a wrathful enlightened being. Visualizations of herukas often include these nine iconographical elements—three for body, three for speech, and three for mind: (1) charming, gracious (S: śṛṅgāra; T: sgeg-pa)—beautified with ornaments and radiant; (2) brave (S: vīra; T: dpa'-ba)—posing and strutting; (3) threatening, repulsive (S: bībhatsa; T: mi-sdug-pa)—with rolling eyes, wrathfully grimacing; (4) laughing (S: hāsya; T: dgod-pa)—smiling and making the laughing sound of "ha, ha"; (5) fierce, terrible, cruel (S: raudra; T: drag-shul-can)—with mocking laughter, making the sound of "hi, hi, hūṃ, phaṭ"; (6) fearful, terrifying (S: bhayānaka; T: 'jigs-su rung-ba)—grinding the teeth, bending the neck, holding up a weapon; (7) compassionate (S: kāruṇya; T: snying-rje)—with bloodshot eyes and youthful skin; (8) awesome, impressive, outrageous (S: adbhuta; T: rngam-pa)—with gaping mouth and clicking tongue; (9) peaceful (S: śānta; T: zhi-ba)—supple, gently gazing at the tip of the nose.

Mount Meru and the four continents (T: gling bzhi ri-rab dang bcas-pa) Ancient Indian Buddhist cosmology describes the world as being a single great four-sided mountain surrounded in the cardinal directions by four "continents." There are two smaller subcontinents in the intermediate directions, on either side of the main continents. The planet Earth, accordingly, would correspond roughly to the southern continent, Jambudvīpa. Meru is the central mountain. The four large continents are: East, Pūrvavideha (T: shar gyi lus-'phags-pa); South, Jambudvīpa (T: lho'i 'dzam-bu-gling); West, Aparagodānīya (T: nub kyi ba-glang-spyod); and North, Uttarakuru (T: byang gi sgra-mi-snyan). *See also* Jambudvīpa.

mudrā (T: phyag-rgya; sign, symbol, gesture) A mudrā may be any sort of symbol. For instance, the white dharmacakra is a mudrā of Vairocana, the hooked knife is a mudrā of Vajravārāhī. Specifically, mudrās are symbolic hand gestures that accompany sādhana practices. They are used to state the quality of different moments of meditation. More generally, mudrā is the provocative color of apparent phenomena. Mudrā is self-evidencing, and the symbol and symbolized are inseparable.

Mudrā can also refer to the consort of a deity or yogin. Karmamudrā (T: las kyi phyag-rgya) is a tantric practice involving the union of male and female, and is associated with the third abhiṣeka (prajñājñānābhiṣeka).

nāḍī, prāṇa, and bindu (T: rtsa, rlung, thig-le) According to the yogic teachings of the path of skillful means (S: upāyamarga; T: thabs-lam), realization is attained through the synchronization of body and mind. This may be achieved through meditating on nāḍī, prāṇa, and bindu—the psychic components in the illusory body. Prāṇa is the energy, or "wind," moving though the nāḍī, the channels. Bindu is the quintessence secreted within the body. As is said, "Mind consciousness rides the horse of prāṇa on the pathways of the nāḍīs. The bindu is mind's nourishment."

Because of dualistic thinking, prāṇa enters the lalanā (T: rkyang-ma) and rasanā (T: ro-ma), the left and right channels. This divergence of energy in the illusory body corresponds to the mental activity that falsely distinguishes between subject and object and leads to karmically determined activity. Through yogic practice, the prāṇas can be brought into the central channel (S: avadhūti; T: dbu-ma), and therefore transformed into wisdom-prāṇa. Then the mind can recognize its fundamental nature, realizing all dharmas as unborn.

This belongs to advanced practice and can only be learned through direct oral transmission from an accomplished guru. Once the meditator is well established in the experience of the fundamental nature of mind, he can meditate on it directly, dissolving the nāḍī, prāṇa, and bindu visualization. Meditation using the concept of psychic channels belongs to the category of "sampannakrama with signs." The formless practice, which contemplates the nature of mind directly, is "sampannakrama without signs."

nāga (T: klu; snake) A class of deities with human torsos and serpent-like lower bodies, said to inhabit low-lying marshy areas and bodies of water. They are associated with jewel-treasures and with knowledge. They are said to have guarded the *Prajñāpāramitā-sūtras* until the great teacher Nāgārjuna took custody of them. *See also* levels, three.

Nāgārjuna (T: klu-grub) A famous Indian master of the first century A.D., and founder of the Madhyamaka school. There is also a tantric master of the same name who was a teacher of Tilopa. Traditional sources claim that these two are one and the same. His name comes from the legend that he retrieved the *Prajñāpāramitā* literature from the nāgas.

Nairātmyā (T: bdag-med-ma; nonego) The consort of Hevajra. Hevajra was the principal yidam of Marpa, and it is said that Marpa's family of one main wife and eight consorts was a manifestation of the Hevajra maṇḍala. His wife's name, Dagmema, is the Tibetan for Nairātmyā. *See also* emanation devīs (of Hevajra), nine.

Naktso Lotsāwa Tsültrim Gyalwa of Naktso (T: Tshul-khrims rgyal-ba, Nag-tsho; b. 1011 ?) is perhaps best known for his role in helping to persuade Atīśa to come to Tibet. He then traveled with Atīśa for nineteen years, attending him and studying with him. Just before his death, Atīśa sent Naktso to receive the famous paṇḍita Jñānakara (*see* Ākarasiddhi) in Kungthang. Naktso translated several texts with Jñānakara as well as many others with other paṇḍitas. There are over twenty translations attributed to him in the Bka'-'gyur and Bstan-'gyur.

nirmāṇakāya *See* kāya.

nirvāṇa (T: mya-ngan las 'das-pa) *See* enlightenment.

nonvirtues, ten (S: akuśala; T: mi-dge-ba) Killing, stealing, sexual misconduct, lying, slander, abusive words, idle gossip, covetousness, ill-will, and wrong views. Acts are nonvirtuous or unwholesome when they result in undesirable karmic effects. Thus, this list of ten unwholesome acts occurs generally in discussions of the functioning of karma. The first three are actions of body, the next four of speech, and the last three of mind.

nyagrodha tree A fig tree.

obscurations (S: āvaraṇa; T: sgrib-pa) There are two classes of obscurations or, veils—kleśāvaraṇa and jñeyāvaraṇa (conflicting emotions and primitive beliefs about reality). The first stems from belief in "me" and "mine" and the resulting emotional reactions. The second obscuration stems from more subtle conceptualization, and corresponds to the ego of dharmas—believing that objects of experience are substantial and possess an independent existence. Both obscurations can be seen through by means of prajñāpāramitā.

offerings (T: mchod-pa) The principle of offering has several levels of application, generally based on generosity and surrendering one's ego-clinging. Outer (material) offerings of anything desirable in the world are given as expressions of gratitude, appreciation, and nonattachment. Inner offering is giving up the attachment to one's body. Secret offering is surrendering the ego reinforcement that we derive from dualistic emotions. The "fourth" offering is recognizing the inseparability of offerer, offering, and the recipient in things as they are. All the above offerings are referred to as "faith offerings" (T: dad-zas) and are made from devotion to a guru or a deity.

oral instructions (S: upadeśa; T: gdams-ngag, man-ngag) In vajrayāna, the guru personally communicates the essence of meditation practice to his students. In this manner, both the literal instructions and their intuitive sense are conveyed to the student. Even if the student came across the instructions in written form, it would still be necessary for him to receive them directly from the mouth of his teacher. *See also* hearing lineage.

paṇḍita A scholar; a title often given to one who has mastered the five sciences. Paṇḍita usually refers to an Indian scholar and/or one learned in Sanskrit.

pāramitā (T: pha-rol-tu phyin-pa; transcendent, perfection, "gone to the other shore") The six pāramitās are the main practices of the mahāyāna. They are generosity (S: dāna; T: sbyin-pa), discipline (S: śīla; T: tshul-khrims), patience (S: kṣānti; T: bzod-pa), exertion (S: vīrya; T: brtson-'grus), meditation (S: dhyāna; T: bsam-gtan), and knowledge (S: prajñā; T: shes-rab). They are called "transcendent" or, more literally, "gone to the other shore," because they carry us across the ocean of saṃsāra to enlightenment. Moreover, these practices are described from the point of view of the other shore, enlightenment. Most ethical principles are expressed in dualistic language, invoking conventional distinctions of good and bad, perfect and imperfect, ideal and actual. The pāramitās are conceived from the beginning as being founded on a nondualistic approach to behavior. They transcend karmic entanglements of conceptualized virtue.

pardo (S: antarābhava; T: bar-do; existing in between) Traditionally, there are said to be six different pardos, or intermediate states: 1) the pardo of the place of birth (T: skye-gnas bar-do), 2) the pardo of dream (T: rmi-lam bar-do), 3) the pardo of meditation (T: bsam-gtan bar-do), 4) the pardo of the moment of death (T: 'chi-kha'i bar-do), 5) the pardo of dharmatā (T: chos-nyid bar-do), and 6) the pardo of becoming (T: srid-pa'i bar-do). It is this last one, the pardo of becoming, or of seeking rebirth, that is most commonly referred to by the word pardo. This pardo is the intermediate state after death and before the next birth, and is said to usually last forty-nine days.

pātrī and **śruva** (T: dgang-gzar, blugs-gzar) Utensils used in performing the ritual fire offering (S: homa; T: sbyin-sreg). The śruva is a ladle with a handle several feet in length. Clarified butter (ghee) is poured from the śruva into the pātrī, a hearth-shaped receptacle, also on a long handle. Through an opening in the pātrī, the ghee can be poured onto the fire as an offering.

permission-blessing (T: rjes-su gnang-ba) A type of empowerment for a student to practice or study a particular text or sādhana. It is often given for an abbreviated sādhana or for a practice that has no abhiṣeka connected with it. A permission-blessing is often given as a reading transmission. *See also* reading transmission.

piṭaka (T: sde-snod; basket) The Buddhist scriptures are divided into three "baskets," or piṭakas: the sūtra-piṭaka (T: mdo-sde'i sde-snod), which contains discourses of the Buddha; the abhidharma-piṭaka (T: mngon-pa'i sde-snod), which contains the analytical works on Buddhist psychology; and the vinaya-piṭaka (T: 'dul-ba'i sde-snod), which contains the texts on monastic discipline and attitude.

plakṣa tree The waved-leaf Indian fig tree—a large and beautiful tree that bears small white fruit.

poisons, five, three (T: dug) Poison is synonymous with kleśa. The three root poisons are rāga (T: 'dod-chags; passion), dveṣa (T: zhe-sdang; aggression), and moha (T: gti-mug; delusion). The five poisons include the above three plus mānas (T: nga-rgyal; arrogance) and īrṣyā (T: phrag-dog; envy). *See also* realms, lower or higher.

Practice Lineage (T: sgrub-brgyud) A name for the Kagyü lineage, which emphasizes its strong allegiance to meditation practice.

prajñā (T: shes-rab; knowledge) Prajñā is the natural sharpness of awareness that sees, discriminates, and also sees through conceptual discrimination. "Lower prajñā" includes any sort of worldly knowledge (e.g., how to run a business, how to cook a meal). "Higher prajñā" includes two stages: seeing phenomena as impermanent, egoless, and suffering; and a higher prajñā that sees śūnyatā—a direct knowledge of things as they are. *See also* prajñāpāramitā.

prajñā, three kinds of (S: trividhā-prajñā; T: shes-rab rnam-pa gsum) Three aspects of knowledge, resulting from the three stages of learning in the Buddhist path: hearing, contemplating, and meditating. The student begins by hearing the teachings and developing from this an attitude of openness and intellectual understanding of the dharma. This is called *prajñā resulting from hearing* (S: śruta-mayī-prajñā; T: thos-pa las byung-ba'i shes-rab). This knowledge is contemplated so that it can be profoundly understood and applied to everyday life. This is the *prajñā resulting from contemplating* (S: cintā-mayī prajñā; T: bsam-pa las byung-ba'i shes-rab). Finally, one meditates on the truths that were studied and contemplated so that they can be directly experienced with naked insight. In this way the student finally comes to identify with the dharma. This is called *prajñā resulting from meditating* (S: bhāvanā-mayī-prajñā; T: bsgom-pa las byung-ba'i shes-rab).

prajñāpāramitā (T: shes-rab kyi pha-rol-tu phyin-pa; perfection of knowledge) The sixth pāramitā. Prajñā is considered to be the eyes without which the other five transcendent actions would be blind. According to Gampopa, prajñāpāramitā is the awareness that the whole of reality is without origination or basis. It sees through any solid existence as well as through any nihilistic interpretation of reality. Even the duality between saṃsāra and nirvāṇa is transcended and, therefore, prajñā gives birth to more active and energetic upāya (seventh pāramitā).

Prajñāpāramitā is called the mother of all the buddhas, and is sometimes depicted as a youthful, smiling deity. The *Prajñāpāramitā-sūtras* describe prajñā and the other pāramitās.

In vajrayāna, prajñā corresponds to the feminine principle of space, the mother of all wisdom and manifestation. *See also* ḍākinī, prajñā.

prāṇa (T: rlung; wind) *See* nāḍī, prāṇa, and bindu.

prātimokṣa *See* individual liberation.

pratyekabuddha (T: rang-sangs-rgyas; solitary buddha) In the early texts, one who attains liberation from saṃsāra without the benefit of a teacher and does not teach others. In the Tibetan tradition, the pratyekabuddha became a symbol of a certain stage of enlightenment. He concentrates on individual liberation through examining the twelvefold chain of dependent co-origination, pratītyasamutpāda. It is also the name of the second of the nine yānas.

Regarded positively, he is worthy of veneration as among the awakened ones. Regarded negatively, his spiritual arrogance and fear of saṃsāra prevent him from completely developing skillful means and compassion. Hence, his enlightenment is only partial.

precious substances, six (T: bzang drug) Various medicinal substances: yellow myrobalan (T: a-ru; Terminalia chebula), beleric myrobalan (T: ba-ru; Terminalia belerica), emblic myrobalan (T: skyu-ru; Emblica officinalis), bamboo manna (T: cu-gang), musk (T: gla-rtsi), and solidified elephant bile (T: gi-wang).

preta (T: yi-dvags; hungry ghost) Pretas inhabit one of the three lower realms of saṃsāra. They suffer the obsession of hunger and craving. It is said that even if they came upon a lake of pure fresh water, due to their heavy karmic obscurations, they would experience it as an undrinkable pool of pus. Pretas are depicted with very large bellies and very thin necks.

qualities, eight (T: yan-lag brgyad-ldan) These qualities describe the virtuous properties of water. They are: (1) coolness (T: bsil-ba), (2) sweetness (T: zhim-pa), (3) lightness (T: yang-ba), (4) softness (T: 'jam-pa), (5) clearness (T: dvangs-pa), (6) free from impurities (T: dri-ma med-pa), (7) when drunk, soothes the stomach (T: 'thung-na lto-bar 'jam-pa), and (8) clears and soothes the throat (T: mgrin-pa sang dang bde-ba).

qualities that please the senses, five (S: pañca-kāma-guṇāḥ; T: 'dod-pa'i yon-tan lnga) Five substances, often used as offerings, that please the senses—one for each of the sense faculties: seeing, hearing, smelling, tasting, and touching.

qualities, three (T: gsum-ldan) Although the Tibetan text merely states that Marpa "possesses the three," not indicating what three he has, these are most likely the three qualities of wisdom (T: mkhyen), compassion (T: brtse), and power (T: nus). These three correspond to the three principal bodhisattvas: Mañjuśrī, lord of prajñā; Avalokiteśvara, lord of compassion; and Vajrapāṇi, lord of power.

rakta (T: khrag; blood) The feminine counterpart of śukra (T: khu-ba; semen, sperm). It is symbolic of bodhicitta.

rasāyana (T: bcud-len; extracting the essence) Rasāyana can have a broad range of meanings. Traditionally, it has been connected with the alchemical practices of metallurgy, medicine, and magic. In the vajrayāna tradition, it has generally been applied to different practices that serve to strengthen the health and vitality of the body. For example, there is an ascetic practice in which one takes only prepared food pills as sustenance. The food pills form a graded regimen. One starts with pills made of vegetable matter and gradually works up to pills made entirely of minerals. At other times, rasāyana can refer to the nāḍī, prāṇa, and bindu practice or to the karmamudrā practice.

In *The Life of Marpa,* the general meaning of rasāyana, as something that brings strength and life, seems to be the one used.

reading transmission (T: lung) A ceremony in which a master reads through a sādhana or liturgy, usually quite rapidly, thereby empowering the disciples to practice it. It is a type of permission-blessing. A lung may also be given on a text to be studied. *See also* abhiṣeka, permission-blessing.

realms, lower or higher (S: ṣaḍgati; T: 'gro-ba rigs drug) All beings of saṃsāra belong to one of the six "gates," or realms. The higher realms include: deva (T: lha; god), asura (T: lha-ma-yin; jealous god), and nara (T: mi; human). The lower realms include: tiryak (T: dud-'gro; animal), preta (T: yi-dvags; hungry ghost), and naraka (T: dmyal-ba; hell).

In each realm, there is a typical psychophysical pattern of recreating your experience, based on a predominant kleśa: pride (god), paranoia or jealousy (asura), passion or dissatisfaction (human), ignorance (animal), craving (preta), and aggression (hell). The karmic momentum in most of the realms is so intense and overlapping that exiting from the realms only comes about when a being's karma in that realm happens to wear thin. Our human realm is considered very fortunate because the maintenance of ego is somewhat haphazard. Therefore, there is the possibility of altering our situation by cutting the cycle of saṃsāra.

regent (S: yuva-rāja; T: rgyal-tshab) Traditionally, a tantric lineage-holder guru chooses one of his disciples to be his regent—to serve as a repository of all the guru's teachings and transmissions, and often to lead the guru's other disciples. It is the regent's task to hold the teachings intact and uncorrupted for the next generation of disciples. This takes on a special significance when the guru plans to have his rebirth discovered, as is the case with the Tibetan tülku lineages. In this case, the regent holds the lineage during the minority of his guru's reincarnation, returning to him at the proper time all the learning he had held in his previous lifetime.

rinpoche (T: rin-po-che; precious one) An honorific term for a Tibetan guru.

ritual traditions (T: phyag-len) Details of liturgical practice passed on from generation to generation—mainly orally. Phyag-len is also an honorific term for spiritual practice itself.

root downfalls, fourteen (S: mūlāpatti; T: rtsa-ba'i ltung-ba) These fourteen root downfalls are the basic transgressions that destroy one's samaya vow. As such, they destroy the root of one's path and intensify confusion and suffering. They are: disparaging one's guru, not obeying what the Buddha said, having contempt for one's vajra brothers and sisters, forsaking kindness toward all sentient beings, abandoning bodhicitta, disparaging the dharma, proclaiming secret teachings to those who are unripe, denouncing one's body, doubting the purity of all dharmas, loving enemies and harmful beings, having the wrong realization of the dharma which is beyond words, causing someone to lose their faith, not keeping with oneself necessary articles for one's samaya vows, and disparaging women.

royal treasures of a universal monarch, seven (T: rin-chen, rgyal-srid sna bdun) These are the precious: wheel (S: cakra; T: 'khor-lo), wish-fulfilling gem (S: cintāmaṇi; T: yid-bzhin nor-bu), queen (S: strī; T: btsun-mo), minister (S: gṛhapati; T: blon-po), elephant (S: hastin; T: glang-po), steed (S: aśva; T: rta-mchog), and general (S: pariṇāyaka; T: dmag-dpon).

ṛṣi (T: drang-srong) Ancient Indian patriarchal sages or seers to whom the Vedic hymns were revealed. The Tibetan translation interprets ṛṣi as meaning "the straighforward or righteous one."

rūpakāya (T: gzugs kyi sku; form body) *See* kāya.

sacred outlook (T: dag-snang) Awareness and compassion lead the practitioner to experience śūnyatā. From that comes luminosity, manifesting as the purity and sacredness of the phenomenal world. Since the sacredness comes out of the experience of śūnyatā, the absence of preconceptions, it is neither a religious nor a secular vision—that is, spiritual and secular vision could meet. Moreover, sacred outlook is not conferred by any god. Seen clearly, the world is self-existingly sacred.

sacred places, twenty-four (S: pīṭha; T: yul; country, seat) Names of twenty-four geographical places and the psychic centers in the body that they represent. The names of the twenty-four countries correspond to parts of the body, veins, dhātus within the body, gods, goddesses, and so on. The twenty-four countries are: Pullīramalaya, Jālandhara, Uḍḍiyāṇa, Arbuda, Godāvarī,

Rāmeśvara, Devīkoṭa, Mālava, Kāmaru, Oḍra, Triśankuni, Kośala, Kaliṅga, Lampāka, Kāñci, Himālaya, Pretādhivāsinī, Gṛhadevatā, Saurāṣṭra, Suvarṇadvīpa, Nagara, Sindhu, Marudeśa, Kulatā.

sacred representation (T: rten; that which holds, supports) Ritual objects such as icons, scepters, and tormas are representations or "vessels" of divine principles. These are the sacred objects placed on shrines and used in liturgical practices. They are considered vessels, or supports, of the actual deities being visualized, because they aid the practitioner in relating directly to these divine principles and also are thought to be blessed by them and contain their energy. There are, for example, the sacred representations of body, speech, and mind, which stand for the body, speech, and mind of the Buddha—the three kāyas. Thus, a crystal ball or stūpa could be the representation of dharmakāya; a holy scripture, of sambhogakāya; and a statue of the buddha or a deity, of the nirmāṇakāya.

Sadāprarudita (T: rtag-tu rngu; ever-weeping) The name of a bodhisattva, renowned for his unwavering perseverance in seeking enlightenment. He appears in the *Prajñāpāramitā* literature. His teacher was Dharmodgata, whom he met in the city of Gandhavatī.

sādhana (T: sgrub-thabs) A type of vajrayāna ritual text, as well as the actual meditation practice it sets out.

Śākya A tribe of ancient India into which Gautama, the historical Buddha, was born. The Buddha is known as Śākyamuni (sage of the Śākyas), and also as lord of the Śākyas and king of the Śākyas.

Śākyamuni *See* Śākya.

salu rice (= T; S: śāli) A kind of wild rice.

samādhi (T: ting-nge 'dzin; fixing the mind, meditative absorption, concentration) A state of total involvement in which the mind rests unwaveringly, and the content of the meditation and the meditator's mind are one. There are many different kinds of samādhi, depending on whether the meditation is developed with a certain mental image, a principle such as compassion, or with the mind itself as the object of meditation, for example.

Samādhi refers to the principle of absorption in meditation, but does not specify the degree of insight (vipaśyanā, prajñā) that is present. Thus, it could refer to a conditioned state of concentration in the six realms in which the sense faculties are halted, or to an unconditioned, flowing, and unobstructed experience.

Samantabhadra (T: kun-tu bzang-po; all-good) One of the eight great bodhisattvas, he is an emanation of Vajrasattva. He is also known as the primordial, dharmakāya buddha, particularly within the Nyingma lineage.

samaya (T: dam-tshig; S: coming together; T: sacred word or vow) The vajrayāna principle of commitment, whereby the disciple's total experience is bound to the path. When the vajra master performs abhiṣeka, the disciple's being is bound together with the master and the deities of the maṇḍala. The disciple becomes irrevocably committed to regard his master as an embodiment of enlightenment, and to retain sacred outlook in all his experience. During the abhiṣeka ceremony, the disciple formally takes the samaya oath. However, in some sense, the samaya principle becomes active as soon as master and student establish a vajrayāna relationship.

The samaya vow is experiential and can be violated in a moment of thought. As Atīśa said, "Keeping samaya is like keeping a mirror polished—as soon as you have cleared it, dust begins to alight." The most important samaya is a proper attitude toward one's root guru. Besides that, the principal points are maintaining the essence of hīnayāna and mahāyāna discipline, and extending sacred outlook throughout one's experience. *See also* root downfalls, fourteen.

samaya substance (T: dam-tshig gi rdzas) Blessed substances offered at a gaṇacakra—meat, torma, and other food, along with liquor. Sometimes "samaya substance" refers specifically to the liquor offered during such a feast.

sambhogakāya *See* kāya.

sampannakrama (T: rdzogs-pa'i rim-pa; completion, perfection stage or practice) One of the two stages of sādhana practice. In sampannakrama, the practitioner dissolves the visualization of the sādhana and meditates formlessly. This breaks any fixation that may have developed from the visualization. Sampannakrama is the key practice that defines the nontheistic approach. Utpattikrama arises from sampannakrama. Visualization being based on nonego allows the deities to arise naturally from the practitioner's mind. *See also* utpattikrama.

saṃsāra (T: 'khor-ba) In contrast to nirvāṇa, saṃsāra is the vicious cycle of transmigratory existence. It arises out of ignorance and is characterized by suffering.

sang (T: srang) See *sho.*

saṅgha (T: dge-'dun) The third of the three jewels of refuge. In the narrow sense, saṅgha refers to Buddhist monks and nuns. In a mahāyāna sense, the mahāsaṅgha, or greater saṅgha, also includes the lay community. The vajra saṅgha includes vajrayāna practitioners who may be living as householders or as solitary yogins. The noble saṅgha, as an object of refuge, may also refer to the assembly of bodhisattvas and arhats, those who have attained realization.

Sāṅkhya (T: grangs-can-pa) One of the earliest Hindu philosophical schools to be thoroughly systematized, Sāṅkhya provides the metaphysical and epistemological view that underlies the classical eight-limbed yoga of Patañjali. In this system, reality is comprised of two principles: prakṛti, which emanates the physical world, and puruṣa, which is eternal, unconditioned awareness.

Śāntibhadra Another name for Kukkurīpā, a mahāsiddha and one of the main teachers of Marpa.

śarīra (T: ring-bsrel) Tiny pill-sized relics found among the cremated remains of saints. Śarīra is one type of relic; it is said to be very hard and to shine with five different colors.

śāstra (T: bstan-bcos; treatise) A type of Buddhist text; generally a commentary or a philosophical treatise.

Śavari One of the eighty-four mahāsiddhas, Śavari was known as a hunter and as a hermit. Thus he is referred to in *The Life of Marpa* as the hermit (T: ri-khrod) or the Lord of Hermits (T: ri-khrod dbang-phyug). Tāranātha's *Bka'-babs bdun-ldan* places Śavari in the lineage of mahāmudrā as the disciple of Nāgārjuna and the guru of Maitrīpa.

sciences, five (S: pañca-vidyā-sthānāni; T: rig-pa'i gnas lnga) A classical list of five fields of study appropriate to a completely educated person. According to the *Mahāvyutpatti,* these are: (1) the science of language (S: śabda-vidyā; T: sgra'i rig-pa), (2) dialectics (S: hetu-vidyā; gtan-tshigs kyi rig-pa), (3) spiritual science (S: adhyātma-vidyā; T: nang gi rig-pa), (4) medicine (S: cikitsā-vidyā; T: gso-ba'i rig-pa), and (5) mechanical arts (S: śilpa [-karma-] sthāna-vidyā; T: bzo'i gnas kyi rig-pa).

secret mantra (S: guhyamantra; T: gsang-sngags) A term for vajrayāna emphasizing the fact that the teachings on the practice of Buddhist tantra are secret and withheld from students who would not properly understand them.

sevenfold service (T: yan-lag bdun) A standard mahāyāna liturgy, including prostration, offering, confession, rejoicing in the merit of others, requesting the teacher to teach, asking the teacher to remain and not pass into nirvāṇa, and dedicating the virtue of one's practice to all sentient beings.

sho (T: zho) A Tibetan measure, often used in measuring gold. It has been figured variously as a dram, 1/10 ounce, or, as a coin, 2/3 rupee. There are 10 *sho* in one *sang*, which is thus equal to about one ounce.

siddha (T: grub-thob; accomplished) A term for enlightened masters in the tantric tradition. Siddha has the connotation of one who, besides being realized on the absolute level, is in tune with the magical possibilities of the phenomenal world.

Tilopa, Nāropa, and Maitrīpa are among the famed eighty-four mahāsiddhas. "Mahāsiddha" has also come to refer generally to an accomplished or enlightened being. *See also* Introduction, pp. xxix-xxxiv.

siddhi (T: dngos-grub; accomplishment) Siddhis, or accomplishments, are either ordinary or supreme. The eight ordinary siddhis involve mastery over the phenomenal world. Supreme siddhi is enlightenment.

signs, ten (T: rtags bcu) Ten signs of advancement in the mastery of the caṇḍālī practice. The first five signs indicate progress in controlling prāṇa—the experience of smoke, a mirage, a glowworm, a flame, and a cloudless sky. These are the five ordinary signs.

The last five "special signs" indicate the attainment of permanent mastery or confidence in controlling prāṇa—seeing clearly sun rays, moon rays, lightning, rainbows, and finally, the combined light of the sun and the moon.

sindūra maṇḍala This refers to a maṇḍala representation, drawn on a mirror-like surface, often polished silver. The surface is coated with sindūra, a powdered substance consisting of red lead or vermilion. The maṇḍala is then drawn in the sindūra, thus revealing the mirror-like surface.

skandha (T: phung-po; heap) The five skandhas are aggregates of dharmas, which make up the individual and his experience. They are form (S: rūpa; T: gzugs), feeling (S: vedanā; T: tshor-ba), perception (S: saṃjñā; T: 'du-shes), formation (S: saṃskāra; T: 'du-byed), and consciousness (S: vijñāna; T: rnam-par shes-pa).

In the confused state, we cling to one or another aspect of these five as a concrete self. When the skandhas are actually seen, no self is found in them, singly or taken together. Moreover, one does not find an individual apart from them. In vajrayāna, they are correlated to the five buddhas of the maṇḍala.

śrāmaṇera (T: dge-tshul) A novice monk who has taken the vow of pravrajyā, or renouncing family life, and who observes 36 precepts. A full monk (S: bhikṣu; T: dge-slong) would vow to observe 253 precepts.

śrāvaka (T: nyan-thos; hearer) Originally, a disciple who actually heard the teachings of the Buddha directly. It is also the name of the first of the nine yānas, in which the practitioner concentrates on basic meditation practice and an understanding of basic Buddhist doctrines such as the four noble truths.

śrī (T: dpal; glorious) A common honorific.

śruva *See* pātrī and śruva.

stages, five (S: pañcakrama; T: rim lnga) The five stages are a description of the process of vajrayāna meditation. They are: (1) solitude of body (T: lus-dben), (2) solitude of speech (T: ngag-dben), (3) solitude of mind (T: sems-dben), (4) luminosity (T: 'od-gsal), and (5) unity (T: zung-'jug). One interpretation of these five stages is that the first two are connected with utpattikrama, the visualization of a deity, whereas the last three are connected with sampannakrama, formless meditation. These five stages are expounded in the cycles of Guhyasamāja, Hevajra, and Cakrasaṃvara.

In particular, there is an important commentary on the *Guhyasamāja-tantra* called the *Pañcakrama,* which was written by Nāgārjuna. Here the five stages are given different names: (1) vajra recitation (S: vajra-jāpa), (2) purification of mind (S: citta-viśuddhi), (3) self-blessing (S: svādhiṣṭhāna), (4) perfect enlightenment (S: abhisaṃbodhi), and (5) unity (S: yuganaddha), all of which are considered part of sampannakrama. Nāropa also wrote down instructions on the *Guhyasamāja* concerning the five stages. *See* "List of Translations by Marpa Lotsāwa."

stages (of yoga), two Utpattikrama and sampannakrama.

stūpa (T: mchod-rten) Originally, a memorial mound containing the relics of the Buddha, symbolizing the mind of the Buddha, the dharmakāya. Later, the relics of other enlightened beings, scriptures, statues, and so on, were included in stūpas. Stūpas are objects of veneration and range from simple altar pieces to very large structures that may be seen for miles around.

Subhaginī A teacher of Tilopa, also known as Sumati.

sugata (T: bde-bar gshegs-pa; well gone) An epithet for a buddha.

śūnyatā (T: stong-pa-nyid; emptiness) A doctrine emphasized in mahāyāna, which stresses that all conceptual frameworks, including the dharma system of the hīnayānists, are empty of any "reality." As a realization, it grows out of the awakening of prajñā. First, at the hīnayāna stage, one's personal existence is seen through. Subsequently, the experience to which one clings is also dissolved through awareness. This is the realization of egolessness of self and a portion of egolessness of dharmas. At the mahāyāna level, through prajñā and compassion, the practice of the pāramitās, the practitioner cuts through the remaining subtle watcher. In vajrayāna, śūnyatā is equivalent to the feminine principle—unborn, unceasing, like space.

sūtra (T: mdo; juncture) The sūtras are those hīnayāna and mahāyāna discourses in the Buddhist canon that are attributed to Śākyamuni Buddha.

Sūtra means meeting point, junction, referring to the meeting of Buddha's enlightenment and the student's understanding. A sūtra is usually a dialogue between the Buddha and one or more of his disciples, thus elaborating a particular topic of dharma.

svabhāvikakāya *See* kāya.

svatantra-madhyamaka (T: dbu-ma rang-rgyud) Madhyamaka is a school of Buddhist philosophy whose methods are based on a radical criticism of any thesis that takes an ontological stand. To assert that something is, or is not, is to fall into one of the extremes of nihilism or eternalism. The prasaṅga-madhyamaka (T: dbu-ma thal-'gyur) school is famous for attempting to carry this approach to its ultimate point. Using reductio ad absurdum as their logical method, the prāsaṅgikas destroy any philosophical thesis and refuse to assert any point of their own.

Svatantra-madhyamaka is a competing school of thought in which one uses reductio ad absurdum on philosophical opponents, but also dares to make independently (svatantra) true statements about the nature of reality. Bhāvaviveka is a famous early proponent of svatantra. There developed several varieties of svatantra. In Tibet, the most well known was the svatantra-yogācāra-madhyamaka, which was brought to Tibet by Śāntarakṣita in the eighth century. In this philosophical schema the principles of the Yogācāra school of mind-only are held to be relatively true, whereas the critical approach of Madhyamaka exposes the ultimate truth.

tantra (T: rgyud; continuity) Tantra may refer to many different kinds of texts. For instance, there are medical tantras, astrological tantras, and so on. More specifically, tantras are the root texts of the vajrayāna and for the systems of meditation they describe. Each tantra usually deals with the maṇḍala of a specific deity or enlightened principle. Tantras, similar to sūtras, are attributed to Śākyamuni, who sometimes manifests as Vajradhara, Vajrasattva, and so on.

The "four orders of tantra" refer to the four yānas: kriyā, upa (caryā), yoga, and anuttara. The tantras themselves have been categorized variously as father, mother, and nondual tantras.

The mother tantras present deities associated with the transmutation of passion into enlightened energy. *Cakrasaṃvara* is an example of a mother tantra. Father tantras are associated with the transmutation of aggression, *Guhyasamāja* being an example. Nondual tantras relate to the transmutation of ignorance, such as the *Kālacakra-tantra.*

Tantra means continuity, and refers to continuity throughout the ground, path, and fruition of the journey. Continuity of ground means that the basic nature, whether it is called suchness, ground mahāmudrā, or tathāgatagarbha, remains like the sky, encompassing everything from sentient beings to buddhas—luminous and untainted by habitual patterns. Although never departing from its own nature, it gives birth to infinite possibilities. Thus, it is the basis for the arising of the skandhas and, in general, impure saṃsāra. It is also the cause for the trikāya of buddhahood. For the practitioner, it means that body, speech, and mind, in all their confused and wakeful manifestations, are included in the path.

Path tantra means applying profound techniques to overcome basic ego. Because the skillful means are based on the ground perspective, they are profound and progress in stages, from dealing with the crude experience of beginners up to the complete realization of Vajradhara.

Fruition tantra means finally realizing who and what you are. You realize your being as one with the body, speech, and mind of the tathāgatas. That is, you realize the ground that was there continuously, from the beginning.

tāntrika (T: sngags-pa; one who does mantra) One who practices tantra, or vajrayāna.

Tārā (T: sgrol-ma) An emanation of Avalokiteśvara, she is said to have arisen from one of his tears. She embodies the female aspect of compassion and is a very popular deity in Tibet. Her two common iconographic forms are white and green.

things as they are (T: gnas-lugs) The phenomenal world directly seen from sacred outlook, once the obscurations have been cleared.

times, three (T: dus gsum) The past, the present, and the future.

tira Ḍākinī code-word for corpse.

torma (S: bali) A sculpture made out of tsampa and molded butter, used as a shrine offering, a feast offering substance, or as a representation of deities. There are traditional designs for each of the many types of torma.

transmission (T: ngo-sprod) The major teachings of tantra transcend verbal expression and must be communicated from guru to disciple in a more direct manner, through the meeting of minds beyond words. Known as transmission, this mystical form of teaching is often achieved through gesture and symbol and usually involves some sense of empowerment.

transmissions, four special (T: bka'-babs bzhi) *See* note on p. xxxii.

trials, twelve major and twelve minor (T: dka'-chen bcu-gnyis, dka'-phran bcu-gnyis) Nāropa underwent twelve minor trials while seeking his guru, Tilopa. These visionary experiences consisted of being exhorted by Vajrayoginī, who appeared in the form of an ugly old hag, to go to Tilopa; leaping over a leper woman without hands and feet, who blocked his path; jumping over a stinking bitch crawling with vermin; not wanting to associate with a man playing tricks on his parents; not wanting to help a man who was tearing the intestines out of a human corpse and then cutting them up; refusing to help a rascal who had opened the stomach of a live man and was washing it with warm water; being entreated to marry a king's daughter in order to hear of Tilopa's whereabouts from the king; refusing to kill a deer with a bow and arrow given to him by a dark man with a pack of hounds; refusing to eat fish and frogs offered by a strange old couple; refusing to help a man cruelly killing his parents; having actually met Tilopa, refusing Tilo's request to kill a handful of lice; and lastly, meeting many one-eyed people, a blindman who could see, an earless one who could hear, a man without a tongue who spoke, a lame man running about, and a corpse gently fanning itself—thus pointing out the symbols of mahāmudrā.

The twelve major trials that Nāropa underwent as a student of Tilopa: jumping off a tall building; jumping into a fire; receiving a beating upon ruining the food of those refusing to give alms; being attacked by leeches as he attempted to build a bridge; being burned by hot reeds at the hand of Tilopa; chasing an apparitional man to the point of exhaustion; receiving a beating upon attacking a minister; receiving a beating upon attacking a queen; receiving a beating upon attacking a prince; the dissatisfaction in his relationship with his consort and his job, as well as hitting his penis with a rock; having his consort beaten by Tilopa; and the dismembering of his body for use as a maṇḍala. Nāropa underwent these trials at the insistence of Tilopa over the course of twelve years. After each trial, Tilopa conveyed a particular teaching to Nāropa and was able to rectify the physical hardships that Nāropa experienced.

trikāya (T: sku gsum; three bodies) *See* kāya.

tsampa (T: rtsam-pa) A flour used throughout Tibet as a staple food—ground, roasted barley. It is often mixed with tea and butter into a thick porridge.

Uḍḍiyāṇa (T: o-rgyan) Birthplace of Padmākara (Padmasambhava) and also said to be the region in which Tilopa resided. Geographically, Uḍḍiyāṇa probably lies in the area between Afghanistan and Kashmir. It is also regarded as the realm of the ḍākinīs.

upāya (T: thabs; skillful means) Generally, upāya conveys the sense that enlightened beings teach the dharma skillfully, taking into consideration the various needs, abilities, and shortcomings of their students. Upāya is an expression of compassion. In the bodhisattva's discipline, it corresponds to the first five pāramitās and to relative bodhicitta. By prajñā alone, without upāya, the bodhisattva is fettered to a quietistic nirvāṇa. By upāya without prajñā, one remains bound to saṃsāra. Therefore the practitioner must unify them.

In vajrayāna, upāya arises from śūnyatā. It is joined with prajñā and represents the male, form aspect of the union of form and emptiness.

upāyamarga (T: thabs-lam; path of skillful means) Although all Buddhist yānas employ numerous techniques (S: upāya) for gaining realization, vajrayāna particularly is called the path of skillful means because of its great variety of powerful and often highly specialized techniques. Within vajrayāna, there is also a twofold division between meditation practices with form, called "path of skillful means" and meditation practices without form, which are called "path of liberation." Within the practices with form, the practices of karmamudrā were even more particularly called upāyamarga.

utpattikrama (T: bskyed-pa'i rim-pa; arising,developing stage or practice) One of the two stages of sādhana practice. In utpattikrama the practitioner develops and meditates with the visualization that is the focus of the sādhana. This stage has an emphasis on form, so that the practitioner appreciates the luminous and active nature of emptiness. *See also* sampannakrama.

vaiḍūrya Lapis lazuli.

vajra (T: rdo-rje; adamantine, diamond, indestructible, thunderbolt) One of the five buddha families, the vajra family is associated with the buddha Akṣobhya of the eastern direction. Its quality is pristine clarity, indestructibility. In general, the term vajra conveys the sense of what is beyond arising and ceasing and hence indestructible. A vajra is also a ritual scepter used in vajrayāna practice.

vajra brothers and sisters (T: rdo-rje lcam-dral, rdo-rje mched-lcam-dral) Fellow disciples who have received abhiṣeka and other vajrayāna transmissions together.

Vajradhara (T: rdo-rje-'chang; vajra holder) The name of the dharmakāya buddha. He is depicted as dark blue, and is particularly important to the Kagyü lineage, as it is said that Tilopa received vajrayāna teachings directly from Vajradhara.

vajra holder (T: rdo-rje 'dzin-pa) Can either refer to Vajradhara or to a vajra master.

vajra master (S: vajrācārya; T: rdo-rje slob-dpon) One who is accomplished in the vajrayāna teachings and capable of transmitting them to others.

Vajrasattva (T: rdo-rje sems-dpa'; vajra being) A buddha of the vajra family, Vajrasattva is white and is associated with purity.

Vajravārāhī (T: rdo-rje phag-mo; diamond sow) A ḍākinī, she is the consort of Cakrasaṃvara. She and Vajrayoginī are aspects of the same deity. Vajravārāhī is marked by a sow's head protruding above her left ear. The sow represents Vairocana buddha —ignorance and passion, dharmadhātu wisdom and compassion.

Vajrayoginī (T: rdo-rje rnal-'byor-ma) A semiwrathful yidam in the Cakrasaṃvara cycle. She is red, with one face and two arms, young and beautiful, but enraged and wearing ornaments of human bones. She represents the transformation of ignorance and passion into śūnyatā and compassion. In the Kagyü tradition, her sādhana is often given as the students' entry into anuttarayoga practice.

Vetālī (T: dud-sol-ma) A mahākālī who has been a traditional protector of the Practice Lineage since the time of Nāropa and Marpa. She is dark blue, wearing the skull crown and bone ornaments. She wields in her four arms a skull cup, scorpion-handled sword, triśūla, and khaṭvāṅga. She rides over a blood lake on a donkey with a white blaze.

Victorious One(s) and sons of (S: jina; T: rgyal-ba) Originally an epithet for a buddha, it has come to be used in connection with enlightened beings generally. The capitalized "Victorious One" refers to Śākyamuni Buddha and lower case "victorious ones" to buddhas generally. When "victorious one" is used in connection with a teacher's name, the implication is that he is to be viewed as a buddha.

views, six (S: ṣaṭkoṭi; T: mtha' drug) Six perspectives on the teachings that a Buddhist student uses in understanding them: literal meaning (S: neyārtha; T: drang-don), true meaning (S: nītārtha; T: nges-don), implied (S: saṃdhyā-bhāṣā; T: dgongs-pa-can), not implied (S: na saṃdhyā-bhāṣā; T: dgongs-pa-can ma-yin-pa), explicit (S: yathāruta; T: sgra ji-bzhin-pa), and not explicit (S: na yathāruta; T: sgra ji-bzhin-pa ma-yin-pa). These are often used in conjunction with the "four methods."

His Holiness Dingo Khyentse, Rinpoche composed the following dohā to explain the meaning of these ten terms:

The *literal meaning* mainly expresses relative truth with appearance.
Disciples are gradually shown the true meaning.
The *true meaning* shows naked absolute truth beyond appearance.
This is the oral instruction for fortunate ones with sharp faculties.

To cut the root of existence, it is said, "Kill your parents."
The meaning itself—cultivating and refraining from attachment—is *implied*.
The real meaning is said to be "conquering with remedies the cultivation of attachments."
Not implied is said to show this clearly with words.

In each of the four orders of tantra, beginning with the maṇḍala, fire offering, and so forth,
Explicit dharma language is proclaimed.
Bound by signs not proclaimed by śāstras in the world,
Not explicit is bound by words difficult to understand.

The actual root texts are explained word-for-word with definitions, according to syntax.
That is the *meaning of words.*
The path of mantrayāna, the perfection of ground, path, and fruition,
Is only proclaimed in anuttara; this is the *general meaning.*

The extraordinary union and destruction, āli, kāli, and so on,
Are shown by code words; this is the *hidden meaning.*
The unsurpassable secret of the actual path and fruition
Is clearly shown by both words and meaning; this is the *ultimate meaning.*

vihāra (T: gtsug-lag-khang) A monastery, temple, or Buddhist residential complex.

virtues, ten (S: kuśala; T: dge-ba) The opposites of the ten nonvirtuous actions. *See* nonvirtues, ten.

what has been told and what has been realized (T: lung gi chos, rtogs-pa'i chos) The dharma that has been told are the teachings that one listens to, studies, and contemplates. The dharma that has been realized are these same teachings, fully understood and experienced through meditation.

wisdoms, five (S: pañca-jñāna; T: ye-shes lnga) The wisdoms of the five buddha families: dharmadhātu wisdom (S: dharmadhātuviśuddhi-jñāna; T: chos kyi dbyings kyi ye-shes), mirror-like wisdom (S: ādarśa-jñāna; T: me-long lta-bu'i ye-shes), wisdom of equanimity (S: samatā-jñāna; T: mnyam-pa-nyid kyi ye-shes), discriminating-awareness wisdom (S: pratyavekṣana-jñāna; T: so-sor rtogs-pa'i ye-shes), and the wisdom that accomplishes all actions (S: kṛtyānuṣṭhāna-jñāna; T: bya-ba nan-tan-du grub-pa'i ye-shes). *See also* buddha families, five.

yāna (T: theg-pa; vehicle) The vehicle that carries the practitioner along the path to liberation. On different yānas, the landscape of the journey, the nature of the practitioner, and the mode of transportation are seen differently. There is a distinctive outlook, practice, action, and fruition in each yāna. Presenting a particular yāna depends on the evolutionary readiness of the student and the accomplishment of the teacher.

In vajrayāna teachings there are three yānas—hīnayāna, mahāyāna, and vajrayāna. They can be practiced simultaneously. Sometimes "one yāna" is spoken of, referring to this simultaneous practice, and to the fact that no matter what the teachings, the student must make a gradual journey from confusion to enlightenment.

According to the Rime (ecumenical) and the Nyingma traditions, there are a total of nine yānas: śrāvakayāna and pratyekabuddhayāna (together comprising hīnayāna), mahāyāna, and six tantric yānas—kriyā, upa (caryā), yoga, mahāyoga, anuyoga, and atiyoga. *See also* hīnayāna, mahāyāna.

yantra (T: srung-'khor) A protection amulet worn around the neck. Yantra contain mantras and sometimes pictures of deities.

yidam (T: yi-dam) The vajrayāna practitioner's personal deity, who embodies the practitioner's awakened nature. Yidam is explained as a contraction of yid kyi dam-tshig, "samaya of mind." Yidams are sambhogakāya buddhas, which are visualized in accordance with the psychological makeup of the practitioner. The student first develops intense devotion toward his guru. This relationship makes it possible for the student to experience intuitive kinship with the lineage and then with his yidam. Identifying with the yidam means identifying with his characteristic expression of buddha nature, free of distortions. Through seeing his basic nature in this universalized way, all aspects of it are transmuted into the wisdom of the spiritual path. This leads directly to compassionate action—skillful and lucid.

Peaceful yidams inspire the student's gentleness, awakening openness. Semiwrathful yidams are the union of vajra passion and anger in the transcendental sense—simultaneous magnetizing and destroying as an expression of the awakened state. Wrathful yidams are associated with the dynamic energy of "vajra anger," the primordial compassion that cuts through hesitations of idiot compassion and disbelieving in one's buddha nature. The male yidam (peaceful: bhagavat; semiwrathful: ḍāka; semiwrathful and wrathful: heruka) signifies awakened energy, skillful means, and bliss. The female yidam (peaceful: bhagavatī; semiwrathful and wrathful: ḍākinī) signifies compassion, emptiness, and prajñā. This emptiness is fundamental accommodation and ultimate fertility. Through union with the heruka, the ḍākinī can give birth to enlightenment.

yogas, three (T: rnal-'byor gsum) *See* note on p. 19.

yogas of Nāropa, six (T: nā-ro chos drug) Six special yogic practices received by Nāropa from Tilopa. They are the yogas of caṇḍālī (T: gtum-mo), illusory body (S: māyādeha; T: sgyu-lus), dream (S: svapna; T: rmi-lam), luminosity (S: prabhāsvara; T: 'od-gsal), ejection of consciousness (S: saṃkrānti; T: 'pho-ba), and the pardo (S: antarābhava; T: bar-do).

yoga tantra (T: rnal-'byor rgyud; union tantra) The third of the tantric yānas, which emphasizes the union of the expansiveness of all apparent phenomena and the profundities of meditative experience. As a particular expression of this tantra, the practitioner is seen as the embodiment of a great prince and the deities are seen as part of that manifestation.

yogic applications (T: las-tshogs) Special practices that are connected with a particular yidam cycle and usually have more worldly achievements as their goals. Practicing the sādhana of a particular yidam usually aims to connect the disciple with the enlightened principle (supreme siddhi) represented by that deity. Having done this, the student may go on to gain specific "ordinary" siddhis, such as the ability to cure "infant death," cause storms, or bring physical wealth. This is done through techniques that are special applications of the previously perfected yidam practice.

yogic discipline (S: vrata; T: brtul-zhugs) Generally a term for religious practice, moral vows, or acts of penance. But in Tibetan tantra, it takes on a special meaning and refers to particular practices where even seemingly negative or immoral behavior can be transmuted into enlightened action. The tāntrika cannot reject anything as inherently impure, and must even be able to transmute such activities as drinking and sexuality. Today, practices of yogic discipline are often performed symbolically or psychologically; but in ancient times they were taken more literally.

yogin (T: rnal-'byor-pa) A male practitioner.

yoginī (T: rnal-'byor-ma) A female practitioner.

INDEX

This Index does not include items found in the "List of Translations by Marpa Lotsāwa" and the "Glossary." Many terms and names indexed here are also included in the Glossary. Please refer to the Glossary for definitions and explanations.